"In her thoroughly researched and ... sor Jung has provided her readers ... wisdom and profound spiritual in... authentic relationships and godly spiritual guidance, praying fervently for God's renewing touch on their lives and in their communities, *Godly Conversation: Rediscovering the Puritan Practice of Conference* provides instruction, inspiration, and hope."

— GARTH ROSELL, Professor of Church History,
Gordon-Conwell Theological Seminary

"Dr. Joanne Jung has done a great service to the church by bringing back to our attention the long-forgotten Puritan spiritual practice of 'conference' in all its various forms. Not content merely to explore this practice on an academic level (although her thorough exploration of Puritan materials would be reason enough for this book), Dr. Jung takes the next step and shows how this discipline connects with the contemporary church as an antidote to the now moribund small group movement. *Godly Conversation: Rediscovering the Puritan Practice of Conference* is a welcome and valuable addition to the now growing literature on spiritual formation."

— RICHARD PEACE, Robert Boyd Munger
Professor of Evangelism & Spiritual Formation,
Fuller Theological Seminary

"There is a strong resurgence of interest in the history of Christian spiritual practices, yet too few are familiar with the important contributions made by the Puritans. In this book, Joanne J. Jung provides a wonderful addition to the literature by exploring the Puritan practice of conference, a vital and varied aspect of Puritan spirituality that is not widely enough known. Not only does this study offer historical insight, it also suggests the contemporary relevance of conference for believers today."

— KELLY M. KAPIC, Professor of Theological
Studies, Covenant College

"Our understanding of Puritan spirituality gets another boost from Joanne Jung in this fine study of a significant cluster of devotional practices. While personal experience of God's grace was essential to that seventeenth-century movement, Puritanism also fostered spiritual growth in the covenanted community, through godly conversation and 'conference' meetings. The book will find appreciative readers among scholars of religious history as well as pastors and other Christian leaders. These spiritual practices developed in the seventeenth century will provide depth to today's emphasis on small group ministry, Bible study, mentoring, and spiritual direction."

— CHARLES HAMBRICK-STOWE, Senior Minister of the First Congregational Church, Ridgefield, Connecticut

"With one eye constantly on the needs of the contemporary church, practical theologian Joanne Jung has recovered an important aspect of Christian community from old and neglected Puritan sources. This stimulating and important study examines the gathering of the saints in informal settings, or 'conferences,' where Scripture and sermons were discussed and 'ingested' to nurture the spiritual life. The cumulative effect of Jung's research is to put the topic of conference at the top of the list of important Puritan disciplines, thereby redressing the popular misconception that Puritans were individualists. The book offers us a detailed taxonomy of the types of Puritan conference, and it expounds for the first time the important role that women played in fostering the practice. The study is based on extensive original research in primary sources, and the author's infectious passion for the church and its history clearly demonstrates that the 'old' can illumine the 'new' and inform and guide the church today."

— JAMES E. BRADLEY, Geoffrey W. Bromiley Professor of Church History, Fuller Theological Seminary

GODLY
CONVERSATION

GODLY
CONVERSATION

rediscovering the Puritan practice of conference

Joanne J. Jung

Foreword by J. I. Packer

Reformation Heritage Books
Grand Rapids, Michigan

Godly Conversation
© 2011 by Joanne J. Jung

All rights reserved. No part of this book may be used or reproduced in any manner whatsoever without written permission except in the case of brief quotations embodied in critical articles and reviews. Direct your requests to the publisher at the following address:

Reformation Heritage Books
2965 Leonard St. NE
Grand Rapids, MI 49525
616-977-0889 / Fax 616-285-3246
orders@heritagebooks.org
www.heritagebooks.org

Printed in the United States of America
12 13 14 15 16 17/10 9 8 7 6 5 4 3 2

Library of Congress Cataloging-in-Publication Data

Jung, Joanne J.
  Godly conversation : rediscovering the Puritan practice of conference / Joanne J. Jung ; foreword by J.I. Packer.
      p. cm.
  Includes bibliographical references and index.
  ISBN 978-1-60178-133-8 (pbk. : alk. paper) 1. Spiritual life—Puritans. 2. Spirituality—Puritans. I. Title. II. Title: Rediscovering the Puritan practice of conference.
  BV4501.3.J86 2011
  248—dc22
                         2011016231

For additional Reformed literature, request a free book list from Reformation Heritage Books at the above regular or e-mail address.

Contents

Foreword by J. I. Packer vii
Preface. xi
Acknowledgments. xiii

1. In Search of Piety's Forgotten Discipline. 1
2. A Royal Conflict over Prophesyings and the Origins
   of Puritan Conference 21
3. Scripture for Puritan Eyes: The Word Read 53
4. Scripture for Puritan Ears: The Word Heard 69
5. Holy Conference: "A Kinde of Paradise". 91
6. Holy Conference: Categorized and Exercised. 124
7. Puritan Conference for the Contemporary Church. 156

Bibliography. 181
Subject Index 199

Foreword

The people who were called Puritans in sixteenth- and seventeenth-century England had a bad press in their own day, and on the whole still do. They were, and are, pictured as folk who lived on the edge of fanaticism, driven by a combative God-centeredness and having a crushing sense of duty that pressed down upon every aspect of their lives. They were, and are, imagined as austere extremists, rigid and censorious, perhaps visionaries, perhaps neurotics, certainly a company of grim and gritted-teeth solitaries, each battling his or her way to heaven essentially unaided and alone. We today, as children of the secular, relativistic laissez-faire culture that surrounds us, find it hard to appreciate humanity of the historic Puritan type, shaped fundamentally as it was by a belief in a holy God who addresses us all via Bible and pulpit, who crisscrosses all our life activities with commands and prohibitions, whose hatred of sin and resolve to punish it are nightmarishly real, and who calls us to unceasing conflict against the evils of the world, the flesh, and the Devil. The fact that Puritans generally, not only leaders but also rank and file, though serious-minded, were ordinarily cheerful souls, living in the joy of knowing that their sins were forgiven through Christ's cross and they themselves were securely in covenant with God, and the further fact that they were extremely sociable, with hearts wide open to family and friends, seems to many simply incredible. But this is how it was—or, should I say, how they were.

During the past two generations, an academic cottage industry of studying Puritan faith and experience in terms of the Puritans' own writings (mostly printed sermons) has developed, and at point after point the truth on these matters has been brought into focus, mostly in high quality doctoral theses. The present book is one such venture in wiping the mud off the face of Puritanism so that its real features may be properly seen. It explores one aspect of the fellowship that Puritans conscientiously practiced as a God-given means of grace.

Did the Puritans believe that "holy conference"—edifying conversation, that is, about spiritual things—was a prescribed Christian duty? Yes, as a body they did. Richard Baxter was one of the many who pressed the point. Having urged in general terms the need for such conversation, even for those who fear they will not be very good at it, he proceeds in his typical, rather overwhelming way to give two lists. List one is of what we would call conversation starters. You may, he says, choose to talk about "1. ...the last sermon that you heard, or of someone lately preached that nearly [i. e., deeply] touched you. 2. Or of something in the last book you read. 3. Or of some text of Scripture obvious [i.e., relevant] to your thoughts. 4. Or of some notable (yea, ordinary) providence which did lately occur. 5. Or of some examples of good or evil that are fresh before you. 6. Or of the right doing of the duty that you are about."[1] Then list two is of things that are always worth talking about.

> Let the matter be usually, 1. Things of weight, and not small matters. 2. Things of certainty, and not uncertain things. Particularly the fittest subjects for your ordinary discourse are these: 1. God himself, with his attributes, relations and works. 2. The great mystery of man's redemption by Christ; his person, office, sufferings, doctrine, example, and work; his resurrection, ascension, glory, intercession, and all the privileges of his saints. 3. The covenant of grace.... 4. The workings of the Spirit of Christ upon the soul.... 5. The ways and wiles of Satan, and all our spiritual enemies.... 6. The corruption and deceitfulness of the heart; the nature and workings, effects and signs of

---

1. Richard Baxter, *A Christian Directory* (Grand Rapids: Soli Deo Gloria Publications, 2008), 465.

ignorance, unbelief, hypocrisy, pride, sensuality, worldliness, impiety, injustice, intemperance, uncharitableness, and every other sin; with all the helps against them all. 7. The many duties to God and man which we have to perform, both internal and external.... 8. The vanity of the world, and deceitfulness of all earthly things. 9 The powerful reasons used by Christ to draw us to holiness.... 10. Of the sufferings which we must expect and be prepared for. 11. Of death…and how to make ready for so great a change. 12. Of the day of judgment.... 13. Of the joys of heaven.... 14. Of the miseries of the damned.... 15. Of the state of the church on earth, and what we ought to do in our places for its welfare. Is there not matter enough in all these great and weighty points, for…conference?[2]

Undiscerning critics have spoken of Bunyan's Christian, in *Pilgrim's Progress* part one, as an example of the ethos of solitary struggle that they take to be Puritanism's essence devotionally. But a closer look reveals that this is not even half the story. Bunyan gives Christian two traveling companions, with each of whom he enjoys edifying conversations that the author records at length. First came Faithful, later martyred in the town of Vanity; once he and Christian had met up, "they went very lovingly on together; and had sweet discourse of all things that had happened to them in their pilgrimage."[3] Then came Hopeful, to whom Christian said as they crossed the enchanted ground (the land of spiritual sleepiness), "To prevent drowsiness in this place, let us fall into good discourse"; whereupon he quizzed Hopeful thoroughly, as he had previously interrogated Faithful, about his conversion.[4] Conversation in which spiritual experience was shared (as distinct from the sort of hollow blathering that Bunyan puts into the mouths of Talkative and Ignorance) was embraced as a major means of grace, both because of the enhanced sense of divine goodness that it brings and also

---

2. Baxter, *Christian Directory*, 466.
3. John Bunyan, *The Pilgrim's Progress* (Oxford: Oxford University Press, 1945), 85–93.
4. Bunyan, *Pilgrim's Progress*, 165–73.

because it preempts satanic invasions of the mind. Bunyan comments in a couplet:

> Saints' fellowship, if it be manag'd well,
> Keep them awake, and that in spite of hell.[5]

Professor Jung pilots us authoritatively through this dimension of Puritan spiritual discipline. All will benefit from what she has written here.

—J. I. Packer

---

5. Bunyan, *Pilgrim's Progress*, 165.

Preface

A friend once told me, "Puritans always get a bad rap." That moment, my own presuppositions were challenged. In the years that followed, I would discover the Puritans' world, culture, devotion, and heart. I found their pursuit of God inspiring, their love for His Word unparalleled, and their commitment to community contagious. Equipped with sound biblical knowledge, the Puritans nurtured community by inquiring about the state of one another's souls, seeking to nourish receptive souls and help impoverished ones. The popular means of grace called *conference* served them well. It was common because—though few modern-day scholars make mention of it—evidence supports sixteenth- and seventeenth-century Puritan pastors frequently advising and encouraging their congregants to converse with one another on issues of biblical knowledge as it relates to the health of the soul.

The opportunity presented itself to me to uncover more on this practice called *conference*. What were its beginnings, its uses and users, its structure and benefits? And might it be possible to apply its guiding principles to twenty-first-century spiritual formation, perhaps strengthening current church communities? This irrepressible hope became a driving force in the reading, researching, data inputting, thinking, writing, and publication of my dissertation work.

The database Early English Books Online (EEBO), which I accessed through the libraries of Fuller Seminary and Biola University, provided images of primary sources found only in the archival stacks of prestigious libraries on both sides of the Atlantic. My visits to the Huntington Library in San Marino, California, afforded the opportunity to peruse a number of treasured Puritan works. There was no lack of material to investigate.

My research revealed that conference was exercised in many venues of community. Laboriously reading through numerous treatises on conference, however, was like wading through a cluttered garage. To help organize the information, I created a rubric for categorizing the various types of conference. Each was categorized into its proper place, providing a helpful tool for future research.

In *Godly Conversation,* you are invited to come and take a walk through my "garage." Each step will take you through the pages of history, where you will discover the personal sacrifice of an archbishop, evidence of the Puritans' commitment to knowing God's Word, and contributions from Puritan pastors and congregants who found this means of grace an integral part of developing community, growing closer to God and to one another.

Godly Conversation presents Puritan spirituality as a significant contribution to the contemporary discussion of spiritual formation. The mission of this book is to explore a historical segment of Protestant heritage, a time when people were serious about God and their walk with Him, the truth of Scripture, care for souls, and the journey-sustaining power of community. Today, those serious about community—pastoral and ministry staffs, small group Bible studies, or families—will be surprised to find how a movement in sixteenth- and seventeenth-century England can impact their biblical literacy and help them influence the development of a thriving community today.

Acknowledgments

Countless times I would face a blank computer screen and wonder to God how it would be filled with the necessary thoughts and words that would most clearly convey what I had been discovering. The book you have in your hands is evidence of God's kindness, provision, and purpose. *Godly Conversation* would not have been possible had it not been for the wisdom, encouragement, and involvement of many.

Dr. James Bradley was my mentor throughout the entire Ph.D. program at Fuller. Whether by phone or in person, his words of encouragement and guidance were always seasoned with courage and grace. With skill and mastery, Dr. Bradley, one of the finest church historians, established essential parameters that allowed great freedom in research and writing. He helped me discover and cultivate the nerdy researcher part of me I did not fully know existed.

My colleagues at Talbot School of Theology—Dennis Dirks, Mike Wilkins, Moyer Hubbard, Michelle Lee-Barnewall, and Matt Williams, just to name a few—have each, in their unique ways, ensured I did not become a recluse in my studies but maintained a healthy and engaging relationship with God, family, students, friends, and ministry. Their wise counsel, prayers, humor, and caring words, especially when I'd hit that proverbial wall, reminded me of the mission of this work.

My friends in "The Gang" and W.I.L.D. and my mentor, Pat Schiltz, journeyed with me and gave me proof that growing in godliness is an ordained community lifestyle. Thoughts of them continue to bring a smile to my heart.

My family continues to give unspeakable joy. Norm has been the life partner who has been committed to his words, "You need to do this." Four of my favorite friends, our now-grown children, Adriane, Ashley, Cami, and Tyler, have kept me humorously and gratefully tethered to reality. God has been kind to place us in each other's lives as family and beyond that as beloved friends.

I have learned, as the Puritans knew, that Christian fellowship is more than friendship; it is a walking together in godliness. Jonathan Mitchel, a Puritan, penned, "If you have a friend with whom you might now and then spend a little time, in conferring together, in opening your hearts, and presenting your unutterable groanings before God, it would be of excellent use: Such an one would greatly strengthen, bestead, and further you in your way to heaven."[1]

God has made this journey worth taking. The gift of these friends and family reminds me so. They have shaped and influenced me—and therefore my research and writing. God has carved a place in my heart for these and more. I am honored to receive the gift of walking with them together in godliness.

---

1. Jonathan Mitchel, *A Discourse of the Glory* (London: Printed for Nathaniel Ponder, 1677), 15.

CHAPTER ONE

In Search of Piety's Forgotten Discipline

The English Puritans are experiencing a twenty-first-century revival. Periodic name-dropping of some better known Puritans such as John Owen, Richard Baxter, or John Bunyan has been on the rise. Waves of published primary works from, and secondary sources about, these saints of Protestant evangelical heritage continue to find their way onto bookshelves and Internet sites. Decades of historical and theological attention to these saints of the past have formed a solid foundation for the present renewed interest in their lives, printed works, and practices.

Though not completely ignoring the religious perspectives, historians have tended to explore the sociological, political, ecclesiastical, intellectual, and economic perspectives of English Puritanism. Over the last seventy years, these aspects of Puritanism have captivated the interest of such scholars as William Haller, Patrick Collinson, and Christopher Hill, who have surveyed the Puritan landscape. These scholars are profoundly acquainted with the spectrum of Puritan influence and impact in their cultural, political, ecclesiastical, social, and economic spheres.[1] The classic works of these men are foundational to a multifaceted understanding of the Puritan movement.

---

1. William Haller, *The Rise of Puritanism: Or, the Way to the New Jerusalem as Set Forth in Pulpit and Press from Thomas Cartwright to John Lilburne and John Milton, 1570–1643* (New York: Harper, 1957); Patrick Collinson, *The Elizabethan Puritan Movement* (London: Cape, 1967); Christopher Hill, *Intellectual Origins of the English Revolution–Revisited* (Oxford: Clarendon Press, 2001).

Proponents who have recaptured the magnitude and relevance of Puritan spirituality include Geoffrey Nuttall, Horton Davies, Gordon Wakefield, Charles Hambrick-Stowe, and J. I. Packer. Their outstanding scholarship offers a strong religious complement and has buoyed interest in the Puritans.[2] Geoffrey Nuttall understands Puritanism as "a movement towards immediacy in relation to God" with a tradition of faith and experience.[3] He analyzes and identifies the Puritan doctrine of the Holy Spirit as the hallmark that served as the unifying element of Puritanism. Puritanism, then, is perceived as the movement along a spectrum toward a greater emphasis on the testimony of the Spirit.[4]

Adding another perspective, Horton Davies asserts that Puritanism in England was a liturgical movement.[5] He sees the movement as seeking to restore English worship to the simplicity, purity, and spirituality of the primitive church while rejecting the Romanish symbols by which the Catholic Church expressed its character. Though Puritanism began as a liturgical reform, Davies saw it as a development into a distinct attitude toward life.[6] This attitude broadens the scope to include the political and social contexts of the movement and the impact of other traits critical to a broader understanding of Puritanism. Davies, in keeping with a distinctly historical perspective while including the religious, defines Puritanism as "the outlook that characterized the radical Protestant party in Queen Elizabeth's day, who regarded the Reformation as incom-

---

2. Gordon S. Wakefield, *Puritan Devotion: Its Place in the Development of Christian Piety* (London: Epworth Press, 1957); Horton Davies, *The Worship of the English Puritans* (Morgan, Penn.: Soli Deo Gloria, 1997); Charles E. Hambrick-Stowe, *The Practice of Piety: Puritan Devotional Disciplines in Seventeenth-Century New England* (Chapel Hill: Univ. of North Carolina Press, 1982).

3. Geoffrey Fillingham Nuttall, *The Holy Spirit in Puritan Faith and Experience* (Chicago: Univ. of Chicago Press, 1992), 134.

4. Peter Lake, introduction to *The Holy Spirit in Puritan Faith and Experience* by Geoffrey Nuttall (Chicago: Univ. of Chicago Press, 1992), 20.

5. Davies, *Worship of Puritans*, 8.

6. Davies, *Worship of Puritans*, 9.

plete and wished to model English church worship and government according to the Word of God."[7] The Scriptures formed the basis for Puritan spirituality and way of life.

Gordon Wakefield asserts, "Puritanism starts from the absolute sufficiency and supreme authority of Scripture."[8] He confirms the Puritans' foundational dependence on the Word of God, regarding Scripture as "the supreme and final authority. Like a wind from heaven the Bible seemed able to sweep away the corruptions and accretions of the unreformed Church."[9]

Charles Hambrick-Stowe offers this insight: "At its heart... Puritanism was a devotional movement, rooted in religious experience," and that "the rise of Puritanism and the settlement of New England ought to be understood as a significant episode in the ongoing history of Christian spirituality."[10] Hambrick-Stowe's definition was penned nearly three decades ago about a formidable Christian movement whose adherents consistently related life to a Bible-based theology.

J. I. Packer understands the emphasis the Puritans placed on the soul's connection between sound theology and expressed spirituality. His regular appeals to explore their scripturally informed spiritual formation appear throughout his writings, as he has plumbed the depths and breadth of their works over the past number of decades. His time-honored *Quest for Godliness* is a mainstay in understanding the Puritan view of sanctification, or spiritual formation.[11]

A Missing Link

Even with these contributions and the rising interest in revisiting ancient practices employed by the saints of the past for purposes

---

7. Davies, *Worship of Puritans*, 1.
8. Wakefield, *Puritan Devotion*, 13.
9. Wakefield, *Puritan Devotion*, 12.
10. Hambrick-Stowe, *The Practice of Piety*, 25.
11. J. I. Packer, *A Quest for Godliness: The Puritan Vision of the Christian Life* (Wheaton, Ill.: Good News/Crossway Books, 1990).

of incorporating and adapting them for contemporary use, Christian scholarship has been slow to consider Puritan spirituality for such purposes. When sources that focus on the topic of spiritual formation are examined, they are found to have largely ignored contributions from the Puritan movement, choosing instead to highlight the practices of other Christian traditions, even of the same period.[12] There appears to be a historical marginalizing when it comes to exploring Puritan sources that reflect the spiritual movement of that era, especially in the area of the communal aspects of Puritan practices of piety.

The practice of "spiritual formation," a term presently accepted, has been recognized under other phraseology. Robin Maas and Gabriel O'Donnell state in their introduction to *Spiritual Traditions for the Contemporary Church* that what Christian tradition has called asceticism, or piety, is twofold. It encompasses virtues, habits, and attitudes that are required to know God, as well as the ridding of vices, harmful attitudes, and destructive habits that make it impossible to be perfect or, in modern-day vernacular, authentic.[13] After exploring the roots of contemporary Western spirituality in their book, Maas and O'Donnell identify distinctive spiritual and theological traditions. Similarly, John Tyson's *Invitation to Christian Spirituality: An Ecumenical Anthology*, offers a compendium of selections from significant historical figures of Christian church history from the period of the ancient church to contemporary times. Yet, both these works lack any significant input from a group known for their spiritual piety, the Puritans. There are no contributions from a Puritan figure from either side of the Atlantic.

The Puritans are briefly mentioned in Howard G. Hageman's "Reformed Spirituality" in Kenneth Collins's *Exploring Christian*

---

12. Robin Maas and Gabriel O'Donnell, eds., *Spiritual Traditions for the Contemporary Church* (Nashville: Abingdon, 1990), passim; see also John R. Tyson, ed., *Invitation to Christian Spirituality: An Ecumenical Anthology* (New York: Oxford Univ. Press, 1999), and Kenneth J. Collins, ed., *Exploring Christian Spirituality: An Ecumenical Reader* (Grand Rapids: Baker, 2000).

13. Maas and O'Donnell, *Spiritual Traditions*, 16.

Spirituality: An Ecumenical Reader. Richard Lovelace's contribution to this book briefly addresses Puritan spirituality, its goal of "the power of godliness," and its impact on subsequent spiritual movements.[14] Lovelace, in a fuller account, describes the genesis, bearings, and vitality of the spirituality of the Puritans. He then invites his readers to explore their literature more deeply and intentionally, for their "veiled" devotion can aptly influence our modern times.[15]

The Study of Spirituality, edited by Cheslyn Jones, Geoffrey Wainwright, and Edward Yarnold, includes an eight-page contribution, "The Puritans," by Gordon Wakefield.[16] Brian Armstrong's contribution in *The Spirituality of Western Christendom, II,*[17] offers his own renewed perspective on Puritan spirituality. He has "become increasingly impressed by the relatively greater emphasis placed by the English Puritans upon piety, upon inward religion, than by the French and Swiss Calvinists."[18] Armstrong explores two crucial elements of Puritan spirituality: "Religious experience, or a lively encounter with God" and the "strong emphasis on the Bible as the living, convicting, healing, word of God."[19] A decade later, the spirituality of the Puritans appears in a one-page summary by Bradley Holt in *Thirsty for God.*[20]

---

14. Richard F. Lovelace, "Evangelical Spirituality: A Church Historian's Perspective," in *Exploring Christian Spirituality,* ed. Collins (Grand Rapids, Baker, 2000), 218–22.

15. Richard Lovelace, "The Anatomy of Puritan Piety: English Puritan Devotional Literature, 1600–1640," in *Christian Spirituality: Post-Reformation and Modern,* ed. Louis Dupré and Don E. Saliers (New York: Crossroad, 1989), 294–323.

16. Gordon Wakefield, "The Puritans," in *The Study of Spirituality,* ed. Cheslyn Jones, Geoffrey Wainwright, and Edward Yarnold (New York: Oxford, 1986).

17. Brian G. Armstrong, "Puritan Spirituality: The Tension of Bible and Experience," in *The Spirituality of Western Christendom, II: The Roots of the Modern Christian Tradition,* ed. E. Rozanne Elder, Cistercian Studies Series 55 (Kalamazoo, Mich.: Cistercian, 1984), 229–48.

18. Armstrong, "Puritan Spirituality," 229.

19. Armstrong, "Puritan Spirituality," 243.

20. Bradley P. Holt, *Thirsty for God: A Brief History of Christian Spirituality* (Minneapolis: Augsburg Fortress, 1993), 85–86.

The "Classic Texts: An Engagement" section in Alister McGrath's *Christian Spirituality: An Introduction* offers a historical range of representative texts of writers from Gregory of Nyssa to J. I. Packer (with an accompanying guide with which the reader can engage).[21] The Puritans are not represented, proving that current sources have failed to cite a major theological group. McGrath includes an honorable mention of them, however, in a work he co-edited with Timothy George.[22] More recently, Evan Howard's *Brazos Introduction to Christian Spirituality*[23] casts a positive light on the Puritans as a movement with which to be reckoned.

The intermittent attention given to the Puritans and their spirituality over the past few decades stands in contrast to the current swell of publications focused on the Puritan movement and ethos. Francis Bremer and Tom Webster have co-edited *Puritans and Puritanism in Europe and America: A Comprehensive Encyclopedia*.[24] The first of this two-volume work consists of a collection of biographies of those who were unmistakably Puritan, those with Puritan sensitivities, and those opposing the movement—all of whose lives helped shape, define, or direct this movement. The second volume, which includes "Ideas, Events, and Issues" and an offering of select primary sources, provides the reader and researcher with invaluable points of reference to subjects pertaining to, positions held by, and historical events surrounding the Puritans.

---

21. Alister E. McGrath, *Christian Spirituality: An Introduction* (Oxford: Blackwell, 1999), 141–73.

22. Alister E. McGrath, "Loving God with Heart and Mind," in *For All the Saints: Evangelical Theology and Christian Spirituality*, ed. Timothy George and Alister McGrath (Louisville: Westminster, 2003), 16–18.

23. Evan B. Howard, *Brazos Introduction to Christian Spirituality* (Grand Rapids: Brazos, 2008).

24. Francis J. Bremer and Tom Webster, eds., *Puritans and Puritanism in Europe and America: A Comprehensive Encyclopedia* (Santa Barbara, Calif.: ABC-CLIO, 2006).

Joel Beeke's *Puritan Reformed Spirituality*[25] brings renewed insights to the spiritual formation discussion by way of addressing the biblical spirituality of the Reformed and Puritan traditions. Beeke and Randall Pederson's *Meet the Puritans*[26] introduces the reader to more than 120 English and American Puritans. Each entry provides a biographical sketch of the author as well as a review of the author's volumes that have been reprinted within the last fifty years. These works, along with the works of Kelly Kapic and those he edited with Randall C. Gleason or Justin Taylor,[27] promote further reading and a deeper understanding of the Puritans for both the scholar and general public, thus paving the way for exploring further the spirituality of the Puritans.

The recent surge in Puritan interest and scholarship, coupled with the evangelical quest to uncover practices that can be applied to dimensions of spiritual formation in evangelical churches, is fueling a greater appreciation for this segment of Protestant tradition and a realistic application for present-day spiritual formation. Puritan piety, or spirituality, is proving to be a plenteous source from which spiritual insights can be mined.

An uncovering of the long ignored Puritan practice of conference may prove a timely discovery that will help shape the current spiritual atmosphere. Few researchers address the communal means of Puritan conference in any great length. Those who do recognize it as a commonly used means of Puritan piety. None, however, further the discussion of the communal means of conference as a viable discipline with contemporary relevance, and none have simultaneously

---

25. Joel R. Beeke, *Puritan Reformed Spirituality* (Grand Rapids: Reformation Heritage, 2004).

26. Joel R. Beeke and Randall J. Pederson, *Meet the Puritans: With a Guide to Modern Reprints* (Grand Rapids: Reformation Heritage, 2006).

27. Kelly Kapic, *Communion with God: The Divine and the Human in the Theology of John Owen* (Grand Rapids: Baker, 2007); Kelly Kapic and Randall C. Gleason, eds., *The Devoted Life: An Invitation to the Puritan Classics* (Downers Grove, Ill.: InterVarsity, 2004); Kelly Kapic and Justin Taylor, eds., *Overcoming Sin and Temptation* (Wheaton, Ill.: Good News/Crossway, 2006).

connected it with its Puritan roots. O. R. Johnston finds that though Puritan writings often allude to the means of conference, it is usually in passing.[28] This may be due to its acceptance as a common and regular practice. Further research may confirm its familiarity and functionality.

To date, there is no work that takes a serious, in-depth look at the Puritan discipline of conference and its application to contemporary spiritual formation. The revisit of Puritan conference found in this treatment seeks to highlight a dormant Puritan practice in hopes that the evangelical public would benefit from its rediscovery and re-incorporation. This recapturing of conference as a spiritual discipline—with its two-part foundation of the Word and the intention to nurture its expression in life—has potential to impact spiritual guidance, to increase biblical literacy, and to further the dynamics of Bible study small groups as a source of spiritual growth in godliness. The revival of the Puritan practice of conferencing can serve to alleviate more of the reservations many modern-day evangelicals have over spiritual formation, and also provide a vehicle for soul care that is found within their own tradition.

A Rediscovery in Puritan Spirituality

It remains difficult to rid even scholarly minds of the unrelenting stereotype caricaturing Puritans as grim, kill-joy Christians, fanatics in black steeple-hats, the antithesis of Roman Catholic, or indifferent to humanity and the splendors of this world. Not only is this branding no longer tenable, but also its retention blinds the Christian to the wealth of material relevant to Christian spirituality for the individual and for the individual in community. To compound this problem, our present society's pejorative usage of "piety" has negatively influenced the understanding and use of this word. The Puritans, however, used the word "piety" in primarily a positive sense while abhorring false piety, which promoted self-deception and legalism.

---

28. O. R. Johnston, "The Means of Grace in Puritan Theology," *Evangelical Quarterly* 25 (October 1953): 217.

Methods consistent with the disciplines of historical research in tandem with those consistent with practical theology will be applied toward the purpose of uncovering the Puritan discipline of conference. This involves the careful analysis and evaluation of numerous primary and secondary sources in the process of uncovering this aspect of spirituality as exercised by the English Puritans.[29]

The word "conference" is commonly used in present-day vernacular. It is typically used to denote a meeting of a number of people for the purpose of discussion or consultation, as in "conference room" or "conference call." A meeting can sometimes last several days, in which people with a common interest participate in discussions or listen to lectures to obtain information, such as a "leadership conference." The primary definition of conference focuses around a meeting to discuss serious matters. The *Oxford English Dictionary* identifies the sixteenth-century use of the term as, "The action of conferring or taking counsel,…always on an important or serious subject" and notes that formerly in a more general sense it meant "conversation or discourse; a meeting or rendezvous for conversation."[30]

Two definitive works, Wakefield's *Puritan Devotion* and Hambrick-Stowe's *Practice of Piety*, have offered clear scholarship in the area of two specific practices of Puritan piety. Wakefield cites, from Bayly's *Practice of Piety,* that prayer and meditation should accompany reading. The devout Puritan held all that is read in Scripture must be applied either to confirm faith or increase repentance. Each passage was addressed to the particular reader as if God, who was standing at his side, spoke the words.[31] Hambrick-Stowe observes that parents, ministers, and all saints had an obligation to watch over the spiritual welfare of their family members and neighbors.

---

29. Authors of primary sources were those identified as Puritans or had Puritan sympathies. Their works range from collections of sermons and lengthy treatises to shorter printed works, diaries, and letters.

30. *Oxford English Dictionary*, 2nd ed., s.v. "conference," accessed 6 July 2004, http://www.dictionary.oed.com.

31. Wakefield, *Puritan Devotion*, 22.

This took on a number of different forms—one of which was conference. He devotes five pages to the means of private conference and includes bibliographic sources from which more research can be explored.[32]

Engaging in conference furthered one's understanding of Scripture and its application toward growth of godliness in the life of the conferee. One's knowledge and discernment of God's Word was foundational to one's relationship with God through His Son and in His Spirit. Conference done well required one to "first have the word within us; and that not lightly floating in our braine, but deeply setled and hidden in our hearts."[33] Puritan submission to Scripture was the litmus test. As the Puritan minister and writer Thomas Watson states:

> The Rule by which a Christian must try himself, is the Word of God. Phancy and opinion are false Rules to go by. We must judge of our spiritual condition by the Canon of Scripture.... Let the Word be the Umpire to decide the controversie whether we have grace or no. We judge of colours by the Sun. So we must judge of the estate of our souls by the light of Scripture.[34]

Conference combined the two elements of biblical interpretation and care for the soul; minds were engaged even as souls were tended.

E. Glenn Hinson's contribution on Puritan spirituality, in Frank Senn's *Protestant Spiritual Traditions*, includes commonly practiced disciplines. He draws attention to the Puritan position on the sovereignty of God and election and attributes acute problems to the Puritan practice of self-examination. He adds that it was worsened, "since the Puritans made no special provision for spiritual direction which could mitigate the harsh and capricious aspects of

---

32. Hambrick-Stowe, *Practice of Piety*, 150–55.

33. Nicholas Bownd, *Sabbathum Veteris Et Noui Testamenti: Or the True Doctrine of the Sabbath* (London: By Felix Kyngston, 1606), 394.

34. Thomas Watson, *Heaven Taken by Storm* (London: Printed by R. W., 1670), 56–57.

self-criticism."[35] His argument continues with the example of John Bunyan and proceeds to describe the "manic depression" Bunyan was flung into by exercising such reflection. Yet Hinson's mention of spiritual guides placed in Bunyan's life, who may have aided in his conclusion of assurance over judgment, actually demonstrates the presence of others in a community who served to offer direction and care. The opportunity for spiritual guidance that presents itself in the form of conference was an integral part of Puritan spirituality. This communal activity of "private means" proved to have been of great benefit for many Puritans.

The Practice of Conference

The word "conference" retained formal and informal meanings; both were employed in the sixteenth century. Its formal use denoted a formal meeting for consultation or discussion, usually between representatives of societies or parties. "Conference" was also employed in a more general, informal sense by means of conversation, discourse, or talk.

According to Hambrick-Stowe, conferences, or consultations with a spiritual mentor or director, were considered practices of private devotion and expressions of the membership of each believer in the covenant. Conference was exercised among parents with children, masters with apprentices, teachers and Harvard tutors with students, and older women with girls and young women. All had a responsibility to care for the spiritual welfare of others. Ministers were expected to be engaged in spiritual counseling as part of their calling, but conference with other spiritually mature believers was also to be sought. "Although one most often sought such a relationship in time of spiritual struggle, crisis, or melancholy, diary entries also attest to high spiritual attainment resulting from intimate sharing and guidance."[36] Richard Baxter writes:

---

35. E. Glenn Hinson, "Puritan Spirituality," in *Protestant Spiritual Traditions*, ed. Frank C. Senn (New York: Paulist, 1986), 168.

36. Hambrick-Stowe, "Puritan Spirituality in America," in *Christian*

> Another help to this Heavenly life, is, To be much in serious discoursing of it, especially with those that can speak from their hearts, and are seasoned themselves with an heavenly nature. Its pitty, that Christians should ever meet together, without some talk of their meeting in Heaven, or the way to it before they part.... Methinks we should meet of purpose, to warm our spirits with discoursing of our Rest.... Get then together, fellow Christians, and talk of the affairs of your Country and Kingdom, and comfort one another with such words. If worldings get together, they will be talking of the world, when wantons get together they will be talking of their lusts, and wicked men can be delighted in talking wickedness and should not Christians, then, delight themselves in talking about Christ? and the heirs of heaven in talking of their inheritance? This may make our hearts revive within us.[37]

Baxter and other Puritan divines encouraged this discourse, or conference.

Many manuals pointed out that believers ought to seek out "much conference, especially with Ministers and other experienced Christians." In John Bunyan's *Pilgrim's Progress*, private conference is what makes Christian's journey practicable. Time and again, as destruction is imminent, the advice and comfort of a fellow pilgrim enabled him to press on. Private spiritual counseling guided individuals through the conversion experience as it screened church members and led them to make a public profession of faith. In families, it enabled parents to bring their children and servants to experience grace. In "A letter…to His Friend," Jonathan Mitchel (1624–1668) urged:

> If you had a friend with whom you might now and then spend a little time, in conferring together, in opening your hearts, and presenting your unutterable groanings before God, it would be of excellent use: Such an one would greatly strengthen, bestead,

---

Spirituality: Post-Reformation and Modern, ed. Louis K. Duprae and Don E. Saliers, World Spirituality, vol. 18 (New York: Crossroad, 1989), 347.

37. Richard Baxter, *The Saints' Everlasting Rest*, (London: Printed by Rob White for Thomas Underhill and Francis Tyton, 1650), 675.

and further you in your way to Heaven. Spend now and then [as occasions will permit] an hour [or so] with such a friend more then ordinary [sometimes a piece of a day, sometimes a whole day of extraordinary fast, in striving and wrestling with God for everlasting mercy.] And be much in quickning *conference* (author's emphasis), giving and taking mutual encouragements and directions in the matters of Heaven! Oh! the life of God that falls into the hearts of the Godly, in and by gracious Heavenly conference. Be open hearted one to another, and stand one for another against the Devil and all his Angels. Make it thus your business in these and such like ways, to provide for Eternity while it is called today.[38]

The mutual encouragement and direction given and received in the exercise of conference served to attend and strengthen souls.

Puritan Spirituality and the Bible

Paramount to Puritan spirituality was knowing and understanding the Bible, the Word of God. Engaging in faithful Bible reading and meditation upon it was the essential device of Puritan piety. The text under consideration for meditation could either be the text preached on the previous Sabbath or the text of the day in a regular program of Bible reading. For Puritan writers the Bible was authoritative, and the loyal adherence to using biblical language in each text disclosed the ultimate authority of Scripture. The Bible was, above all, "a devotional book" for Puritans.[39]

The Word was also central to the sermon. The Word heard was even more important in Puritan piety than the Word read.[40] The preaching and hearing of the sermon were central acts of Puritan worship. John Owen observes: "The best of men, the most holy and spiritually minded, may have, nay ought to have, their Thoughts of

---

38. Jonathan Mitchel, "Letter to a Friend," appended to *A Discourse of the Glory* (London: Printed for Nathaniel Ponder, 1677), 15–16.
39. Hambrick-Stowe, *Practice of Piety*, 8.
40. Dewey D. Wallace, Jr., ed., *The Spirituality of the Later English Puritans: An Anthology* (Macon, Ga.: Mercer Univ. Press, 1987), 27.

spiritual things excited, multiplyed and confirmed by the preaching of the Word."[41]

O. R. Johnston recognizes the sermon preached was one of three public means of spiritual formation for the Puritan: ministry of the Word, administration of the Sacraments, and prayer with thanksgiving and psalms.[42] The rhetorical style was "plain" in that sermons were to follow an accepted outline, be clearly understood, and be replete with biblical imagery and allusions. Perry Miller, relying on William Perkins's *The Art of Prophesying* and Richard Bernard's *The Faithful Shepherd*, emphasizes the rationality of Puritan sermons and describes them much like a legal brief.[43] Indeed, there was a specific order and structure to a Puritan sermon. Following the reading of the Bible, the selected text was "opened" in exegesis. Doctrines were extracted and theoretical objections were refuted. The final and most elaborate portion of the sermon was applications, or "uses" of comfort, warning, or exhortation.[44]

The Puritan preacher hoped that every auditor would be affected by the words. Theology sanctioned the clergy's influence, and the laity accepted the ministry's calling as a conduit of the Spirit's activity in the Word. Although attendance at sermons was mandatory, the personal meetings with ministers were credited as instrumental in the spiritual lives of their auditors. The Puritans' eager attendance at sermons, a benchmark of righteous behavior, multiplied the opportunities ministers were given to impact their auditors.

Sometimes a minister, in the course of his preparation and memorization of his message, wrote a fairly complete copy of it.[45]

---

41. John Owen, *Phronema Tou Pneumatou, or, the Grace and Duty of Being Spiritually-Minded Declared and Practically Improved* (London: Printed by J. G. for Nathaniel Ponder, 1681), 23–24.

42. Johnston, "Means of Grace," 203.

43. Perry Miller, *The New England Mind: The Seventeenth Century* (Cambridge: Harvard Univ. Press, 1963), 332.

44. Hambrick-Stowe, "Puritan Spirituality in America," 346.

45. Babette May Levy, *Preaching in the First Half Century of New England History*, ed. Matthew Spinka and Robert Hastings Nichols, Studies in Church History, vol. 6 (New York: Russell & Russell, 1967), 82.

More often, printed versions of sermons were usually prepared from notes, whether those of the minister or listener.[46] The devout were encouraged to take notes on the sermon, and members of the congregation often came equipped with inkhorn and paper to do so. Fortunately, many thick notebooks with sermon abstracts closely written by laymen have survived.

Even a system of shorthand had been specifically devised for recording as much of the sermon as possible. Schoolchildren were able to combine their writing ability with their religious indoctrination by taking notes on the Sunday sermon.

Nevertheless, a minister's impact was never an assumed fact. John Sill refused to take an aspect of Thomas Shepard's sermon seriously until, reading over some sermon notes with other people, he saw "there was more in them than I [had] apprehended."[47] The devout listened to and took notes on the sermon so as to spend the following week reflecting on what they had heard and recorded. In pious families, the sermon was reviewed and children were catechized on the main points.

The Puritan family also exhibited a strong and clear spirituality. The head of the household was perceived as minister of the home, and he was given the inalienable responsibility to care for the souls of the household, including family members as well as servants. What set Puritans apart from their contemporaries was their exceptional emphasis on church attendance, reading, prayers, self-examination, family instruction, and conference that formed the household curriculum to lead children and servants to faith.[48] Fathers served as interceding "priests," although mothers and other adults also shared in the responsibility of leading family worship.[49]

---

46. Levy, *Preaching*, 83.
47. Thomas Shepard, *Confessions*, ed. George Selement and Bruce C. Woolley (Boston: Colonial Society of Massachusetts, 1981), 47.
48. John Morgan, *Godly Learning: Puritan Attitudes towards Reason, Learning, and Education, 1560–1640* (New York: Cambridge Univ. Press, 1986), 150.
49. Hambrick-Stowe, "Puritan Spirituality in America," 347.

Householders who shunned this responsibility denigrated the souls of their dependents before God. Catechetical instruction, which included psalm singing, devotional reading of the Bible, devotional manuals or published sermons, and family prayer, comprised the substance of these morning and evening sessions. Prayers before and after eating comprised daytime devotions.

Ministers spent any available time monitoring the progress of family devotions in their churches by periodically visiting to offer advice on how best to conduct the sessions. One pastoral activity was to call on families, examining them on the sermon of the previous Sunday by applying its lessons to them practically.[50] Interpretation of Scripture involved ministers in relationship with the members of their congregation and was not given over to the individual. None of the spiritual brotherhood believed in the right of every man to interpret Scripture for himself. Pastors were to be spiritual fathers, tutors, physicians, and soul friends. Richard Baxter (1615–1691), in Kidderminster, England, followed up the Sunday sermon with a Thursday evening study group at his house where "one of them repeated the Sermon and afterwards they proposed what Doubts any of them had about the Sermon, or any Case of Conscience, and I resolved their Doubts."[51]

Interactions with Puritan clergy were typical and outnumbered other types of interface.[52] Though mainstream, it is clear there was no monopoly on instructing and counseling. Family, friends, and acquaintances also performed that task. Together, these played an essential role in the means of grace of conference with its use of Scripture obtained by way of the minister, his sermons, the auditor's sermon notes, or private Bible reading.

---

50. Wallace, *Spirituality of Later English Puritans,* xxvii.
51. Richard Baxter, *Reliquiae Baxterianae* (London: Printed for T. Parkhurst, 1696), 83.
52. Charles Lloyd Cohen, *God's Caress: The Psychology of Puritan Religious Experience* (New York: Oxford Univ. Press, 1986), 164.

Means of Grace

In view of the extremes of medieval superstition and tradition, the Puritans sought to cultivate a biblical worldview by maintaining a high view of Scripture, depending on the Holy Spirit, and committing to develop a holistic, working theology of the spiritual life. This was accomplished by specific means of grace.

Puritan John Preston says concerning the effectiveness of means:

> You must take heed of depending upon the meanes without GOD. For know that the meanes without God, is but as a penne without Inke, a Pipe without water, or a scabbard without a sword. They will not strengthen the inward man without God: for it is the Spirit that puts life in the meanes, and yet you must not cut off the pipe from the well-head: you must not depend on God without the use of the meanes, but you must use both: that is, first seeke to God, and depend on him for the strengthning of the inward man, and withall use the meanes constantly, because as water is carried from the Well-head unto the pipe, and so from the pipe unto many places, so the meanes are as pipes to carry grace into the soule.[53]

These means of grace were channels that enabled one to be more receptive and ready to grow in faithfulness as God leads. Richard Baxter adds,

> All the means of Grace, and all the working of the spirit upon the soul, and all the gracious actions of the Saints, are so many evident Mediums to prove, that there remaineth a Rest to the people of God.... All these means and motions, implie some End to which they tend, or else they cannot be called means, nor are they the motions of Wisdom or Reason.... God would never have commanded his people to repent and beleeve, to fast and pray, to knock and seek, and that continually, to read and study, to conferr and meditate, to strive and labor, to run and fight, and all this to no purpose.[54]

---

53. John Preston, *Saints' Spiritual Strength* (London, 1637), 113–14.
54. Richard Baxter, *Saints' Everlasting Rest,* 171.

As people of God, it was critical that living lives pleasing to Him meant their practices should reflect and strive to that end of honoring their God. It is also important to recognize that the Puritan practice of religion was as much a social experience as it was a private religion. The social aspects of Puritan life were no less significant than its interiorized religion. In the minds of many of their neighbors, the "closet duties" of prayer and self-examination and the exercising of conference with other saints were among the qualities of the Puritan that constituted a "visible saint."[55]

Private, devotional means of grace, termed "closet" or "secret" exercises, included the reading and studying of Scripture, meditation, and prayer. Indeed, whenever Puritan piety is taken to task, attention tends to be drawn to these individual forms of pious practices.

Hambrick-Stowe credits John Eliot in his delineation of "the way of godly conversation" in expanding and including other formal religious exercises that constituted the private devotional life of New England Puritans.[56] Secret exercises consisted primarily of reading, meditation, and prayer, usually conducted in that order.

Although these secret exercises exhibited the highest degree of privacy, other means of grace were performed in a variety of settings: private meetings of believers in homes, family exercises, and private counseling and prayer sessions with a trusted mentor. Private meetings consisted of neighborhood or occupational groups formed from the congregation by the pastor. Although the minister was often present at these meetings, laypersons usually led the exercises.

Diary entries by both clergy and laity testify to the devotional importance in spiritual growth in the home meetings for both men and women. It was in this setting that laity exercised their abilities to pray and counsel one another.[57] The discourses laypeople held with God, their friends, and themselves marked out activities that were uniquely theirs. Coupled with the preeminent role of preachers

---

55. John Spurr, *English Puritanism 1603–1689* (New York: St Martin's Press, 1998), 37.

56. Hambrick-Stowe, *Practice of Piety*, 136.

57. Hambrick-Stowe, "Puritan Spirituality in America," 346–47.

in guiding the experience of conversion and spiritual growth, the rest of the community had an integral role in the functioning of a multifaceted Christian experience.

Conclusion

The Puritans knew their Bible. Throughout their treatises are margins laden with Scripture references that lend support for many given points. The centrality of Scripture was evident not only in the proof texts found throughout these treatments on conference, but also in the constant effort displayed in asserting the guidance received through Scriptures. Biblical knowledge was to be applied to life for the purpose of growth in holiness.

With regard to Puritan means of grace, Johnston charges, "The amount of material available when dealing with these topics is staggering. The riches seem inexhaustible." His article could shed some light upon "this vast spiritual treasure."[58] In dipping into it, the functional and practical qualities of conference in Puritan piety and the various forms in which it presented itself are demonstrated. By exploring select Puritan confessions or conversion narratives, letters, diaries, and manuals, the methods, contents, and benefits of the Puritan means of conference will be described in subsequent chapters.

The historical origins of the conference as traced through the continental "exercise of prophesying" are explored in the next chapter. One of Elizabeth I's archbishops, Archbishop Grindal, is highlighted as one whose uncompromising position in favor of prophesying made possible the eventual practice of conference. This view, however, also cost him his position. Chapter 3 establishes the Puritan view of Scripture and the authority God's Word. The Word of God, whether in written or spoken form, was the critical basis for the discussion and care that took place in conference. Chapters 4 and 5 present the results of researching the primary material on this discipline and a proposed rubric for cataloging the various types of conference. Examples of men and women who exercised conference

---

58. Johnston, "Means of Grace," 223.

are offered at the close of chapter 5. The final chapter presents the recommendations for the application of conference for the twenty-first-century church. Implications from conference, ranging from incorporation into contemporary Bible study, small groups, and spiritual direction, are explored in that chapter as well.

Not only will the profitable discipline of conference be uncovered, but so will the joy and satisfaction found in this exercise of affirming growth in Christlikeness. Nicholas Bownd sums up the mutual benefits experienced from conference: It is by *"the conferring and talking with others of that which we have in the word read or heard:* especially seeing both it is commended unto us in the Scripture, & also by experience we shall finde the profit of it to be so great, to our selves and others."[59] May we echo these sentiments of Ezekiel Culverwell:

> By musing upon that which often the Scriptures doe teach us concerning love, that it is the *fulfilling of the Law*, and *to give all wee have to the poore without love is nothing*, and *when our faith and hope shall cease, love shall remaine and most flourish in the life to come*, I doe grow to an admiration of the excellencie thereof, the sense whereof I most feele, when as by some good meanes (as some sweete conference) my affection is enlarged to any of Gods Saints, mee thinkes I taste of the happinesse to come, then which, what more delectable?[60]

Conference enlarges the capacity of the heart toward God and others in community.

---

59. Bownd, *Sabbathum Veteris*, 391.
60. Ezekiel Culverwell, *Time Well Spent in Sacred Meditations* (London: Printed by T. Cotes, 1635), 208–9.

CHAPTER TWO

A Royal Conflict over Prophesyings and the Origins of Puritan Conference

The process of uncovering the neglected discipline of Puritan conference would be amiss without making acute observations on its historical context. By appropriately assessing the framework within which Puritan conference finds its origin, the church historian, practical theologian, and common laity can more aptly apply this means of grace with greater understanding and respect. Methodologically sound approaches will afford the practitioner greater skill in appropriating the knowledge and application of this spiritual discipline employed by the English Puritans.

Events that Precede the Emerging Puritan Movement
Henry VIII
Early in the sixteenth century, Henry VIII (1509–1547), in an effort to secure stability for the Tudor dynasty, became frustrated by the failure to produce a male heir. This led him to perform a kind of marital gymnastics in order to secure an annulment of his marriage to Catharine of Aragon, seven years his elder, and to marry his latest infatuation, eighteen-year-old Anne Boleyn. The Protestant inclinations of Anne Boleyn were as serious as Catherine's devotion to the papal church.[1] This required the pope to be discharged from his jurisdiction and authority with the intent to place Henry himself as the head of the Church of England, a move that was more politi-

---

1. G. R. Elton, *Reform and Reformation-England, 1509–1558* (Cambridge: Harvard Univ. Press, 1977), 105–6.

cal than ecclesiastical. After separating the English church from the pope of Rome, the Act of Supremacy (1534) was passed and recognized the king as the supreme head of the church in England. The simultaneous "corruption of the Preaching Friars and Monastic Brotherhoods and their eventual dissolution"[2] allowed for the continuing Reformation that had begun on the Continent.

Another contributing factor in Henry VIII's reign, facilitating the growth of Reformation, was the humanist outlook of the Continental Reformer Desiderius Erasmus. His views were shared by members of Anne Boleyn's faction and Thomas Cromwell, the First Earl of Essex and one of the strongest proponents of the English Reformation. It was Cromwell who masterminded the legislation that severed Roman ties. Concurrent with the decline of the Roman Catholic influence was the advent of Calvinism in England. Simplified forms of worship replaced the more superstitious practices of worshiping relics and images. Preaching became more important, and the laity was allowed greater access to English translations of the Bible. These changes made it conducive for Protestantism to take hold.

Cromwell believed in giving the Bible to the common man and led the way in departing from the policy of keeping the Scriptures only for the learned. Even before Henry VIII made a political break from Rome, Cromwell persuaded him to permit placing English Bibles in the churches.[3] He sought a vernacular version of the Bible, which meant he would rely on the work of Reformer and Bible translator William Tyndale (ca. 1494–1536). Defying the laws that prohibited Bible translating and leaving England without the king's permission, Tyndale accomplished most of the work of translating the Bible into English on the Continent, preparing *two* editions of his New Testament instead of one.[4] A translation ascribed to a ficti-

---

2. Irvonwy Morgan, *The Godly Preachers of the Elizabethan Church* (London: Epworth Press, 1965), 2.

3. A. G. Dickens, *The English Reformation*, 2nd ed. (University Park, Penn.: Pennsylvania State Univ. Press, 1991), 21.

4. Brooke Foss Westcott and William Aldis Wright, *A General View of the History of the English Bible*, 3rd ed. (New York: Macmillan, 1905), 32;

tious Thomas Matthew, an actual work of Tyndale, became available in 1537.[5] God's Word was finally in a language the nation could understand, and this would impact all levels of English society.[6]

The later years of Henry VIII's reign saw the Reformation moving backward. With Henry as supreme head, he carried his regal power to the limit. No bishop or spiritual person would be allowed to preach any doctrine but what the king approved. Several leaders of the Reformation in England were driven into exile and were brought into close contact with the Continental Swiss Reformation. Those who returned to England after Henry's death in 1547 propagated Calvinist views during the reign of Henry's son, Edward VI.

Edward VI

An era of confusion and conflict followed Henry's reign. Edward VI (1547–1553) came to the throne at age ten. In his brief yet calculated reign, Edward steered the nation rapidly and sharply toward Protestantism. The authority of Parliament was greatly increased; no longer could the church be controlled or manipulated by one individual. The first Book of Common Prayer (1549) evolved from medieval orders of service that prescribed some of the traditional vestments: the cope, vestment, tunicle, and alb for the priest; rochet, surplice, and hood for the bishop. These were met with objections from many including Martin Bucer, a Protestant Reformer exiled to England from his base in Strasbourg. By 1550 even Nicholas Ridley, Bishop of Rochester, and Thomas Cranmer (1489–1556), Archbishop of Canterbury, were eager to have all vestments abolished. The second Book of Common Prayer (1552) constituted a departure from the first; neither alb, nor vestment, nor cope was to be used; the bishop was to wear a rochet; the priest or deacon, only a surplice.[7]

David Daniell, *William Tyndale: A Biography* (New Haven: Yale Univ. Press, 1994), 334.
    5. Elton, *Reform and Reformation-England*, 274–75.
    6. Dickens, *English Reformation*, 21.
    7. Everett H. Emerson, *English Puritanism from John Hooper to John Milton* (Durham, N.C.: Duke Univ. Press, 1968), 5.

Only forms of worship that could be derived from Scripture were instituted. Cranmer's Book of Homilies (1547), Book of Common Prayer (1552), and Forty-Two Articles of Religion (1553) introduced the Church of England to the theology of Luther and Calvin and brought England closer to the Continental Reformation.

A critical tenet of the Reformation was preaching. Preaching was the chosen means employed by adherents of Protestantism to persuade the English people of its validity. The prominence placed on the sermon, preached or printed, though not a Reformation innovation, was primary. The intention to restrict unapproved preaching in May 1548 led to a decree that inhibited all preachers (Sept. 1548), including those with an approved license.[8] The Book of Homilies was produced to appease the people's desire for preaching during the shortage of preachers. The first Book of Homilies was published in 1547 and included twelve contributions from several individuals. Copies were placed in each parish to help foster conformity of teaching. The homilies varied in content from one to the next, depending upon the theme and the writer. They addressed many aspects of the Christian faith and life, outlining the human predicament of sin and the way of salvation, and exhorting the hearer to obedience, charity, and discipleship in the face of worldly temptations.[9] Though the homilies met the immediate need for Sunday instruction, repeated readings of the homilies may have brought more tedium than learning; one cannot assume any long-term efficacy. Edward's brief reign, which ended with his death at age fifteen in 1553, furthered the establishment of the English Reformation and Protestant structure of the Church of England.

Mary I

Protestant reforms instituted by Edward VI, however modest, were repealed by Parliament during the bloody reign of Mary I, Edward's

---

8. Patrick Ferry, "Preaching, Preachers, and the English Reformation under Edward VI: 1547–1553," *Concordia Journal* 18 (October 1992): 368.

9. Ferry, "Preaching," 369.

half-sister. This essentially reversed the country to its pre-1548 religious state. During the reign of Mary I (1553–1558), the nation veered harshly back toward Rome.[10] She refused the title of Supreme Head of the Church of England but, nevertheless, kept and enjoyed the power granted to the position. Mary was a devout Roman Catholic. She brokered a marriage with the Roman Catholic Philip of Spain, and steps were then taken to formalize the restoration with Rome. She instituted the English parallel of the Catholic Reformation by reinstating the Latin mass and lending the supremacy of the English church to the jurisdiction of the Roman pope. This set the stage for religious persecution of those refusing to accept these changes: married clergy were deprived of their livings, and leading Reformers who did not choose to hide or go into exile were imprisoned. Those who chose to hide formed secret congregations,[11] while those Protestants choosing exile fled to the Continent—many to Geneva, Strasbourg, Frankfurt, and Zurich—imbibing the doctrinal tenets of the Continental Reformers. Mary's government did not hinder their emigration.[12] While on the Continent, these Marian exiles were exposed to Presbyterian and Congregational principles and collectively formed eight English congregations.[13] Mary's suppression and persecution of Protestants came at the cost of 270 Protestant martyrs; among them were bishops Hugh Latimer, Nicholas Ridley, John Hooper, and Thomas Cranmer. All were martyred by being burned at the stake. Her approach earned her the infamous nickname Bloody Mary. Rather than stifling the movement, sympathy aroused by these martyrs fueled the cause of Protestantism.

As Mary grew increasingly ill and weak in the last months of her reign, "the exiles in their Protestant fastnesses were preparing for

---

10. Edwin S. Gaustad, "Quest for Pure Christianity," *Church History* 12, no. 41 (1994): 9.

11. Leon Howard, *Essays on Puritans and Puritanism*, ed. James Barbour and Thomas Quirk (Albuquerque: Univ. of New Mexico Press, 1986), 28.

12. Elton, *Reform and Reformation-England,* 383.

13. C. W. Dugmore, *The Mass and the English Reformers* (London: Macmillan, 1958), 207.

their return and concerting things with the secret friends" who had remained in England.[14] When the Catholic monarch Mary Tudor died, the way opened for Protestant reforms to take place in England. Bloody Mary's persecution of Protestant leaders and attempt to restore Catholicism died with her. News of her death was greeted with high expectations for a newly Reformed England. This turn of events fueled the hope of many whose spiritual and intellectual forerunners formed the posture of Puritanism.

The Puritan Movement in the Reign of Elizabeth I

The task before Elizabeth I (1558–1603) was difficult as she ascended the throne at the death of her half-sister, Mary. Mary's Catholic Reformation had been outwardly successful in revoking all the ecclesiastical legislation of Henry VIII and Edward VI and restoring the status and worship of the medieval church. In every other way, however, it had been a disaster. When Mary died and Elizabeth acceded to the throne, all indications were that the Church of England would become more Protestant than it had been at the death of Edward. But England's first experience in many years of a woman on the throne had not given Elizabeth a boost of confidence. At age twenty-five, Elizabeth began to rule a kingdom composed of sharply opposed religious interests that threatened political division and social disturbance. She had to deal with Catholic bishops left from Mary's reign and the returned Protestant exiles.

Elizabeth's first Parliament met late in January 1559. Many of the leading laymen among the exiles had already returned home by the time it opened. Full representation, however, was eclipsed due to the absence of some ecclesiastics, particularly those from Geneva. Those who remained on the Continent intentionally delayed their return, waiting to see the direction the queen and Parliament would take with the church. Nevertheless, lay exiles from the English churches in Switzerland and Germany played a critical role in the parliamentary proceedings with outside support from their clerical

---

14. Elton, *Reform and Reformation-England*, 395.

colleagues.[15] Her Parliament proceeded to pass two acts of utmost importance: the Act of Supremacy and Act of Uniformity, which, together, formed the Elizabethan Settlement.

The Elizabethan Settlement

The Act of Supremacy revived ten acts that Mary's Parliaments had repealed.[16] This new statute abolished the jurisdiction in England of any foreign prince, person, prelate, state or potentate, spiritual or temporal, within the queen's dominions. It also imposed an oath upon all ecclesiastical and lay officials acknowledging the queen alone as the "supreme governor," not as "supreme head," of "this realm, and of all other her highness' dominions and countries, as well as in all spiritual or ecclesiastical things or causes, as temporal."[17] This act nullified much of Mary's legislation and reopened the separation with Rome. The Act of Uniformity explicitly revived the second Act of Uniformity of Edward VI, defining the worship and doctrines of the church. Passing the Act of Uniformity in 1559 allowed for the use of the Book of Common Prayer, a work Cranmer produced during Edward VI's reign. This work, modified to include certain alterations and additions, stressed the use of English rather than Latin in church services, the reading of the Bible, and congregational participation in worship.

The Elizabethan Settlement in religion was an uneasy compromise. It retained a great deal from medieval Catholicism while making concessions to the new Protestantism.[18] In 1562 the Thirty-nine Articles became the official doctrinal creed and confession of the Church of England. It was essentially a renegotiation based on only slight modifications of the highly Protestant Forty-two Articles

---

15. Claire Cross, *Church and People, 1450–1660: The Triumph of the Laity in the English Church* (Atlantic Highlands, N.J.: Humanities Press, 1976), 127–28.

16. Philip Hughes, *The Reformation in England*, rev. ed. (London: Burns and Oates, 1963), 29.

17. Hughes, *Reformation in England*, 31.

18. Hugh Martin, *Puritanism and Richard Baxter* (London: SCM Press, 1954), 15.

of the Edwardian Reformers and served to retain the principles of *via media* and *adiaphora*. Elizabeth tried to secure comprehension, *via media* or the middle way, so that one inclusive religious organization would cover the whole country. The *via media* appealed to the English. They were fond of compromise, disliked extremes, excesses, and over-precise definitions,[19] though religion was not considered optional or voluntary. The Roman Church's argument of *adiaphora*, or "things indifferent," was that the validity of these matters was to be decided by the leaders of the church and government. Issues of rule or manners not specifically addressed in the Scriptures were taken under the authority of the church for judgment. Nevertheless, the Puritans' extreme reliance on Scripture led them to denounce the whole idea that certain religious observations were *adiaphora*. It was this emphasis on the Bible and rejection of *adiaphora* that led Puritans to criticize what they saw as ritualistic and formulaic liturgy in the Elizabethan church.[20] Their efforts to replace it with their own simpler and more attenuated forms of worship seemed inexorable, much to the chagrin of Elizabeth.

Unsettled with the Settlement

Hundreds of Marian exiles returned from Europe with the strong hope of resuming the Protestant Reformation begun under Edward VI. They desired to see the last vestiges of resemblance to the Church of Rome removed from the national church, to rid the Church of England of all evidences of its historic Catholic connection, and to let the New Testament determine church order and worship.[21] As the queen and her supporters tried to determine the character of their new national church, those who passionately sought to make the Protestant Reformation a redeeming reality on all of English life and culture desired to purify it. These came to be called Puritans.

---

19. David Martyn Lloyd-Jones, *The Puritans: Their Origins and Successors* (Edinburgh: Banner of Truth, 1987), 221.

20. Christopher Durston and Jacqueline Eales, *The Culture of English Puritanism: 1560–1700*, Themes in Focus (New York: St. Martin's Press, 1996), 17.

21. Gaustad, "Quest for Pure Christianity," 9.

While their name was initially used as a term of reproach and derision, the English Puritans emerged as a distinct group in the reign of Elizabeth I in the 1560s; their movement began and had intended to remain within the national church. The Puritans did not have any desire to divide or destroy the Church of England but sought Reformation from within and insisted on the liberty to pursue their goal of Reformation. They believed in an educated clergy, dedicated pastors who could expound the Scriptures, win the lost, discipline church members, and be personal examples to the flock. Though Elizabeth did not share their intense sentiment, the roots of Puritanism were firmly planted in the Elizabethan era as it took the form of an organized movement.[22]

Though the Elizabethan Settlement reversed the ecclesiastical trend established by Mary, it was not reforming enough to satisfy the more precise believers, the "hotter" sort of Protestants.[23] Most Puritans differed from their neighbors in the degree of their religiosity; that is, some were more intensely Protestant than their Protestant neighbors or even the Church of England.[24] They were not satisfied with the way the political break had worked out ecclesiastically. Elizabeth's Acts of Uniformity failed to rid England of the clerical vestments, ceremonies, and other visible remnants of Catholicism. The Puritans were convinced the Elizabethan church had abandoned the goal of further Reformation. Its motivation and efforts were half-hearted and, therefore, remained "halfly Reformed," precariously positioned halfway between Rome and Geneva. This fueled their insistence for a more

---

22. Puritanism as a cohesive entity continues to be the subject of considerable debate. See essays in Francis J. Bremer, ed., *Puritanism: Transatlantic Perspectives on a Seventeenth-Century Anglo-American Faith* (Boston: Massachusetts Historical Society, 1993); Patrick Collinson, *The Elizabethan Puritan Movement*, 22–28; Horton Davies, *The Worship of the English Puritans*; William Haller, *The Rise of Puritanism*, 5. Haller recognizes the influence of religious writers on the history of Puritan thought and asserts that historic Puritanism as a movement had begun early in Elizabeth's reign.
23. Collinson, *The Elizabethan Puritan Movement*, 27.
24. Spurr, *English Puritanism*, 4.

complete, fully Reformed church whose doctrines and worship were completely based on the teaching of Scripture alone.

But Elizabeth's actions and reactions reflected her steadfast policy to establish an English church that was neither too Roman nor Genevan[25] even if it meant backpedaling on some royal decisions. Elizabeth was driven by the conservative instincts of a new monarch that resulted in pragmatic compromise. Though she preserved much of the Edwardian Reformation, her approach was less resolute than her brother's. She was content with the mild climate of British Protestantism and even strove to subdue the radically dissident voices by persecution and deprivation of living.

Offended with the Genevan party, those most resistant to compromise,[26] Elizabeth favored the scheduled readings from the Book of Homilies crafted by Cranmer in Edward's reign as a more predictable alternative than the sermons of the Zurich-inspired prophesyings.[27] What had previously been employed as an exception to the rule would now be preferred as the rule; prophesyings would become the explicit context from which the origins of Puritan conference can be found.

The Prophesyings

The insistence upon a "lively preaching ministry" was the one change agreed upon and sought by the Reformers.[28] The revival of preaching under Edward VI was temporarily eclipsed under Mary and revived upon the accession of Elizabeth. The English Reformers advanced the claims of Scripture in opposition to the authority of popes and

---

25. F. Ernest Stoeffler, *The Rise of Evangelical Pietism* (Leiden: E. J. Brill, 1965), 24.

26. Emerson, *English Puritanism*, 9.

27. Susan Wabuda, *Preaching during the English Reformation*, Cambridge Studies in Early Modern British History (Cambridge: Cambridge Univ. Press, 2002), 14.

28. Collinson, *The Elizabethan Puritan Movement*, 23; Timothy George, "The Reformation Roots of the Baptist Tradition," *Review & Expositor* 86 (Winter 1989): 9.

councils, and they substituted the efficacious preaching of the Word for the primary emphasis on the sacraments as vehicles of grace.[29] Elizabethan Protestantism held fast to a preaching ministry.

Returning from the Continent, the Marian exiles found many churches without ministers because of deprivations. In reality the number was small indeed, and the number of ministers remained low until late in Elizabeth's reign.[30] To complicate the situation, the quality of the clergy, at least in the beginning of Elizabeth's reign, was very poor.[31] The clergy were so "ignorant and illiterate, that many who had cure of souls were incapable of preaching, or even of reading to the edification of the hearers."[32] The lack of competent, skilled clergy created an even more critical need in the Elizabethan church. The Puritans appeared more concerned than the queen in augmenting the quantity and quality of preaching. They believed the cause of reform among the English people depended upon the effective use of the pulpit.[33] Their urgent appeals to Elizabeth for an educated preaching clergy stemmed from their conviction that more preachers meant more people would be exposed to the Word of God. The diminished number and inabilities of preachers would impede the progress of reform.[34]

Elizabeth's response to the situation was a demand for strict observance of Cranmer's Book of Common Prayer and Articles of Religion. This did little to satisfy the Puritan longing for the sort of biblical preaching they had experienced in the great Reformed

---

29. Paul S. Seaver, *The Puritan Lectureships: The Politics of Religious Dissent, 1560–1662* (Stanford: Stanford Univ. Press, 1970), 15.

30. Emerson, *English Puritanism*, 7.

31. Alan Fager Herr, *The Elizabethan Sermon: A Survey and a Bibliography* (New York: Octagon Books, 1969), 18.

32. Daniel Neal, *The History of the Puritans: Or, Protestant Non-Conformists; from the Reformation in 1517 to the Revolution in 1688; Comprising an Account of their Principles; Their Attempts for a Further Reformation in the Church, Their Sufferings, and the Lives and Characters of their most Considerable Divines* (1837; repr., Minneapolis: Klock & Klock, 1979), 1:225.

33. Ferry, "Preaching," 362.

34. Ferry, "Preaching," 363.

churches on the Continent. In addition, when Elizabeth preferred and defended the reading of homilies for Sunday instruction, this did little to salve the tension, especially when such temporary expedients became accepted practices. When Puritan ministers were sequestered from their pulpits and deprived of their livings for nonconformity, some of the church's most vigorous Protestant preachers were silenced. Opposition inevitably followed.[35]

The number of parishes in need of ministerial leadership outnumbered the available and qualified clergy who could serve. Some pastors tended as many as four churches. A solution to the scarcity of preachers was found in the establishment of prophesyings—meetings of ministers for theological training, study of the Bible, and preaching expository sermons. This was followed by discussion on sound doctrine, life, and manners. It was the prophesyings that gave the Elizabethan church the appearance of a Reformed church and fostered the hope that, by this means, a full English Reformation would become a reality.[36]

Definition and Origin

The method designed to train ministers to interpret the Scriptures and practiced by some of the Continental Reformed churches was called prophesying. The ancestry of this institution is so called from the Pauline use of the term in 1 Corinthians 14:29–31, "Let the prophets speak two or three, and let the other judge.... For ye may all prophesy one by one, that all may learn, and all may be comforted" and 1 Thessalonians 5:20, "Despise not prophesyings."[37] Its provenance was the New Testament, where "prophesying" appears

---

35. Seaver, *Puritan Lectureships*, 17.

36. Patrick Collinson, "Prophesyings," in *Puritans and Puritanism in Europe and America: A Comprehensive Encyclopedia*, eds. Francis J. Bremer and Tom Webster (Santa Barbara, Calif.: ABC-CLIO, 2006), 495.

37. Patrick Collinson, John Craig, and Brett Usher, *Conferences and Combination Lectures in the Elizabethan Church: Dedham and Bury St Edmunds, 1582–1590*, Church of England Record Society (Woodbridge: Boydell, 2003), 28; Davies, *Worship of the English Puritans*, 189.

as a regular facet of Christian worship. The reappearance of prophesying coincides with the rediscovery of the New Testament at the Reformation.[38] In Zurich, this archetypal biblical conference was employed to train the nongraduate clergy with the proper approach and skill to preach and to maintain a general doctrinal agreement. Its origins are found in the 1520s, when *prophezei* was a daily exercise in the Grossmünster[39] where two or three speakers expounded on the exegesis of a text from the original languages. It was followed by a sermon on the same text of Scripture given in the language and for the benefit of the attending laity.[40] In Geneva, similarly named meetings were held weekly between a congregation and its pastor where the discussion of doctrine was open to all church members. This type of forum allowed any church member to discuss or dispute the doctrine taught by the ministers.[41] Some of the Marian exiles would have attended and observed these types of meetings in the towns where they lived, adopting and implementing them in England.

Prophesying in England

The earliest instance of prophesying in England appears to have been established by John Hooper (d. 1555), an Edwardian bishop and Marian martyr.[42] Having personally experienced the original model in Zurich, he imported this experiment with some modifications. His was a closed clerical exercise. Similar exercises appeared after Elizabeth's accession as some preachers took the initiative in the early 1560s in establishing exercises of prophesying in England. On returning to England from exile, an intentional effort was made

---

38. Nuttall, *The Holy Spirit*, 76.
39. "Great minister"; Huldrych Zwingli initiated the Reformation in Switzerland from his office at the Grossmünster, starting in 1520.
40. Collinson, Craig, and Usher, *Conferences and Combination Lectures*, 28.
41. Collinson, Craig, and Usher, *Conferences and Combination Lectures*, 29.
42. Collinson, "Prophesyings," 494; Collinson, Craig, and Usher, *Conferences and Combination Lectures*, 28.

to include prophesying in service books, where it is variously called "interpretation of the scriptures" and "prophecy."[43]

At St. Albans from 1560, early evidence shows the unlearned clergy meeting for theological training. In 1572, these meetings became public, and up to three speakers expounded before a lay audience.[44] Prophesyings also appeared at Norwich as early as 1564.[45] An operation of the institution in Northampton reveals the workings of the adult education program, where in addition to addressing biblical illiteracy, the tenets of Puritanism could be introduced within the legal limits of the Church of England and with cooperative ecclesiastical and secular authorities.[46] These public assemblies of preachers and aspirant preachers were held in market-town churches[47] and became common throughout England. Prophesying was a favorite exercise among Puritans. In these early days, prophesyings were simply a clerical exercise; preachers met to explore and cultivate the gift of preaching and to be joined together in a common fraternity. These assemblies of the preaching clergy were devoted to systematic biblical exposition, indoctrination, and homiletical training.[48] As supplemental, on-the-job training for the "godly clergy," it eased the transition from an academic training to a pastoral, preaching ministry, especially as the Elizabethan concern changed from an effort to quickly fill the many vacant pulpits to a belief that there was more to a truly Reformed ministry than an academic degree.[49]

---

43. Collinson, *The Elizabethan Puritan Movement*, 169.

44. Archdeacon David Kemp of St Albans to Bishop Edwin Sandys, 6 July 1576, cited in Collinson, Craig, and Usher, *Conferences and Combination Lectures*, 29.

45. Stanford E. Lehmberg, "Archbishop Grindal and the Prophesyings," *Historical Magazine of the Protestant Episcopal Church* 34 (June 1965): 89.

46. M. M. Knappen, *Tudor Puritanism: A Chapter in the History of Idealism* (Gloucester, Mass.: P. Smith, 1963), 253.

47. Collinson, *The Elizabethan Puritan Movement*, 127.

48. Collinson, *The Elizabethan Puritan Movement*, 51.

49. Tom Webster, *Godly Clergy in Early Stuart England: The Caroline Puritan Movement, 1620–1643* (Cambridge: Cambridge Univ. Press, 2002), 23.

The prophesyings also served in the indoctrination and homiletical training offered to ignorant clergy. Improvement was sought as the unlearned and nonpreaching clergy were brought under the tutelage and discipline of the graduate ministers.[50] Whether attended by the learned or unlearned, these exercises were more responsible than any other avenue in establishing and propagating Protestantism in Elizabethan England.

The benefits of having trained clergy in the parishes further popularized this exercise. A group of Puritans of Essex prayed that George Withers, the archdeacon of Colchester, would "erecte some like exercise as was the prophesy for the trialland increasing of mynisters giftes and for the acquaintynge of them together in love."[51] Where they were set up they were very popular, for they were a novelty; as Bishop Cooper of Lincoln once told Archbishop Grindal, "Gentlemen and gentlewomen will come in good…6 or 7 miles to a conference, that will hardlie come to a learned mans sermon."[52] None of the written orders for prophesying seems to have originated with the bishops who sanctioned them. Under a bishop who had empathy and sympathy for the preachers in this situation, however, there was a tendency for these exercises to come under Puritan influence, and equally for Puritan experiments to receive episcopal sanction.[53] The popularity and growth of prophesyings can be attributed to the official and semiofficial projects for clerical improvement, but more particularly to the spontaneous enterprise of the Puritan preachers themselves.[54] Preachers were responsible for the prophesying "both for their better exercise and also for the education of the people."[55] So effective was this means to improve the quality and skill of the clergy, that even with the queen's latter suppression of the prophesyings and the accompanied waning of

---

50. Collinson, *The Elizabethan Puritan Movement*, 210–11.
51. Morgan, *The Godly Preachers*, 70.
52. Lehmberg, "Archbishop Grindal and the Prophesyings," 124.
53. Collinson, *The Elizabethan Puritan Movement*, 174.
54. Collinson, *The Elizabethan Puritan Movement*, 170.
55. Collinson, *The Elizabethan Puritan Movement*, 172.

the bishops' interest, the godly clergy remained committed to its use. The enterprise of the Puritan ministers inspired, sustained, and propagated the prophesyings.

As the prophesyings evolved, they became an avenue to involve the laity in godly life. Consequently, the word "brother," first adopted by the preachers to describe their company or brotherhood, came to be applied to the laity who followed them.[56] This association may have proven significant in the attractiveness of the exercise as well as the solidarity formed in their communities.

Format of Prophesyings

The exercise of prophesying as practiced on the Continent was scholastic and intellectual in nature and was usually conducted in Latin. It was described as "a weekly exercise yearly from Easter to Michaelmas of all the ministers dwelling within 7 or 8 miles of the town. Upon a Monday they met about 9 a.m. Two were appointed to answer some question of divinity, and all the rest oppose each in his course or order."[57]

A high value was placed on sermons found in preaching conferences, or prophesyings. These religious exercises involved ministers meeting at a central church to exercise themselves in the exposition of Scripture. In England, this weekly practice found the preachers meeting at nine in a church convenient enough where many could attend. It would begin with some part of morning prayer, as set forth by law, and would lead into singing a hymn to the Holy Ghost.[58] A junior or youngest divine would first enter the pulpit where, for approximately half an hour, he would "contract his meditations, treated upon a portion of Scripture, formerly by a joint agreement assigned to him."[59] Four or five other divines followed who

---

56. Irvonwy Morgan, *Puritan Spirituality: Illustrated from the Life and Times of the Rev. Dr. John Preston* (London: Epworth Press, 1973), 107.

57. Morgan, *The Godly Preachers*, 70–71.

58. Morgan, *The Godly Preachers*, 88.

59. Thomas Fuller, *The Church History of Britain: from the Birth of Jesus Christ until the Year 1648* (London: T. Tegg, 1837), 3:6.

explained the meaning of the same passage. Finally, a more grave or experienced divine summed up the previous findings and added his own comments. As was a common practice in Zurich, the proceedings were brought to a close with a vernacular sermon preached to a lay audience. Prayer was then offered from the Book of Common Prayer for the whole church, the queen's majesty, and the realm. The session closed with the singing of a psalm.

The ministers then withdrew for conference in fraternal censure of the doctrine delivered and reflection of their own lives and conducts. The unlearned clergy who were not free to speak in the exercise were examined in the progress of their study. Attendees also took the time to share personal testimonies and to discuss issues from a range of matters.[60] Lastly, as a gathered community, the next meeting was determined, texts assigned, preachers deputed, and either a new moderator was selected or the previous one continued.[61] The high-level of interaction and accountability could not help but stimulate all levels of the clergy toward advancing in their studies and preaching skills.

Where an auditory was permitted, the godly sat with opened Geneva Bibles, searching the texts as cited by the preachers. This provided fertile instructional grounds for their learning. While the clergy met for conference, the laity could be found fervently discussing what they had heard among themselves: "all of them, men and women, boys and girls, labourers, workmen and simpletons."[62] This type of discourse possibly fueled the occasion for conference among the laity.

The Cambridge Version of Prophesyings

At first these prophesyings had no necessary connection with the universities and in many centers were established long before Laurence Chaderton became master of Emmanuel College at Cambridge.

---

60. Collinson, *The Elizabethan Puritan Movement*, 171–72.
61. Fuller, *Church History of Britain,* 122.
62. Collinson, *The Elizabethan Puritan Movement*, 175.

Sometimes called the "pope of Cambridge Puritanism," Chaderton drafted a model of an exercise that called for divinity students to integrate an extracurricular exercise in addition to their regular studies. The model, dating from the mid-1580s, is entitled, 'An order to be used for the trayning upp and exercising of Students in Divinitye whereby they may be made fitte and meete to discharge the dewties belonging to that profession.'[63] The two means of attaining the gifts necessary for a successful ministry were given: first, "mutual conference" on passages of Scripture, and second, disputation.

Chaderton's order includes an exposition of the correct form for such exercises, based firmly on the Pauline models, particularly 1 Corinthians 14:29. Hence, the common root of both the Emmanuel order and the Elizabethan prophesyings is provided in the same Pauline exhortation.[64] As the Puritan colleges began to provide a flow of preachers for churches, these regular gatherings of clergy perpetuated a godly familiarity first introduced to them in the university.[65]

Prophesyings Draw Concern from Elizabeth
By the 1570s, prophesyings were a common[66] and familiar practice to all. In some towns, Monday was "the day of the common exercise"; in others it was Saturday. Some towns had a regular pattern of prophesyings, while for others it was a novelty. There were congregational varieties and academic varieties. Sometimes prophesyings took the form of weekly meetings between pastor and congregation to discuss doctrine, or learned expositional labors conducted in Latin among scholars and students. Prophesyings were intended to assimilate graduate clergy, improve ignorant clergy, or promote a Puritan agenda. A lay audience could be present or completely absent. The prophesyings could be organized by an archdeacon or

---

63. Webster, *Godly Clergy*, 17.
64. Webster, *Godly Clergy*, 17–18.
65. Collinson, *The Elizabethan Puritan Movement*, 127.
66. Spurr, *English Puritanism*, 53.

initiated by the Puritan preachers themselves meeting weekly, fortnightly, or monthly. Some bishops were interested in, approved of, and encouraged the "good and godly" practice of prophesyings; others, because they lacked an understanding of the exercise, disapproved of them. Separatists as well as conformists employed the exercise of prophesyings.

There was, however, potential for abusing the practice and evidence of those who did. It was known that some slighted the preachers who regularly attended these exercises. The intended harmony within the group was open to jarring comments and internal conflict. Pastors sometimes included "impertinent excursions" in their sermons, using this forum to voice their displeasure over the authority or governing of the church.[67] The promoting of selfish agendas causing divisions and censuring could certainly prejudice an observer.

Perhaps it was the many variations of the exercise and the reported abuses that heightened Elizabeth's suspicions. In her eyes, these were not standardized exercises that produced predictable sermons or preachers that would conform to her program. In addition, the name, *prophesying,* "carried a whiff of chiliasm" for those who did not like the sound of it, including Queen Elizabeth.[68] Greater than the fear that the frequency and format of these exercises presented was the trepidation that rabid, nonstandardized preaching and preachers would breed a rebellious intellectualism. Prophesyings were problematic for Elizabeth, who remained committed to *via media* and *adiaphora*. She would not abandon her goal for a totally comprehensive church. Elizabeth sought to quell the potential for upheaval or unrest by suppressing the exercise. To do so required the enlistment of her archbishops.

---

67. Fuller, *Church History of Britain,* 122.
68. Collinson, Craig, and Usher, *Conferences and Combination Lectures,* 28.

The Queen and Her Archbishops

Elizabeth's decision to steer a middle course for her reign is apparent in her appointment of archbishops. Her control of the church would be extended through these select bishops. The queen had to accept a more Protestant religious settlement than she seemed to have intended, and she had to select bishops to enforce that settlement: men whose decidedly Protestant convictions ran counter to her more conservative tastes. To her disappointment, almost none of the bishops who served under Mary would serve in her church after the passing of the Acts of Supremacy and Uniformity.[69] Nevertheless, once episcopal subordination to the crown had been established, Elizabeth's interest was set in preserving the power of her bishops through whom she sought to control her church.[70]

Archbishop Matthew Parker

The deprivation of the Marian bishops caused numerous vacancies, especially in the higher levels of the church. The process of filling the vacant positions was slow and tedious. All the bishoprics were without active episcopal leadership for more than one to two years after Elizabeth's accession. The formidable task before Elizabeth was to find enough exceptional men whose philosophy of ministry resonated with hers; quality and quantity were of greatest importance. Though the vast majority of candidates were committed Protestant clergy who had gone into exile in the previous reign and experienced life in Reformed congregations on the Continent, the choice of her first Archbishop of Canterbury, Matthew Parker (1504–1575), was an exception. Virtually every other major bishopric went to former exiles.

Parker had a brilliant academic career and was a good scholar and administrator. He was moderate and tolerant in doctrine and, by personal taste, an antiquary rather than a theologian.[71] A merci-

---

69. Cross, *Church and People*, 131–32.
70. Cross, *Church and People*, 130.
71. A. G. Dickens, *Reformation and Society in Sixteenth-Century Europe* (London: Thames & Hudson, 1966), 186.

ful man, he did his best to avoid bloodshed.[72] Yet, he was not afraid to stand up to the queen if he thought her policy was mistaken. Much of Parker's primacy was devoted to superintending the production of the Bishops' Bible.[73] In the autumn of 1564, it was rumored that the queen was considering severe measures to enforce conformity in the church regarding the dress of the clergy and the use of the prayer book. The storm broke with the publishing of Archbishop Parker's *Advertisements* (1566).[74]

In January 1565, Elizabeth had remonstrated with Parker over the lack of outward conformity in the church. She ordered that the vestments clause of the Act of Uniformity be strictly observed. This led Parker to draw up his *Advertisements,* assuming they were to be issued as royal injunctions, approved by the queen. Though Elizabeth was unmistakably Protestant, she could be capricious, especially in the determination of church policy.[75] She refused to commit to the *Advertisements* and withdrew herself, leaving the archbishop and his fellow bishops with the *Advertisements* issued in his own name and the unpleasant task of attempting to dragoon the parochial clergy into obedience.[76] Both the Puritans and their orthodox brethren admitted that the Vestments or Vestiarian controversy, as it came to be called, was concerned not with fundamentals of faith and practice but with indifferent matters. These matters would be those that could be settled by the ministers themselves.

---

72. John R. H. Moorman, *A History of the Church in England* (London: A. and C. Black, 1961), 212.

73. Peter Newman Brooks, "The Principle and Practice of Primitive Protestantism in Tudor England: Cranmer, Parker and Grindal as Chief Pastors, 1535–1577," in *Reformation Principle and Practice,* ed. Peter Newman Brooks (London: Scolar Press, 1980), 125–26. Matthew Parker may have desired one of two intended objectives: (1) to reduce the circulation of the remarkably successful Geneva Bible, with its decidedly "presbyterian" understanding of ministry and thereby trump the Puritans, or (2) it may have been a skillful attempt by the primate to sharpen the biblical scholarship of his fellow bishops.

74. Morgan, *The Godly Preachers,* 33.

75. Emerson, *English Puritanism,* 7.

76. Cross, *Church and People,* 137.

In response to Parker's pleas of *adiaphora*, the recusants argued that if the wearing of surplices constituted a matter indifferent, then the bishop could have no justification in forcing them on those with tender consciences. Because the *Advertisements* were not issued with the queen's expressed authority, her subjects did not feel necessarily bound to use them. Archbishop Parker's attempts to enforce uniform practice led a number of Puritan clergymen to withdraw from their clerical posts, and their lay supporters angrily protested on their behalf.[77] Elizabeth's bishops learned very early in the reign the extent to which they depended upon the royal will. They discovered that not only in matters of discipline, but also doctrine, they had little power to act without at least the implicit authorization from the queen.[78]

The Queen, Archbishop Parker, and the Prophesyings
One matter in which Queen Elizabeth and Parker were in full agreement was the exercise of prophesying. Seen largely as a Puritan enterprise, they agreed these exercises were not part of the authorized infrastructure of the established church and her program for conformity. Even before these activities attracted unfavorable attention from those in authority, there was evidence of a church within the church. Elizabeth's suspicions toward the exercise prompted her to order them suppressed whenever she was reminded of their existence.

In 1574, reports of the activities of suspended Puritan preachers in two of the Norfolk prophesyings had led to the issuing of a general order to all bishops by Archbishop Parker for the suppression of "these vain exercises." This was at the queen's command,[79] but the clergy held that without instruction there was no hope that the country would accept any high standard of moral discipline.

---

77. Seaver, *Puritan Lectureships*, 4.
78. Cross, *Church and People*, 136.
79. Patrick Collinson, *Archbishop Grindal, 1519–1583: The Struggle for a Reformed Church* (Berkeley: Univ. of California Press, 1979), 235.

Without freedom of teaching, the whole structure would collapse. These gatherings of clergy, though they appeared to be for credible purposes, smacked of conspiracy against her throne. Elizabeth adamantly insisted on obedience, fearing the intellectual pursuits of her subjects would breed preposterous notions of equality or, worse, spiritual autonomy. Even with the shortage of trained ministers, the threat of "wild and uneducated preaching"[80] and any perceived potential for dissension and schism were enough to prompt the queen's prejudice against the prophesyings. She sought conformity of her subjects in standardized religious practices as the guarantee of stability and followed through with the orders for the regular reading of printed homilies.

The homilies presented by church administrators were read aloud by appointed lay or clerical readers. Together with official measures designed to suppress preaching, they reflected the government's desire to exercise control over the theology of the clergy.[81] The Puritans, the more uncompromising of the Reformers, believed that a homily read by a minister too ignorant to be licensed to preach was a poor substitute for the zealous expounding and application of the Scriptures by an educated clergyman.[82] The Reformers concluded that under Elizabeth's system the only uniformity was that of "dull ignorance."[83] The reading of homilies seemed to spur prophesyings as the movement reached its height in 1574 to 1576.

Archbishop Edmund Grindal

After Archbishop Parker's death in May 1575, Edmund Grindal (1516/20–1583) was nominated as successor in November and confirmed in February 1576. He was a Marian exile—the only one to serve as Archbishop of Canterbury—who had lived in Strasbourg, one of the chief settlements of English refugees. He occasionally

---

80. Davies, *Worship of the English Puritans*, 64.
81. Ferry, "Preaching," 363.
82. Seaver, *The Puritan Lectureships*, 17.
83. Knappen, *Tudor Puritanism*, 252–53.

visited other places, spending some time at Wassalheim, Spires, and Frankfort.[84] As Bishop of London, Grindal sympathized with the Puritans in their desire to abolish the remnants of popery. Still, he carefully enforced the queen's orders for uniformity, especially in the matter of clerical vestments. In 1570, he was elevated to the Archbishopric of York and seemed the natural successor to Matthew Parker. While he was Archbishop of York under Elizabeth, his initial visit to the diocese revealed the continuing ineptness of the clergy. He contended that where the clergy were incompetent, "by a necessary consequence the people cannot be well instructed."[85]

His nomination to Canterbury was urged upon the queen by her chief advisor, Lord Burghley, who shared Grindal's sympathy for the Reformers. Grindal had successfully ascended to places of prominence and distinction in the church, but his final and highest advancement would bring about the most troubling time of his life. As archbishop, he continued to observe the ignorance of the clergy and the great need of more frequent preaching for the people in the foundational truths of religion. He followed closely in the tradition of those Edwardian Reformers who emphasized preaching as a primary function of the ministry and had the closest sympathies to the Puritans of all the prelates. Consequently, he was familiar with the exercise of prophesying and found great value in its use. Grindal understood the energizing force that drove the persistence of the godly preachers and the need for evangelical preaching in the church. He firmly believed with the Puritans that the "public and continual preaching of God's word is the ordinary mean and instrument of the salvation of mankind."[86] As Archbishop of Canterbury,

---

84. Edmund Grindal, *The Remains of Edmund Grindal: Successively Bishop of London and Archbishop of York and Canterbury*, ed. William Nicholson and Great Britain Ecclesiastical Commissioners for England (Cambridge: Printed at the Univ. Press, 1843), 3.

85. Cited in Patrick Collinson, "Reformer and the Archbishop: Martin Bucer and an English Bucerian," *Journal of Religious History* 6 (December 1971): 327.

86. Morgan, *The Godly Preachers*, 92.

Grindal sought to execute certain reforms and continued his policy of improving clerical education by urging his clergy, many of them decidedly "puritan," to attend prophesyings. He looked with a favorable eye upon the exercises, "considering they might, notwithstanding certain incidental inconveniences, be made, in the main, subservient to the cause of true religion."[87] Under the archbishop's auspices, prophesyings continued to flourish.

Noting the need to redress the indiscretions and "mischiefs," Grindal devised a brief set of rules for the regulation of the exercises, thereby protecting them from the objections of the court. He redressed the irregularities and mischiefs[88] by setting down rules and orders for the more useful management of these exercises. It bore this title: *Orders for reformation of abuses about the learned exercises and conferences amongst the ministers of the church*. It is possible Burghley consulted with the archbishop in the framing of these directions.

Within six months of Grindal's serving as Archbishop of Canterbury, Elizabeth voiced her displeasure at his encouragement of the prophesyings. She feared the potential for abuse of such gatherings: that they would serve as opportunities for the dissemination of Puritan doctrine and the outbreak of civil disturbance and prove to be "the bane of the church and commonwealth."[89] Grindal maintained that with proper regulations in place, they posed no such danger and that they were indispensable means for the formation and maintenance of a more learned ministry. The queen would not be convinced; rather, she believed:

> [These meetings] gave encouragement to novelty, made people ramble in their fancy, and neglect their affairs. That their curiosity was too much indulged, and their heads over-

---

87. Brooks, "The Principle and Practice," 181.
88. John Strype, *The History of the Life and Acts of the Most Reverend Father in God, Edmund Grindal…to which is Added an Appendix of Original Mss*, Burt Franklin Research and Source Work Series, Philosophy and Religious History Monographs 145 (New York: B. Franklin, 1974), 220–21.
89. Fuller, *Church History of Britain*, 2.

charged with notions by these discourses; and that by raising disputes, and forming parties, things might possibly grow up to a public disturbance.[90]

Fearful that the prophesyings would "occasion dissensions and unquiet disputes,"[91] she held that the kingdom was over-furnished with such instructions.

By the summer of 1576, she commanded that the exercise of prophesying be suppressed.[92] The queen also preferred the number of preachers to be reduced and preached sermons be replaced by read homilies: "that it was good for the Church to have few preachers, and that three or four might suffice for a county; and that the reading of homilies to the people was enough."[93] She expected her archbishop to follow through with peremptory orders that aligned with her commands, earning her title of "supreme governor" of the church.

In Defense of Prophesyings

As Archbishop of Canterbury and Chief Pastor, Grindal felt compelled to lead the ministry by defending a critical Reformation principle against infringement from the crown. Anxious to convince the queen that the prophesyings should continue, he sent letters surveying his diocesan bishops. They were asked to describe the status of the exercise being held in each ordinary jurisdiction and to communicate their assessments concerning them. The bishops' responses, dated from July through December, reveal much on the religious climate in Elizabethan England, especially with regard to the prophesyings.[94]

Encouraged and enlivened by the support of the bishops, Grindal asked the queen to allow the continuation of the exercises. When a personal audience with the queen proved futile, the archbishop chose

---

90. Grindal, *Remains of Edmund Grindal*, 11.
91. Grindal, *Remains of Edmund Grindal*, 375.
92. Lehmberg, "Archbishop Grindal and the Prophesyings," 87–88.
93. Strype, *History of the Life*, 329.
94. Lehmberg, "Archbishop Grindal and the Prophesyings," 88.

a challenging course of action. On December 8, 1576,[95] Grindal dared to write a lengthy and celebrated letter to the queen arguing for the preaching exercises, and if the queen preferred to replace him, he would offer to resign. His refusal to be the queen's instrument in suppressing the prophesyings was cause for royal dismay.

Queen Elizabeth's order for the suppression of prophesyings prompted this puzzled reply from her archbishop:

> But surely I cannot marvel enough how this strange opinion should once enter into your mind, that it should be good for the church to have few preachers. Alas, Madam! Is the scripture more plain in any one thing, than that the gospel of Christ should be plentifully preached, and that plenty of labourers should be sent into the Lord's harvest; which, being great and large, standeth in need, not of a few, but many workers?[96]

What disturbed the archbishop was the queen's attitude toward both the prophesyings and preaching as a whole. He was dismayed that she thought it was profitable for the church to have few preachers and that the homilies were better for the people than a sermon.

Grindal's indirect response was in defense of preaching

> [as] the ordinary mean and instrument of the salvation of mankind. St. Paul calleth it the ministry of reconciliation of man unto God. By preaching of God's word the glory of God is enlarged, faith is nourished, and charity increased. By it the ignorant is instructed, the negligent exhorted and incited, the stubborn rebuked, the weak conscience comforted, and to all those that sin of malicious wickedness the wrath of God is threatened.[97]

Grindal unwaveringly held that by preaching, "due obedience to Christian princes and magistrates is planted in the hearts of subjects: for obedience proceedeth of conscience; conscience is grounded

---

95. For an explanation of the correct date, often given in error as 20 December, see Collinson, "Reformer and the Archbishop," 391.
96. Grindal, *Remains of Edmund Grindal,* 378.
97. Grindal, *Remains of Edmund Grindal,* 379.

upon the word of God; the word of God worketh his effect by preaching. So as generally, where preaching wanteth, obedience faileth."[98] He asserted that the preaching of God's Word made loyal subjects. He reminded the queen that from Yorkshire, where preaching flourished, a significant number of men served her against rebels, whereas rebellion in the north was fueled by ignorance of God's Word.[99]

He was not alone in supporting the prophesyings that informed this kind of preaching; they were ordained and approved by bishops. His experience showed that these exercises produced a zealous and able ministry and corrected the lay opinion that the clergy were an idle lot. He assured the queen that these exercises were subject to strict rules and then reminded her that in religious matters she should be guided and limited by her clergy, just as in legal matters she was by her judges. He hoped the queen would reconsider her legal authority in ecclesiastical matters, finally reminding Elizabeth of her ultimate position as a mortal creature: "And although ye are a mighty Prince, yet remember that He which dwelleth in heaven is mightier."[100] She was ultimately accountable to God.

The boldness and confidence to write such a letter stemmed from his commitment to such an exercise and also the graciousness that had been extended to him by the queen.[101] But the archbishop stood powerless in persuading the queen to tolerate the prophesyings, no matter how carefully he argued for its regulation. Elizabeth would not tolerate this breach of her program for conformity. Her steely determination to pursue the suppression of the prophesyings was consistent with her commitment to *via media*. In May 1577, seeing that Grindal would not be instrumental in it, Queen Elizabeth bypassed the archbishop and sent her own commandment to the rest of the diocesan bishops. In formal letters she ordered for the suppression of the public exercise by those "pretending to a more

---

98. Grindal, *Remains of Edmund Grindal*, 378–79.
99. Grindal, *Remains of Edmund Grindal*, 380.
100. Knappen, *Tudor Puritanism*, 256.
101. Fuller, *Church History of Britain*, 4.

purity."[102] Grindal's assessment of Her Majesty's policy seemed unbiblical for Elizabeth; it was national preservation. As with the archbishop who preceded him, Grindal found he, too, was no match for Elizabeth.

Defeat for Prophesyings

By June 1577, the queen had decided to order Grindal's suspension and sequestration.[103] By order of the Privy Council, the archbishop was confined to his house and sequestered for six months. Elizabeth never allowed his sequestration to be completely rescinded before his death in 1583. Grindal spent the greater part of his primacy in retirement and disgrace. In January 1578, there was some discussion of depriving him, but the proposal was so poorly received that it was immediately dropped.[104] His relationship with Elizabeth was strained, and although he occasionally received some tokens of Elizabeth's friendly regard, he never entirely emerged.[105] His courageous defense of the means to bring the educational level of ordinary parish ministers to a biblical knowledge requisite for the profitable instruction of the people brought him a reputation for godliness that many Puritan clergy and laity never forgot.[106]

The demise of the prophesyings was greeted with great disappointment from all the godly: "With heavy hearts we will yield to your commandments, giving over this godly exercise until we by prayer and petition may again obtain it," wrote Anthony Gilby (ca. 1510–1585), a Church of England clergyman and one of the translators of the Geneva Bible, and other ministers of Ashby.[107] It was conceivable that this pictured the end of prophesyings, this useful practice for advancing Christian knowledge and piety, at a time

---

102. Emerson, *English Puritanism*, 18–19.
103. Lehmberg, "Archbishop Grindal and the Prophesyings," 92–93.
104. Grindal, *Remains of Edmund Grindal*, 12–13.
105. Grindal, *Remains of Edmund Grindal*, 11.
106. Cross, *Church and People*, 146–47.
107. Cited in Collinson, *The Elizabethan Puritan Movement*, 209.

when both were at low ebb in England.[108] Yet, prophesyings did not suffer the same fate as their most staunch supporter, the archbishop. That the meetings were fully abandoned is doubtful. Though in the southern province they were effectively prohibited, in many other areas where the queen's ban did not extend, the exercises continued, receiving the support of secular and ecclesiastical authorities alike.

Puritan Conference Emerges

Many sympathetic observers were persuaded that private conferences of the clergy, which were a typical addendum to prophesyings, were not covered by the queen's ban.[109] Though prophesyings may have been banned, conferences were allowed to continue. A program of reforms established a monthly exercise that resembled prophesying, except that a single sermon was to replace the multiple ones presented before the people. Lasting for an hour from 9 a.m. to 10 a.m. and followed by a private conference of the ministers until 1 p.m., both the skilled and unskilled clergy assembled for academic and socialization needs. In some places, the life of the Puritan preachers revolved around these regular conferences with their brethren. The doctrinal, homiletical, and expositional exercises drew the ministers together and, combined with conference, nurtured the spiritual brotherhood characteristic of the Puritan clergy.

The meetings of preaching ministers were never put to a stop and were never or could never have been halted by ecclesiastical authority. In communities where the presiding bishops were inclined to support conference, the practice and the spiritual brotherhood flourished. Biblical knowledge and communal care continued to thrive. Where the bishops were less supportive, the meetings became more secretive, being hosted in homes instead of parish churches or inns. The exercise of conference, which succeeded the prophesyings, was private and

---

108. Neal, *History of Puritans*, 1:235.
109. Collinson, *The Elizabethan Puritan Movement*, 209.

always held in the house of one of the brethren.[110] It continued to be a discipline exercised by the clergy, and was adopted by the laity as well.

Richard Greenham describes conference as that which is employed "with Ministers of God, Our equals, Or others."[111] Just as with matters of the natural order, people need assistance; likewise, people should investigate and explore spiritual matters in community. Richard Bernard expounds on conference as the "asking of superiors and Ministers, by reasoning with equals, and teaching inferiours, all in reverence and humility, to understand that I know not, to be resolved in that I doubt of, and to call to memorie what I have forgotten."[112] Further commenting on the profit one gains from this exercise and its importance to growth in godliness, Thomas Watson pens, "Good conference enlightens the mind when it is ignorant; warms it when it is frozen; settles it when it is wavering. A good life adorns Religion; good discourse propagates it."[113]

The use of conference was not only encouraged but was also given as a charge to exercise. This type of religious discourse required

> [that minds be] well furnished with knowledge. Hereby, you will have a Treasure to fetch from.... If you would have your Tongues run fluently in Religion, they must be fed with a spring of knowledge.... So we must first have our Heads filled with knowledge, and then we shall be able to draw out to others in Good discourse.[114]

It could be exercised in small enough gatherings so as to procure "things honest before men, that it may be done wisely, without con-

---

110. Morgan, *The Godly Preachers*, 158.
111. Richard Greenham, *The Workes of the Reverend and Faithfull Servant of Jesus Christ M Richard Greenham* (London: Imprinted by Felix Kingston, 1599), 369.
112. Richard Bernard, *Josuahs Resolution for the Well Ordering of His Household* (London: Printed for John Legatt, 1629), 51–52.
113. Watson, *Heaven Taken by Storm*, 72–73.
114. Watson, *Religion Our True Interest, or, Practical Notes upon the Third Chapter of Malachy the Sixteen, Seventeen and Eighteen Verses* (London: Printed by J. Astwood, 1682), 100.

fusion and destruction: & not by too great a multitude, that wee may affoord our doings before men."[115] A seventeenth-century author further describes those who engaged in this practice as

> those who were thus Convened, were a Select Number of Holy Experience'd Souls, full of Zeal for God's Glory, and Love to each other; being under the Sacred Influences of the Same Spirit, Exciting and Stirring them up, to sequester themselves from the World, and from Sinners; that they might the more freely and mutually discourse of Divine Matters, to each others Edification, and sweet Satisfaction.[116]

This discourse would find its bearings in the Scriptures, as Greenham explains:

> This rule must be kept that conference with our equals must be of those things which we heard of our Ministers, as it must be kept also in meditation, which is conference with ourselves. We must for a time like babes hang at the mouthes of the Ministers, because we cannot runne before we goe: nay we cannot goe without a leader.[117]

Conference was exercised among the clergy, clergy with members of the congregation, and in groups of godly laity. The Puritan view of Scripture and its authority played heavily in conference; the discoveries found in the biblical text, wedded to their piety, fueled this communal practice. From parish to household, whether academic or popular, clergy present or not, conference became a widely accepted means of grace among the godly: it was a form of enabling that was engaged and enjoyed.

---

115. Greenham, *Workes*, 370.
116. Anonymous, *Stated Christian Conference Asserted to be a Christian Duty* (London: Printed for and sold by Will. Marshal, 1697), 14.
117. Greenham, *Workes*, 369.

CHAPTER THREE

Scripture for Puritan Eyes: The Word Read

The plethora of Puritan sermons, treatises, tracts, and theological writings continues to provide ample evidence of the one doctrinal tenet that stands at the head of their theology: the authority of Scripture. The Puritan view of Scripture and its authority played heavily in everyday life; the discoveries found in the biblical text, wedded to their piety, fueled their daily existence. It was central to the piety, sine qua non of the spiritual life: the source of divine wisdom. The revealed Word of God was central to all doctrinal, intellectual, and moral life in the sixteenth and seventeenth centuries.[1] It served as the Puritans' devotional book as well as "a revelation given through things which happened in history, and which it exactly records."[2] In fact, the Bible was the only authority that the Puritan acknowledged in matters of religion: "the booke of bookes."[3]

The contemporary church continues to exhibit signs and symptoms of a void in the understanding and practicality of biblical knowledge. Biblical literacy continues its downward trend, and the church is in need of recapturing the power and impact Scripture affords. Our Protestant predecessors regarded the Word of God, in the form of private and public Bible reading and sermons, as the

---

1. Durston and Eales, *Culture of English Puritanism,* 16; Christopher Hill, ed., *The English Bible and the Seventeenth-Century Revolution* (London: Penguin, 1994), 20.

2. Wakefield, *Puritan Devotion,* 19.

3. Richard Rogers, *Seven Treatises* (London: Printed by the assignes of Thomas Man, 1630), 379.

ultimate authority. As Christians today study these roots of Protestant spirituality, may they likewise find their hearts inflamed with a passion for the Word.

Reformation Roots

The Puritan devotion to and zeal for Scripture was at the very heart of Puritanism. The vitality of the movement was derived from the Puritans' study of the Bible. Because Puritans were united in their dependence upon the Bible as their supreme source of spiritual sustenance and guide for the reformation of life, Puritanism has been regarded as "a Bible movement."[4] Tracing its historical ties to the Reformation will further an understanding of the Puritan view of Scripture; an examination of these roots suggests why they held the Word of God as authoritative. It explains Scripture's role in the sermon and how the Puritan sought to retain the Word preached for growing in godliness. Growth in the understanding and application of God's Word was critical for a growth in godliness.

Though the Protestant Reformation of the sixteenth century created significant doctrinal distancing from Roman Catholic tradition, the inspiration and authority of the Holy Scripture was not a disputed issue between Roman Catholics and Protestants. All of the Reformers accepted both the divine origin and infallible character of the Bible. One of the questions that emerged during the Reformation was how the divinely attested authority of Holy Scripture was related to the authority of the church and the ecclesiastical tradition of the Roman Church. The *sola* in *sola scriptura* was not intended to disregard completely the value of church tradition but, rather, to subordinate it to the primacy of Holy Scripture. While the Roman Church appealed to the witness of the church to validate the authority of the canonical Scriptures, the Protestant Reformers held to Scripture's self-authenticating witness of the Holy Spirit; it was deemed trustworthy on the basis of its own perspicuity evidenced by the internal witness of the Holy Spirit.

---

4. J. I. Packer, "Theology on Fire," *Christian History* 41, no. 12 (1994): 32.

The Bible was authoritative, based on the divine inspiration and testimony of the Holy Spirit and the self-evidencing power of Scripture. Calvin affirms:

> For by a kind of mutual bond the Lord has joined together the certainty of his Word and of his Spirit so that the perfect religion of the Word may abide in our minds when the Spirit, who causes us to contemplate God's face, shines; and that we in turn may embrace the Spirit with no fear of being deceived when we recognize him in his own image, namely, in the Word. God did not bring forth his Word among men for the sake of a momentary display, intending at the coming of his Spirit to abolish it. Rather, he sent down the same Spirit by whose power he had dispensed the Word, to complete his work by the efficacious confirmation of the Word.[5]

The words of Scripture are the very words of God, and the Reformers believed the verity of every word. Calvin states, "Hence the Scriptures obtain full authority among believers only when men regard them as having sprung from heaven, as if there the living words of God were heard."[6] Countering the papacy, he asserts that the Scriptures were given to the apostles and to the early church in a complete and pure form without the requirement of any doctrinal system, creed, laws, or body of authority. The true gospel was obscured by those who claimed to be ministers of the Word, as stated:

> [Those] who not only conceal and encourage the ignorance of the people by their silence, but also take no notice of gross errors and impious superstitions, are impudent in their boasts that they are ministers of the Word. Indeed, that sort of thing is to be found in the Papacy today, where a great many give out sparks of sound doctrine, but do not dare to scatter the darkness of ignorance, and, while a depraved fear of the flesh

---

5. John Calvin, *The Institutes of the Christian Religion*, ed. John T. McNeill (Louisville: Westminster, 1960), 1.9.3.

6. Calvin, *Institutes*, 1.7.1.

keeps them back, they make the excuse that the people are not capable of more solid teaching.[7]

The Reformation was a period of rediscovery of the canonical Scriptures. The conviction that Scripture had been retrieved and restored in true form and meaning was the single most important force in post-Reformation biblical exegesis.[8]

The Continental Reformation grew from the Word and in turn fostered an ardent attention to the Word. As the Reformation spread to England, the "word-centeredness"[9] remained consistent with its Reformation roots. Those who passionately sought to make the Protestant Reformation a redeeming reality on all of English life and culture, thus "purifying" it, came to be known as Puritans. The Puritans sought reformation mostly from within the Church of England, seeking to purge it of all evidences of its historic Catholic connection and to let the New Testament determine church order and worship. Both the Puritans and those opponents in the established church subscribed to the sixth of the Thirty-nine Articles: "Holy Scripture containeth all things necessary to salvation: so that whatsoever is not read therein, nor may be proved thereby, is not required of any man, that it should be believed as an article of Faith, or be thought requisite or necessary to salvation."[10] In general, the established clergy accepted Luther's doctrine of the authority of the Scriptures—that it contained the articles of belief necessary for salvation but did not dictate forms of worship or church govern-

---

7. John Calvin, *The Acts of the Apostles*, ed. David W. Torrance and Thomas Forsyth Torrance, trans. W. Fraser John (Grand Rapids: Eerdmans, 1966), 174.

8. Edward Davidson, "John Cotton's Biblical Exegesis: Method and Purpose," *Early American Literature* 17, no. 2 (Fall 1982): 119.

9. Daniel W. Doerksen and Christopher Hodgkins, *Centered on the Word: Literature, Scripture, and the Tudor-Stuart Middle Way* (Newark: Univ. of Delaware Press, 2004), 26. The meaning of "word-centering," used by Peter Lake, reflects the Elizabethan and Jacobean prominence given to sermons and lectures—the Word preached—many of which found their way into print as well.

10. Mark A. Noll, ed., *Confessions and Catechisms of the Reformation* (Grand Rapids: Baker, 1991), 215.

ment. The Puritans accepted Calvin's conception of the authority of Scriptures for doctrine, forms of church government, and methods of worship. In their view, if the Bible is binding on one issue, it is binding in all issues. Puritans regarded it as inconsistent for the established church to hold the Bible as authoritative in matters of belief and not extend its authority to matters of government and worship. The Puritans, standing on the shoulders of Calvin, were not willing to accept the selective limits that tradition had held.

The Puritan View of Scripture
The place of Scripture in Puritan thought has always received notice. Recent scholarship confirms the continuing interest in the religious and social impact of Scripture in Puritan life.[11] The Puritans regarded Scripture as the supreme and final religious authority. William Ames (1576–1633), a Puritan theologian and university teacher, reflects Calvin's thought: "The Scripture is perfect in its operation in us because it is the vehicle of the Holy Spirit."[12] God has chosen to reveal Himself through the Spirit in the Word. In *The Marrow of Theology*, a theological treatise that comes as close to a systematic theology as any Puritan writing, Ames addresses the questions of the Bible's authority: "What the authors have committed to writing, in terms of its substance and chief end is nothing else than the revealed word of God, which is the rule of faith and morals." Regarding sufficiency, Ames states, "Scripture is not a partial but a perfect rule of faith and morals. And no observance can be continually and everywhere necessary in the church of God, on the basis of tradition or other authority, unless it is contained in

---

11. Davies, *Worship of the English Puritans*; Doerksen and Hodgkins, *Centered on the Word*; Lisa M. Gordis, *Opening Scripture: Bible Reading and Interpretive Authority in Puritan New England* (Chicago: Univ. of Chicago Press, 2003); Hill, *The English Bible*; John Ray Knott, *The Sword of the Spirit: Puritan Responses to the Bible* (Chicago: Univ. of Chicago Press, 1980).

12. William Ames, *Disputatio Theologica, De Perfectione* (Cantabrigia: Ex officina Rogeri Danielis, 1646), 3.

Scriptures."[13] Ames agrees with the usual Reformed assertion that the Bible should be regarded as perfection.

Though the Westminster Confession would not be drawn up until 1643 and completed in 1646, these tenets—echoes of the early Puritans—appear once again. Concerning the Bible, the confession declares that "our full persuasion and assurance of the infallible truth and divine authority is from the inward work of the Holy Spirit, bearing witness by and with the Word in our hearts"(1.5). The Holy Scriptures are the Word of God, the only infallible rule of faith and practice:

> The authority of the Holy Scripture...dependeth not on the testimony of any man or Church; but wholly upon God (who is truth itself) and the author thereof...our full persuasion and assurance of the Holy Spirit, bearing witness, by and with the Word, in our hearts.... Nothing is at any time to be added—whether by new revelations of the Spirit or traditions of men.... The Church is finally to appeal to them.... The infallible rule of interpretation of Scripture is the Scripture itself.[14]

The Bible alone is authority. It was the means of perfection as well as the source of truth. Given its perfect, divine author, Scripture must also be perfect.

The Puritans believed that the primary principle of the Reformation was adherence to the Word of God;[15] they insisted the Scriptures be the only and final authority. The Bible was not authoritative solely because the church declared it so. They regarded tradition with suspicion in its impact on all aspects of the Christian life: corporate, societal, and personal. The distrust for ceremonial religion grew; set prayers and sacraments were incapable of allowing for the fullest movement of the Holy Spirit.

---

13. William Ames, *The Marrow of Theology*, ed. and trans. John D. Eusden, (1629; repr. Grand Rapids: Baker, 1997), 187.

14. Henry Scowcroft Bettenson, *Documents of the Christian Church*, 2nd ed. (London: Oxford, 1963), 347.

15. Davies, *Worship of Puritans*, 8.

The Puritans sought to carry out the Reformation to its logical, though not inevitable, conclusion, and eliminate from the established church the forms, rituals, and ceremonies for which no basis or warrant existed in the Bible. William Bradshaw (bap. 1570, d. 1618), one of the intellectual fathers of the Independents, describes the position he regards as characteristic of the English Puritans:

> IMPRIMIS they houlde and maintaine *that the word of God contained in the writings of the Prophets and apostles, is of absolute perfection, given by Christ, the Head of the Churche, to be unto the same the sole Canon and rule of all matters of Religion, and the worship and service of God whatsoever. And that whatsoever done in the same service and worship cannot bee justified by the said word, is unlawfull. And therefore that it is a sinne, to force any Christian to doe any act of religion or divine service, that cannot evidently bee warranted by the same.*[16]

The inspired Word of God was the source for knowing God's will for the church and for the individual's daily life. From the Bible only could people receive the assurance of salvation. William Perkins (1558–1602), the theologian of the Elizabethan Puritan preachers and "Prince of Puritan theologians," writes, "We must further know that every article and doctrine concerning faith and manners, which is necessary unto salvation, is very plainly delivered in the scriptures."[17] The Puritans sought biblical knowledge, not simply for personal intellectual assent or as a means of advancing material interests, but because salvation and growth in godliness was impossible without it.

The Bible was not relegated as a reference tool for periodic use, but was the living Word of the living God. Holy Scripture was critical for the Puritan; reading it was imperative for it contained the words for life. Puritan reverence for God meant reverence for Scrip-

---

16. William Bradshaw, *English Puritanisme* (London: W. Jones's secret press, 1605), A2.

17. William Perkins, *The Work of William Perkins*, ed. Ian Breward (Abingdon, England: Sutton Courtenay Press, 1970), 339.

ture, and serving Him meant obedience to His Word. The Puritan sought to know and do all that it prescribed. God's Word was the foundation and constant guide in Puritan spirituality.

A Private Means of Grace: The Word Read
Private Bible Reading

Private Bible reading was an essential practice of Puritan piety. It was not only a Christian duty but also a mark of godliness; it was a daily activity so commonplace, so familiar and private, that it often went unrecorded. The Bible was regarded as "indispensable," the reading of which was "deemed necessary to all good Englishmen."[18] The reading of the Scriptures was the heart of Puritan religion.[19] Samuel Crossman (bap. 1625. d. 1684), a Church of England clergyman, states that the godly man is "one that loves and delights indeed in his Bible."[20]

The translation most commonly used was the English-language Geneva Bible, the work of Marian exiles. First published as a whole in 1560, the vernacular Bible of the sixteenth century was still a new thing, bought with martyr's blood.[21] This version introduced the numbering of the verses and included some "most profitable annotations"—marginal notes that clearly reflected the Reformed theology of Geneva.[22] These notes offered interpretations different from those of the Homilies and were supplemented by translations of Calvin's

---

18. Louis B. Wright, *Religion and Empire: The Alliance between Piety and Commerce in English Expansion, 1558–1625* (Chapel Hill: Univ. of North Carolina Press, 1943), 53.

19. Spurr, *English Puritanism*, 74.

20. Samuel Crossman, *The Young Mans Monitor* (London: Printed by J. H., 1664), 131.

21. Wakefield, *Puritan Devotion*, 15.

22. Wakefield, *Puritan Devotion*, 14; Ian Green, *Print and Protestantism in Early Modern England* (Oxford: Oxford, 2000), 73–74. Green finds that the Geneva Bible offered more direction and more specific advice on how to study the Bible. He observes that the marginal notes were exegetical rather than controversial, "assisting the reader in understanding an unusual term or metaphor, or to provide a paraphrase of an otherwise puzzling literal translation."

commentaries and sermons on books of the Bible. English bishops felt compelled to produce their own version without the Calvinistic marginal notes. Even with the advent of the Bishops' Bible in 1568, the Geneva Bible continued to be preferred, read, and studied by all classes of the population.[23] Its popularity continued even after the introduction of the Authorized Version of 1611,[24] but its last edition was printed in 1644.

The radical Protestants' intentions were to publish inexpensive editions of the Bible that were small and pocketable. The failure to print cheap editions of the Bishops' Bible of 1568 aided in making the Geneva Bible the Bible of the people.[25] The printing presses dispersed the new English versions of the Bible that helped meet the demand for copies and helped to foster literacy and the desire for further knowledge. The booksellers' shelves carried large portions of Bibles, collections of sermons, theological treatises, and meditations.[26] The number of Bibles and New Testaments published in England between the Reformation and 1640 has been estimated at over one million,[27] peaking in the 1630s.[28]

Richard Rogers (1551–1618), a Church of England clergyman and author, states that Bible reading is a "helpe to godliness": "For a minde well seasoned before, shall be undoubtedly better seasoned and refreshed, when it shall usually and oft drink the water of life, out of the sweet fountaine of Gods word by reading."[29] Richard Greenham (ca. 1535–1594), a patriarch of the spiritual brotherhood of Puritan preachers and a contemporary of Rogers, encourages the reading of the Word:

---

23. Gerald Lewis Bray, ed., *Documents of the English Reformation* (Minneapolis: Fortress Press, 1994), 355.
24. Hill, *The English Bible*, 56, 58.
25. Hill, *The English Bible*, 17–18.
26. Doerksen and Hodgkins, *Centered on the Word*, 15.
27. C. John Sommerville, "On the Distribution of Religious and Occult Literature in Seventeenth-Century England," *The Library*, fifth series, vol. 29, no. 2 (1974): 223.
28. Green, *Print and Protestantism*, 53.
29. Rogers, *Seven Treatises*, 390.

> [It] helpeth mens judgements, memories and affections, but especiallie it serveth for the confirmation of our faith: which may bee prooved by the example of the men of Berea, Act.17.13. It serveth to discerne the spirits of men, 1.Joh.4. To make sounder confession of our faith, to stop the mouthes of our adversaries, and to answere the temptations of Satan and the wicked.[30]

His appeal for a faithful reading of the Scriptures stems from his understanding of the condition of man:

> But because men sinne, not onely in neglect of hearing and reading, but also in hearing, and reading amisse: therefore the properties of reverent and faithful reading and hearing, are to be set downe, which are these that follow: they be eight in number. 1. Diligence, 2. Wisedome, 3. Preparation, 4. Meditation, 5. Conference, 6. Faith, 7. Practice, 8. Prayer. The three first goe before reading and preaching. The foure next come after them. The last must go before, and be with them, and come after them.[31]

Prayer accompanied their regular reading of the Scriptures with meditation, closely followed by conference.

Lewis Bayly (ca. 1575–1631), a Puritan devotional writer, recommends the Bible to be read three times a day, "a chapter at a time" every morning, noon, and night. Adherence to this program would result in having read the Bible, except for six chapters, in one year. Those remaining chapters were added to the reading task on the last day of the year. Reading, however, was not just an ephemeral exercise as Bayly adds, "One chapter thus read with understanding, and meditated with application, will better feed and comfort thy soul, than six read and run over without marking their scope or sense, or making any use thereof to thine own self."[32]

---

30. Greenham, *Workes*, 381–82.
31. Greenham, *Workes*, 382.
32. Lewis Bayly, *The Practice of Piety Directing a Christian how to Walk*

As Puritans read and studied their Bibles, they were encouraged to cross-reference Scriptures and other books. They annotated and noted as they read.[33] They would also read the Bible until they could literally hear it speak to them:

> One day as I was going up stairs, these words came in with such power upon my soul, *he that loveth my father and keepeth his word, my father will love him, and we will come and take up our abode with him.* This scripture made my heart leap within me for joy.[34]

The heart-imbedded Word fostered a greater receptivity to God.

The Puritan manner of reading and interpreting remained consistent with Reformed thought. The accepted interpretive tool of the Middle Ages was the *quadriga*, which regarded the historical, literal sense of a passage as "the dead and killing letter" and sought to find edification and truth in allegory. The Reformers and the Puritans rejected this. Biblical interpretation involved the understanding of "the vivid use of allegory, parable, analogy, and hyperbole in the Bible—all of which contribute to the force and life of the Scriptures."[35] They recognized allegories as being used in Scripture but avoided allegorizing the literal meaning. William Perkins (1558–1602), a Puritan theologian and Church of England clergyman, argues, "Scripture has only one sense, the literal one. An allegory is only a different way of expressing the same meaning. The anagogy and tropology are ways of applying the sense of the passage."[36] Puritans were keenly aware of the literary devices found in the Bible. Their emphasis on the literal sense was not a dull and

---

that He may please God (Delf, Great Britaine: Printed by Abraham Iacobs, 1660), 162.

33. Spurr, *English Puritanism*, 191.

34. Charles Doe, *A Collection of Experience of the Work of Grace* (London: printed for Chas. Doe, 1700), 17–18.

35. John Dykstra Eusden, introduction to *The Marrow of Theology*, by William Ames (Grand Rapids: Baker, 1968), 62.

36. William Perkins, *The Arte of Prophesying* (London: By Felix Kyngston, 1607), 31.

unimaginative literalism, but a serious reading of the manifest sense, aware of an author's use of imagery, symbolism, and typology.[37]

For the Puritan, the Bible was God's personal instruction to the reader, and to understand the divine text was the Holy Spirit's work of illumination. The Puritan believed that the Spirit who inspired the biblical writer spoke within the reader as it was read. That the religious life was effected by the work of the Holy Spirit meant it was an activity initiated from God's side. As Richard Sibbes (1577?–1635), another Church of England clergyman and leading Puritan theologian, states:

> The same Spirit that inspired holy men to write the word of God, works in us a belief that the word of God is the word of God. The stablishing argument must be by the power of God's Spirit. God, joining with the soul and spirit of a man whom he intends to convert, besides that inbred light that is in the soul, causeth him to see a divine majesty shining forth in the Scriptures.[38]

In the same vein, Perkins asserts, "For we have the voyce of the holy Ghost speaking in the Scripture: who doth also worke in our hearts a certaine full perswasion of the Scriptures, when we are exercised in hearing, reading and meditating of them." He is "the principall interpreter of the Scripture."[39] The Holy Spirit is the cause of this effectual means.

In his understanding of Spirit-enabled reading, Perkins drew on Calvin's assertion that one could not hope to understand the Scriptures clearly without the illumination of the Holy Spirit:

> Indeed, the Word of God is like the sun, shining upon all those to whom it is proclaimed, but with no effect among the blind. Now, all of us are blind by nature in this respect. Accordingly,

---

37. Doerksen and Hodgkins, *Centered on the Word*, 16.
38. Richard Sibbes, *The Complete Works of Richard Sibbes*, ed. Alexander B. Grosart (Edinburgh: J. Nichol, 1862), 427.
39. Perkins, *The Arte of Prophesying*, 19, 31.

it cannot penetrate into our minds unless the Spirit, as the inner teacher, through his illumination makes entry for it.[40]

Divine illumination from the Holy Spirit as well as from within the reader thus closed the gap between the reader and author.[41]

The revealed will of God as found in Scripture became the external criterion by which the Puritan discerned and deciphered the stirrings of his heart.[42] Henry Smith (ca. 1560–1591), a Church of England clergyman often referred to as the "Silver-Tongued Preacher" or "Silver-Tongued Smith" pens:

> [Scripture] is called a lantern, to direct us, Ps. CXIX. 105; a medicine, to heal us; a guide, to conduct us; a bit, to restrain us; a sword, to defend us; water, to wash us; fire, to inflame us; salt, to season us; milk, to nourish us; wine, to rejoice us; rain, to refresh us; a treasure, to enrich us; and the key, to unlock heaven gates unto us.[43]

The question of what benefit is gained by the reading of God's Word is answered in John Turner's (seventeenth-century) treatise addressing the Christian life, "We are informed what we should do, and either confirmed or confounded, in what we have done, that it is good or evil.[44]

A Puritan's submission to Scripture was the acid test: it was against Scripture that one could correctly determine whether grace was received. The light of Scripture determined and judged the estate of the soul. As John Manningham (d. 1622), a lawyer and diarist, pens, "Our soule can never be quiet till it be resolved by the word of God."[45] The words of Scripture had invested them with

---

40. Calvin, *Institutes*, 3.2.34.
41. Gordis, *Opening Scripture*, 23.
42. Spurr, *English Puritanism*, 176.
43. Henry Smith, *The Works of Henry Smith: Including Sermons, Treatises, Prayers, and Poems with Life of the Author*, ed. Thomas Fuller (Edinburgh: J. Nichol, 1866), 494.
44. John Turner, *A Heavenly Conference for Sions Saints* (London, 1645), 26.
45. John Manningham, *The Diary of John Manningham of the Middle*

significance and had made them holy or unholy. God was present in Scripture, in the conscience of a regenerate saint, and in the godly life that flowed from both.[46]

Sights and Sounds of the Bible in Puritan Culture
The Bible influenced Puritan thinking. It supplied the images and metaphors by which they interpreted not only their spiritual lives but also the wider world around them: the world of politics and, in their context, persecution.[47] The Bible was no longer the secret sacred book of the educated elite; it was no longer a mystery accessible only to university-educated Latin speakers. For most men and women, the Bible was their point of reference in all their thinking and the source of virtually all ideas.[48] These ideas were expressed in a Bible-supplied idiom present in the visual world in which they lived, as well as the audible everyday speech of men and women.

The Bible was far from being just a book to be read. It appeared everywhere in the lives of men, women, and children. It was not limited to the church services they were required to attend, but was also prevalent in their daily surroundings. Scripture's influence was inescapable. In Elizabethan England, biblical texts were literally painted on the walls and timber posts of the house. Surviving evidence shows that exhortations such as "Love thi neighbour," "Beware of Pride," and "Feare God," in large black-letter texts on the walls, were widespread. The community, including the less literate, would have had contact with these texts in their churches and also in drinking places, neighbors' dwellings, and even their own homes.[49] Additionally, walls were covered with printed matter:

Temple, 1602–1603, ed. Robert P. Sorlien (Hanover, N.H.: The Univ. Press of New England, 1976), 197.

46. Spurr, *English Puritanism*, 186.
47. Spurr, *English Puritanism*, 176.
48. Hill, *The English Bible*, 34.
49. Tessa Watt, *Cheap Print and Popular Piety, 1550–1640*, Cambridge Studies in Early Modern British History (Cambridge: Cambridge Univ. Press, 1991), 220.

almanacs, illustrated ballads and broadsides, again often on biblical subjects. The presence of a "lokinge [glass]" or "godly tables," in vogue for every Christian home, often contained texts from the Bible—especially the Psalms—as well as prayers, instructions for godly householders, medical information and advice.[50] It is likely that much of the population became acquainted with print and with the Bible through such decorations. These biblical verses and moral inscriptions could have served both didactic and aesthetic purposes.[51] The ubiquity of these visual expressions does not necessarily dictate personal belief, but it does establish the presence of a biblical influence on contemporary society.

Puritan speech was a pastiche of biblical phraseology. It was believed, as Ames pens:

> Speech and action should be completely spiritual, flowing from the very heart. They should show a man well versed in the Scriptures and in pious exercises, who has first persuaded himself and thoroughly settled in his own conscience those things to which he would persuade others, and in whom, finally, there is zeal, charity, mildness, freedom, and humility mixed with solemn authority.[52]

The idiom of the Bible was the Puritan's native tongue, which was used in letters and in conversational speech.[53] One author writes, "And shall not Heaven-born Souls, who Trafick in Heavenly Things, covet as much to meet their Fellow-Travellers, to have a little Discourse of their heavenly Country, and talk one with another in the Language of *Canaan*."[54] Comfortable with "the language of Canaan," Puritans quite naturally expressed their spirituality with it. Perhaps they heeded to Richard Baxter's advice "to get the liveliest picture of them [biblical characters, stories, and situations] that thou pos-

---

50. Watt, *Cheap Print and Popular Piety*, 223–29.
51. Watt, *Cheap Print and Popular Piety*, 217–18.
52. Ames, *The Marrow of Theology*, 195.
53. Martin, *Puritanism and Richard Baxter* 78; Wakefield, *Puritan Devotion*, 8.
54. Anonymous, *Stated Christian Conference*, 23.

sibly canst; meditate of them, as if thou were all the while beholding them, and as if thou were even hearing the *Hallelujahs*, while thou art thinking of them."[55] With almost little thought, Puritans found and identified their own stories with that of God's metanarrative.

As influential as these sights and sounds of Scripture may have been to both users and non-users alike, nothing compared in strength or authority to what was espoused and proclaimed on the Puritan pulpit. The Word read impacted the depth of the individual. The Word heard was intended to reach the depths and cover the breadth of those who thirsted at least weekly for the expounded Word from the pulpit. The minister prepared with diligence and skill for his masterwork: the sermon.

---

55. Baxter, *Saints' Everlasting Rest*, 760.

CHAPTER FOUR

Scripture for Puritan Ears: The Word Heard

Though echoes of the Bible were present in everyday speech, its sounds were most clearly heard in the voice of the minister through his sermons. It would be the Word preached in the sermon that Puritans were most inclined to hear.

A Public Means of Grace: The Sermon

Calvin, in his *Institutes*, exalted the Word of God. In particular, he emphasized that the first and major mark of a true church was the faithful preaching of the Word. "Wherever you see the Word of God purely preached and heard and the sacraments administered according to Christ's institution, there, it is not to be doubted, a Church of God exists."[1] The English Reformers, strongly influenced by Calvin, also held that the Word and sacraments were essential marks of the church. Calvin added:

> It is of no small importance that [the church] is called "the pillar and ground of the truth" and "the house of God" [1 Tim. 3:15]. By these words Paul means that the church is the faithful keeper of God's truth in order that it may not perish in the world. For by its ministry and labor God willed to have the preaching of his Word kept pure and to show himself the Father of a family, while he feeds us with spiritual food and provides everything that makes for our salvation.[2]

---

1. Calvin, *Institutes*, 4.1.9.
2. Calvin, *Institutes*, 4.1.9.

With its roots in the Reformation, the Puritans upheld the prominence given to preaching in the latter part of the sixteenth century and into the seventeenth century.

Puritan Preaching

Church was a part of national life; everyone was expected to attend church services. Puritan preachers dominated the pulpits throughout Elizabethan England; the demand for the clear and articulate exposition of the Word of God came from all sides of the pulpit. Sermons, delivered once or twice each Sunday, were the trademark of visible Puritan spirituality, and Puritans were known to flock eagerly to hear them. It was the "liturgical climax of public worship."[3] Hearing sermons and gadding after them were distinguishing marks of the godly in the minds of many of their neighbors.[4]

The primacy of the preached Word of God was made clear in William Bradshaw's words:

> They hould, that the highest and supreame office and authoritie of the Pastor, is to preach the gospell solemnly and publickly to the Congregation, by interpreting the written word of God, and applying the same by exhortation and reproofe unto them. They hould that this was the greatest worke that Christ & his Apostles did, and that whosoever is thought worthie and fit to exercise this authoritie, cannot be thought unfit and unworthy to exercise any other spiritual or Ecclesiastical authoritie whatsoever.[5]

So highly regarded was the "opening," or the interpretation, of the text by the pastor, that this ability gave credence to the authority held over the church's practices.

The sermon was the clearest and most direct method to appeal to people's hearts and minds. Those who were less literate, or had little leisure for or access to books, could hear the spiritual life pro-

---

3. Packer, *Quest for Godliness*, 281.
4. Spurr, *English Puritanism*, 37.
5. Bradshaw, *English Puritanisme*, 17.

claimed and analyzed in sermons as skilled preachers summoned persons to conversion and holiness.[6] Though the Puritans read or heard the Bible read far more frequently than hearing it preached, they nevertheless embraced preaching as "the most important of the means appointed by God to bring men out of bondage to sin and call together those who were to be his people."[7]

Ames believed preaching was to be "alive and effective so that an unbeliever coming into the congregating of believers should be affected and, as it were, transfixed by the very hearing of the word so that he might give glory to God."[8] Puritan preachers insisted on a lively preaching ministry[9] and emphasized the centrality of the Bible in the Christian life. John Preston (1587–1628), a Church of England clergyman, understood the critical relationship between the preaching pastor and the Word of God:

> First, because Ministers are feeders of the people; *If thou loves me feed my sheep*. The Word of God is the *childrens bread*, and it is unlawful either to defraud them of it, or to give them other instead of it: Now where there can be no feeding, unless the meat be such as is fit for nourishment; for otherwise it will not make them fat. Ministers are the Stewards of the Word of God.[10]

For Puritans, a non-preaching minister was an oxymoron. Richard Greenham established the vital necessity of the sermon in the life of the faithful and offered biblical support for his assertion:

> That preaching is the most principall meanes to increase and beget faith and repentance in Gods people, must be granted, Deut. 18:18, 33:10, Levit. 10:11, Mal. 2:6, 7:2, 2 Chro. 36:15, [Isa.] 50:4, 5, 7, 8, 53:1, 55:10, 11, 57:19, 58:1, 61:1, 62:1, 5, 6, 7, Mat. 13:3, 28, 19:20, Ephes. 4:11, 12, 13, 14, Rom. 10:14, 15, 1 Cor. 1:21, 1 Pet.

---

6. Wallace Jr., *Spirituality of the Later English Puritans*, 27.
7. Owen C. Watkins, *The Puritan Experience: Studies in Spiritual Autobiography* (New York: Schocken Books, 1972), 6.
8. Ames, *Marrow of Theology*, 193–94.
9. George, "Reformation Roots," 9.
10. John Preston, *Riches of Mercy to Men in Misery* (London: Printed by J.T., 1658), 273.

1:23, 25. And where this ordinarie meanes of salvation faileth, the people for the most part perish: Pro. 29:18, Hos. 4:6, 2 Chro. 15:13, Esay 6:9, Mat. 15:14, Luk. 11:52.[11]

Richard Baxter gave perhaps the finest definition of the purpose and position of preaching expressed by the Puritans:

> It is no small matter to stand up in the face of a congregation, and deliver a message of salvation or damnation, as from the living God, in the name of our Redeemer. It is no easy matter to speak so plain, that the ignorant may understand us; and so seriously that the deadest hearts may feel us; and so convincingly, that contradicting cavillers may be silenced.[12]

The sermon carried the weight of being the God-ordained vehicle for salvation and sanctification, serving as the chief means for conversion and growth in godliness.

Private Bible Reading and the Sermon

The critical place the sermon held in the lives of Puritans was intrinsically linked to their reading of the Bible. In his classic description of an English Puritan, John Geree (1601?–1649), a Church of England clergyman, characterized the spiritual and devotional activity of Puritans as he penned these words with regard to their Bible reading and the sermon, "He esteemed reading of the word an ordinance of God both in private and publike; but did not account reading to be preaching. The Word read he esteemed of more authority, but the word preached of more efficacy."[13]

Greenham, in an interactive, question-and-answer-formatted catechism, highlighted the relationship between the Word heard and the Word read:

> *Is it enough to read the Scriptures privately, or with others?*

---

11. Greenham, *Workes*, 381.
12. Richard Baxter, *The Reformed Pastor*, ed. William Brown (Edinburgh: Banner of Truth, 1974), 117.
13. John Geree, *The Character of an Old English Puritan or Non-conformist* (London, 1659), 2.

> No: for God hath also commanded to heare them read publikely in the Church.
>
> *And is it enough to heare them publikely in the Church?*
> No: for he also hath ordained preaching to be used.
>
> *Why must preaching be joyned with reading?*
> Because it is the most principall and proper meanes to beget faith in us.[14]

Greenham cited the evidence of neglecting the God-given means of Bible reading and its negative effect on the listener:

> Reading rather establisheth, than derogatheth from preaching: for none can be profitable hearers of preaching, that have not been trained up in reading the Scriptures, or hearing them read. Many inconveniences come from the neglect of reading as that the people cannot tell when a sentence is alleadged out of the Canonicall Scriptures, when out of the Apocripha, when out of the Scriptures, when out of other writers, that they cannot discerne when he speaketh his owne, or a sentence of the Scripture.[15]

Thus reading establishes preaching, or as Collinson states, the "circular principle at the heart of seventeenth-century biblical culture," where the faithful would hear sermons preached by biblically literate clergy and then prove their truth by reading the scripture themselves.[16] This reading and listening came with both responsibility and benefits, as Thomas Shepard advised:

> Draw near to God in the Word, by looking on it as God speaking to thee. We are far from God, and therefore we cannot hear him: draw near to him when you come to the external Word, when you come to heare the Word, heare it as the voice of God; *You heard the Word as the Word of God*, which you felt in you.

---

14. Greenham, *Workes*, 376.
15. Greenham, *Workes*, 381.
16. Patrick Collinson, review of *The English Bible and the Seventeenth-Century Revolution*, by C. Hill, *Times Literary Supplement* 4697 (April 9, 1993).

> I do not speak that the soule should take everything that Ministers speak as the Word of God, but that which is the Word of God, take it as God speaking. I am not able to expresse the infinite unknown sweetnesse, and mercy, and presence of God, that you shall finde thus coming.[17]

Puritan preaching assumed and depended upon a congregation that knew their Bibles. In a mutually reinforcing way, reading their Bibles augmented the hearing of a sermon. In sermons as well as in other texts of piety, laypeople were exhorted to read the Bible on their own—one was a poor substitute for the other.

Preaching is Prophesying

When Perkins wrote a treatise on the manner and purpose of preaching titled *The Arte of Prophesying*, he gave this definition of prophecy:

> a publique and solemn speech of the Prophet, pertaining to the worship of God, and to the salvation of our neighbour, 1 Cor. 14:3.
>
> Preaching of the Word is Prophesying in the name and roome of Christ, whereby men are called to the state of Grace, and conserved in it. 2. Cor. 5:19.[18]

Through preaching, those who hear are called into the state of grace, and are preserved in it.

Prophesying was a divinely enabled activity in which the minister opened, or interpreted, the text of God's Word to the congregation. Richard Bernard (bap. 1568, d. 1641), a Church of England clergyman and religious writer, pens, "For the Text, it must be Canonicall Scripture: The Minister is Gods mouth, he must then speake Gods word, not onely taking it for his text, but all his words must agree to the written truth, above which he may not presume."[19] The nature

---

17. Thomas Shepard, *Subjection to Christ in All His Ordinances* (London: Printed for John Rothwell, 1652), 189.

18. Perkins, *The Arte of Prophesying*, 1, 3.

19. Richard Bernard, *The Faithfull Shepherd* (London: Printed by Arnold Hatfield, 1607), 17.

of this work required pastors to refrain from relying on their own resources, but on the assistance of the Holy Spirit. The term *prophecying* emphasized the limited human role in opening God's Word. Bernard penned a treatise that complements Perkins' text, giving greater prominence to practical guidance and the minister's impact on his congregation. In his popular preaching manual, *Faithfull Shepheard*, he warns his readers that "preaching should not be a labour of the lippes, or talke of the toong from a light imagination: but a serious meditation of the heart in grounded knowledge by much study and illumination of the Spirit."[20] He emphasized God's role in preaching, insisting that the Spirit of God participates in the preaching of God's Word, and assists the minister both in preparing his sermons and in preaching them. The ultimate effectiveness of preaching is the Spirit's responsibility. The duty of man is to be faithful in teaching the Word. Even with the numerous contributions gleaned from the study of countless books and resources, the preacher was exhorted to conceal this "wisdom." Perkins teaches,

> *Humane wisdome* must bee concealed, whether it be in the matter of the sermon, or in the setting forth of the words....
>
> Artis etiam est celare artem; it is also a point of Art to conceale Art....
>
> The *Demonstration* of the Spirit is, when as the Minister of the word doth in the time of preaching so behave himselfe, that all, even ignorant persons and unbeleevers may judge, that it is not so much hee that speaketh, as the Spirit of God in him and by him. I. Cor.2:4.[21]

Though it was necessary to take the minister's role seriously, because "it is no small matter to meddle with the Secrets of God, to save soules,"[22] ministers were acutely aware of Calvin's warning to recognize that not they, but God, would grant faith to their congregants. God, in ascribing to Himself illumination of mind and renewal of

---

20. Bernard, *The Faithfull Shepherd*, 12–13.
21. Perkins, *The Arte of Prophesying*, 132–33.
22. Bernard, *The Faithfull Shepherd*, 4.

heart, warns that it is sacrilege for man to claim any part of either for himself.[23]

Sermon Preparation
While preaching is prophesying, it is also an "arte," requiring human skill and proficiency. The Puritan minister took seriously the arduous responsibility that came with preaching. To assist his work, he appealed to volumes of exegetical and literary helps. The habit of intensive and extensive spiritual and mental preparation for the pulpit was taken as a matter of course by men who, with Calvin and Luther, tacitly placed the sermon on almost the same respected level as they did Scripture.[24]

The minister's biblical exegesis emphasized the importance of the words in the text of Scripture. This work involved comparing words found in other parts of Scripture as well as exploring the words in their original language. Many preachers were comfortable with and retained their ability to consult original Greek, Hebrew, and Latin texts. They tended to rely on the glosses in the Geneva Bible, which was still a source of information for many Puritans throughout the seventeenth century.[25] In a nearly bookless society, the typical minister's study was equipped with English, Latin, Greek, and Hebrew versions of the Bible. It also had "interlineals," dictionaries, commentaries in Latin and English, concordances of key words and metaphors in the original languages and English. In addition, it included resources of comprehensive systems of divinity from the church fathers, or "ecclesiasticall Historiographers," "Histories of Jewish customs, of their Waights and Measures, and what other matter the learned have written of for the Scriptures especially," encyclopedias of human knowledge, and a range of Protestant ser-

---

23. Calvin, *Institutes*, 4.1.6.
24. Levy, *Preaching in the First Half*, 82.
25. Davidson, "John Cotton's Biblical Exegesis," 121.

mons dating back to the Reformation.²⁶ Bernard recommends that the pastor must have these qualifications:

> Knowledge of Rhetoricke, the Scriptures being full of tropes and figures, with knowledge in the rest of the Liberall Sciences: understanding also in naturall Philosophie, Oeconomicks, Ethicks, Politiques, Geographie, Cosmographie: he may not be ignorant of Antiquities; he is to be acquainted with Histories; and with whatsoever he shall be occasioned to use in the interpretation of the Scriptures; without which no man can worke cunningly upon everie text, if he want the instrument, (that is) the skil of that arte which should helpe him therein.²⁷

The minister was to bring this diversity of knowledge to his reading of the Scriptures, as "many candles to give light to see into his text, both to finde out and lay open such diversitie of matter as lie couched therein; as also to expound and to shew the full meaning of the words."²⁸ He was to be as knowledgeable of the world around him as he was with the Word of God before him. As John Preston (1587–1628) warns, however, preachers must not be like "spiders merely spinning webs to show their skill."²⁹

Sermon Form

The Puritan sermon was set off from all other English preaching by a peculiar homiletical technique known as "the plain style": *plain* in vocabulary, format, subject, and style, and easily understood by all. The Word of God must be presented in a spiritual manner, plain and unadorned, and easy to follow. Words spoken from the pulpit were to be used purposefully, without waste, and were to be chosen so that the "meanest and weakest" in the audience could understand and profit.

---

26. Bernard, *The Faithfull Shepherd*, 38–41; Harry S. Stout, *The New England Soul: Preaching and Religious Culture in Colonial New England* (New York: Oxford Univ. Press, 1986), 32.
27. Bernard, *The Faithfull Shepherd*, 36.
28. Bernard, *The Faithfull Shepherd*, 36.
29. Preston, *Riches of Mercy*, 304.

The plain style is perhaps best known for the simple four-part outline all Puritan preachers used: text, exposition, doctrine, and application. William Perkins summed up the method: He required that a preacher "read the Text distinctly out of the Canonicall Scriptures" and "to give the sense and understanding of it," explaining or opening it up. He should then collect a "fewe and profitable points of doctrine out of the natural sense," which was known as dividing the text. Finally, if the preacher is so gifted, he must apply the doctrine to the life and practice of the congregation in straightforward, plain speech.[30]

After the selected passage is read, the preacher is to analyze or open up the text, explaining one by one the words, ideas, and concepts found within the passage. This involved discussing "the circumstances of the place propounded," or the context of the passage, and explaining its grammatical meanings. It is then prooftexted or "collated" with related passages from other parts of the Bible. Perkins devotes much of *The Arte of Prophesying*, a preaching manual that Puritan ministers consulted to construct sermons, to the theory of exegesis. This emphasis suggests that proper exegesis demanded the greater part of the minister's task.

Drawn from proper interpretation, the sermon then proclaims in a flat, indicative manner the doctrine or doctrines contained in the text or logically deduced from it. Doctrine is the segment of the sermon where the preacher states in a single statement a "theological Axiom, either consisting in the express words of Scripture, or flowing from them by immediate consequence."[31] The doctrine is then "established," or proven to be in harmony with the rest of the Bible, and its general implications explained. This portion of the sermon consists of reasons or proofs, one followed by another with no other transition than a period and a number. The doctrine for each and every sermon, as well as all proofs, rests soundly in the Bible. Proofs

---

30. Perkins, *The Arte of Prophesying*, 148.
31. Allen C. Guelzo, "When the Sermon Reigned," *Church History* 13, no. 1 (1994): 24.

included scriptural support and further arguments for the principle or doctrine explained. Consequently, the body of a sermon usually contained numerous biblical passages and an amalgam of biblical references. Ames explains:

> The discussion of a doctrine consists partly in proofs, if it be questioned by the hearers...and partly in illustration of the things already well proved. Proofs ought to be sought from the clearer testimonies of Scripture, with reasons being added where the nature of the things will allow. But here the treatment must be adapted to the profit of the hearers.[32]

The preacher would refute any objection that could be raised and point out the practical uses of the doctrine for consolation or correction. These were usually stated in the third person.[33]

After the last proof is stated, the sermon ends with the doctrine's applications. Found also in numbered sequence, applications were typically discussed in second person and allowed the minister to inquire whether the auditors had taken the doctrine to heart.[34] Ames states, "To apply doctrine to its use is to sharpen and make specially relevant some general truth with such effect that it may pierce the minds of those present with the stirring up of godly affections."[35] The definition of application is stated here:

> A neerer bringing of the use delivered, after a more generall sort, in the third person, as spoken to persons absent; to the time, place, and persons then present: and uttered in the second person, or in the first, when the Minister, as often the Apostle doth, will enclude himselfe with them.[36]

It is in the application that the contrast between the requirements of the doctrine and the practice of the congregation is made plain, and the challenge delivered. Ames instructs, "Upon this part...great

---

32. Ames, *Marrow of Theology*, 192.
33. Guelzo, "When Sermon Reigned," 24–25.
34. Guelzo, "When Sermon Reigned," 25.
35. Ames, *Marrow of Theology*, 193.
36. Bernard, *The Faithfull Shepherd*, 70.

insistence must be made, since this contains the conclusion and the good of the first part, and is closer to the chief purpose of the sermon, which is the edification of the hearers."[37] It is the device that causes identification on the part of the hearers and helps them know what the passage and the theological precept mean to their own lives. "They sin, therefore, who stick to the naked finding and explanation of the truth, neglecting the use and practice in which religion and blessedness consist. Such preachers edify the conscience little or not at all." After all, application is to be made "for convincing, correcting, instructing, and comforting the present auditorie."[38] It was the use or application of a sermon that gave it its evangelical note, for godly preaching was aimed at the conversion of souls and for their training in holiness.[39]

The sermon ends with a "pithie, forcible, and loving exhortation to move affection," and then moves to thanksgiving and prayer "for a blessing upon that which hath beene spoken."[40] A sermon worth its weight was approximately an hour's length and had practical biblical exposition. Though sermons were many and long—relative to present-day standards—they contained a deep conviction that the nature of the sermon should be practical.

Puritan preachers carefully crafted their sermons for edification of and application by their auditors. They found that the preached Word is most remembered when methodically delivered. Preston asserts that failure to preach without method was equivalent to putting "water into a sieve that will run out." He adds this:

> The end of preaching is not only to stir up the affections, but to enform the judgement, and that is performed when it is remembered, now the memory is strengthened by method.... The end of preaching is to beget knowledge in the people, and

---

37. Ames, *Marrow of Theology*, 192.
38. Bernard, *The Faithfull Shepherd*, 77.
39. Morgan, *Puritan Spirituality*, 14.
40. Bernard, *The Faithfull Shepherd*, 80–81.

this is done by method: for it helps the understanding and the memory."⁴¹

The enduring power of the sermon, as it was preserved in the minds of its hearers, maintained the ability to mold corporate values and personal piety. Responsibility rested heavily on the spiritual maturity and homiletical skills of the pastor, and also on the listening and retentive skills of the auditor.

Tools to Retain the Word Heard

Listening

Listening to the sermon was like meditating upon the Word. A charge to be an attentive auditor comes from Bernard: "When a Minister speaks truly Gods Word, he may speake freely to all: And all must heare him, as if God spake, with reverence."⁴² When it comes to the Word preached, "We come about a business of the highest importance, therefore should stir up our selves, and hear with the greatest of devotion."⁴³ This level of attention was not effortless. Henry Smith (1560–1591) states:

> As there is a foundation, upon which the stones, and lime, and timber are laid, which holdeth the building together; so where this foundation of hearing is laid, there the instructions, and lessons, and comforts do stay and are remembered; but he which leaneth his ears on his pillow, goeth home again like the child which he leadeth in his hand, and scarce remembereth the preacher's text. A divine tongue and a holy ear make sweet music, but a deaf ear makes a dumb tongue. There is nothing so easy as to hear, and yet there is nothing so hard as to hear well.⁴⁴

Attentive and engaged listening helped ensure the preacher's message would take root in the listener.

---

41. Preston, *Riches of Mercy*, 303.
42. Bernard, *The Faithfull Shepherd*, 4.
43. Watson, *Heaven Taken by Storm*, 29.
44. Smith, *Works*, 1:321.

Listening to a sermon was not a passive affair. The hearing of God's Word was vital; it came with guidelines for its practice. Thomas Watson describes how to listen to the Word: (1) give great attention to the Word preached, (2) come with a holy appetite, (3) come to it with a *tenderness* upon your heart, (4) receive it with *meekness*, (5) mingle the Word preached with faith, (6) be not only *attentive* in hearing, but *retentive* after hearing, (7) reduce your hearing to practice, (8) beg of God that He will accompany His Word with His *presence* and *blessings*, (9) make it familiar to you, discoursing of the Word you have heard when you come home.[45]

William Perkins devotes more than a few lines to the correct and specific practice of hearing the sermon in "How to Carry Our Selves in Sermon-time":

> Then after publique prayer, in time of Sermon, when the Word of God is preached before thee, remember the counsell of the Wise-man, *Be neare to heare*; that is, bee attentive, hearken with reverence to that which shall be delivered. Which that thou mayest the better do, observe these directions: have thine eyes fixed most commonly on the Preacher, that so thou mayest keep it and thy thoughts from idle wandring: marke the Text, observe the division; marke how every point is handled: quote the places of Scripture which he allegeth for his Doctrines proofe, fold downe a leafe in your Bible from whence the place is recited, that so at your leasure after your returne from the Church, you may examine it: apply that which is spoken to thy selfe; and endeavour to be bettered by it. Continue in thy attentive hearing, without wearinesse, from the beginning unto the end of the Sermon, and see that thou depart not (unlesse infirmity of health, or some other very necessary occasion call thee away) before with the rest of the Congregation, by after-Prayer & singing of Psalmes thou hast rendred thanks for the comfort and instruction which thou hast received.[46]

---

45. Thomas Watson, *A Body of Practical Divinity* (London: Printed for Thomas Parkhurst, 1692), 406–7.

46. William Perkins, *A Garden of Spirituall Flowers* (London: Printed by R. B[adger], 1638), 116–18.

These helps augmented the great lengths a pastor went to foster the hearing of sermons and to make them as memorable as possible. Richard Rogers adds a reference to two other disciplines that maximize hearing—meditation and conference: "For hearing of the word read and preached, doth little profit, where it is not joyned with preparation to heare reverently and attentively, and where it is not mused on after, yea, and as occasion shall offer, conferred of also."[47]

The faithful and pious of the congregation were conscientious listeners as well as devoted note-takers. Thoughtful listening fostered the ability to make notations of the sermon, which prolonged one's engagement with the Word heard, and provided material for future and further discussions.

Sermon Note-Taking

The format of plain style sermons was not used exclusively by the Puritans. What made a plain style sermon distinctively Puritan was the emphasis placed on the sermon and what the auditor did during and in response to the Word heard. The plain sermon's outline and logical development made it more conducive for memorization and note-taking by the people for review at home. It was part of the duty of a Christian to con[48] the sermons that he or she heard.[49]

Alliteration was one method of fostering the congregation's memory of the headings for the main divisions or doctrines of the sermon. Baxter claims that this device, along with numbering of directions, results in the sermon being more easily retained.[50] Ames cautions preachers to avoid causing confusion between the different parts of the sermon:

> Those who invert and confuse these parts make it difficult for their hearers to remember and stand in the way of their

---

47. Rogers, *Seven Treatises*, 298.
48. An archaic term meaning to get to know; to study or learn…to commit to memory. See *Oxford English Dictionary*, s.v. "con."
49. Davies, *Worship of English Puritans*, 196.
50. Richard Baxter, *A Christian Directory* (London: Printed by Robert White, 1673), 575.

edification. Their hearers cannot commit the chief heads of the sermon to memory so that they may afterwards repeat it privately in their families; and when this cannot be done, the greatest part of the fruit, which would otherwise be made available to the church of God through sermons, is lost.[51]

Logical order served as a helpful memory aid for the Puritans who, equipped with paper and writing utensils, characteristically recorded notes from the sermon. The following week was typically spent reflecting on what had been heard. Ministers organized their sermons according to the practice of analytic commonplaces and methodic disposition. Listeners took notes, and in their subsequent discussions based upon the notes, learned how to think logically in spatial patterns.[52] The visual appearance of the Puritan style sermon, organized according to logic, rendered it plain to the eyes of those taking notes or reading printed sermons and was a distinction from the oratorical style of Anglican and Counter-Reformation preaching.[53]

Conscientious Puritans often took sermon notes to help facilitate meditation. Most of the note-takers were devout, investing time and attention to this exercise. On the habit of writing down sermons as they were preached, there is no lack of evidence.[54] Samuel Clarke, in his compilation of biographies, *The Lives of Thirty-Two English Divines*, records of Arthur Hildersham, "He was alwaie's a delighted frequenter of the publique Assemblies.... He used often even in his old age to write Sermons in the Church."[55] John Manningham's

---

51. Ames, *Marrow of Theology*, 192.

52. John G. Reichtien, "Logic in Puritan Sermons in the Late Sixteenth Century and Plain Style," *Style* 13 (Summer 1979): 249.

53. Rechtien, "Logic in Puritan Sermons," 250.

54. W. Fraser Mitchell, *English Pulpit Oratory from Andrewes to Tillotson: A Study of Its Literary Aspects* (New York: Russell & Russell, 1962), 30 ff. It has been suggested that in the sixteenth century the practice of taking notes of sermons was an attempt to preserve a corpus of Protestant exegesis. In the seventeenth century the practice became more general, and note-taking was a part of the school training of children.

55. Samuel Clarke, *The Lives of Thirty-Two English Divines* (London: Printed for William Birch, 1677), 122.

Diary affords proof of the remarkable interest with which sermons were attended and their main doctrines meticulously recorded. His careful notes on the sermons take up to five pages of small print. One entry of sermon notes filled nine pages. It is presumed these notes were written in longhand.[56] A large portion of John Manningham's *Diary* is devoted to analyses of the various sermons heard by this lawyer of the period.[57] In a funeral sermon by Edmund Calamy (1600–1666) for Lady Anne Walker, he lists twelve virtues of her life, not so much for commendation but for imitation:

> A diligent attender upon Gospel Ordinances, delighting much in the House of God, and preferring the Word of God above her appointed food. A constant Writer of Sermons, and wrote them in her Heart as well as in her Book, and her life was an exact Commentary upon the Sermons heard. She hath a large Book in Folio written with her own hand, wherein under several Heads of Divinity, she hath registred the Observations of her reading both out of the Scriptures (which were her delight) and out of the Writings of our best Divines, and out of her own experiences.[58]

Sermon notes, when joined with reflections from other readings and personal experiences, fostered a life of piety and godliness. Similarly, Samuel Clarke pens this in a biography of his wife, Katherine:

> Her constant gesture at Prayer was Kneeling, thinking that she would not be too humble before God. Her usual manner was to write Sermons to prevent drowsiness and distractions, and to help Memory, whereof she hath left many Volumes, and her practice was to make good use of them, by frequent reading and Meditating upon them.[59]

---

56. Herr, *Elizabethan Sermon*, 79. It is possible to assume that sermon notes would have been taken in shorthand, as an early English system of stenography appears in 1588, when Dr. Timothy Bright published his *Characterize*, the earliest known English system of stenography.

57. Manningham, *Diary of John Manningham*, 16–17.

58. Edmund Calamy, *The Happinesse of Those Who Sleep in Jesus* (London: Printed by J.H. for Nathanael Webb, 1662), 28.

59. Samuel Clarke, *A Looking-Glass for Good Women to Dress Themselves By* (London: Printed for William Miller, 1677), 15.

Men and women were encouraged to be supplied with a stock of sermons: "Wee must do with Sermons, as the Trades-men do with the mony they get; some of it they lay out for their present use, and some they lay up against the time of sicknesse."[60]

Note-taking was a tool used for recording that which was necessary to capture in the heart and mind of a Puritan believer: God's Word. Sermon notes served as fodder for continued spiritual growth.

Repeating the Sermon

The Lord's Day was sacred to the Puritans. After hearing the sermon, the "food of the soul," they spent portions of the rest of the day secluded with their private devotions, catechisms, family Bible reading, and sermon notes. Sometimes they ventured to one another's homes or their minister's to join in repeating of the content and heads of the sermons heard earlier that day.

Preston understands the dilemma of forgetfulness and offers a catalog of methods to foster understanding and memory of sermons. He includes repeating sermons as a method where "one thing is linked to another. And this is needful because we have more then a natural forgetfulnesse in good things."[61] Repeating the sermon, or at least the heads of the sermon, was an important discipline for retaining what was heard. Preston cautions:

> Not repeating the Word of God after it is preached, doth quench the spirit, and that is sin.... Now it is quenched thus, In the time of preaching (for that is the time when the Holy Ghost breaths into our hearts...) when he stirs up motions and we let them die, and recall them not, we quench and grieve the spirit.... Not repeating is the cause that many are always learning, but never come to the knowledge of the Truth.[62]

---

60. Edward Calamy, *The Godly Man's Ark* (London: Printed for John Hancock, 1672), 34.
61. Preston, *Riches of Mercy*, 303.
62. Preston, *Riches of Mercy*, 286, 288.

This exercise encouraged the Puritan to "take opportunity to set our souls in the way of Heaven, to recall the motions which have been stirred up in the inner Chamber of our hearts."[63] Perkins exhorts his readers:

> After thy returne from Church, revive thy memory with a briefe repetition in thy minde of that which thou hast heard before thy sitting downe to dinner: and then with thanksgiving receiving the blessings of God to thy bodily comfort, be mindfull to season the same with good and godly talke to the glory of God, the comfort of thy soule, and the edification of those which are about thee.[64]

Repetition of the "chief heads of the sermon" served as an initial tool for hearers to remember the outline of a message. The Puritans took this exercise to heart. Baxter observes evidence of this familiar practice when he says that on any given Sunday, "You might hear an hundred families singing psalms and repeating sermons as you passed through the streets."[65] Once home, they are encouraged to gather the family, ask for God's assistance and acceptance, sing a psalm of praise, and then repeat the sermon that was heard.[66] Young boys and girls were expected to be able to repeat sermons and were recognized and praised for their abilities.[67]

The repeating of sermons sought to pave the way for truth to enter into the heart. This kind of mindfulness of the sermon throughout the week might have stirred questions or concerns that required explanation or clarification. Baxter opened his home every week for those with such concerns:

> Every Thursday evening my neighbors that were most desirous and had opportunity, met at my House, and there one

---

63. Preston, *Riches of Mercy*, 286.
64. Perkins, *A Garden of Spirituall Flowers*, 118.
65. Baxter, *Reliquiae Baxterianae*, 84.
66. Baxter, *Christian Directory*, 572.
67. Caroline Francis Richardson, *English Preachers and Preaching, 1640–1670* (New York: The Macmillan Company, 1928), 75–76.

of them repeated the Sermon; and afterwards they proposed what Doubts any of them had about the Sermon, or any other Case of Conscience, and I resolved their Doubts.[68]

Repeating the sermon appears as a distinct practice from the discipline of conference and may be focused more intently on the major points of a sermon rather than a discussion of its content.

Isaac Ambrose exhorts his readers to "repeat what we have heard, and confer of it, and examine the Scriptures about the truth of it."[69] Repeating the sermon served as a precursor to another method of remembering and then applying what was heard: the practice of conference.

Conference

The communally practiced private means of conference appears widely used among the Puritans. In conference, participants regularly engaged with one another in discussions on biblical texts. Conference was a means to deepen spiritual truths through discourse exercised "either with Ministers of God. Our equals. Or others."[70] Ministers were directed to incorporate conference as a regular part of their ministerial duties. Baxter observes, "I have found by experience, that some ignorant persons, who have been so long unprofitable hearers, have got more knowledge and remorse of conscience in half an hours close discourse, than they did from ten years public preaching."[71] In conference, one had "an opportunity to set all home for the conscience and the heart."[72]

Conference on spiritual matters was also exercised among fellow Christians and functioned as a very important part of the Puritan's spiritual life. People would meet at one another's homes to discuss the Bible or sermons heard the previous week. In addition

---

68. Baxter, *Reliquiae Baxterianae*, 83.
69. Isaac Ambrose, *Media* (London: printed by T.R. and E.M., 1652), 341.
70. Greenham, *Workes*, 385.
71. Baxter, *The Reformed Pastor*, 196.
72. Baxter, *The Reformed Pastor*, 174.

to discussing sermon notes, parishioners came together to confer over the spiritual state of their souls. Various themes appear to have been topics of conference: the process of conversion, preparation for public profession of faith, church membership, dealing with doubts, difficult cases of conscience, preparing for the Lord's Supper, and continuing in the process of growing in grace and godliness. In addition, ministers encouraged the use of conference within a household. Parents were responsible for the spiritual well-being of all those residing in their home and conference served as a useful avenue for nurturing spirituality.

Adding to the ubiquitous sounds of the Bible in this Puritan era, conference served to weave a believing community together. Conference was a means of grace that was promoted and exercised by both clergy and laity. From parish to household, whether academic or popular, clergy present or not, conference was a widely accepted means of grace among the godly: a form of enabling that was encouraged and enjoyed.

Conclusion

Whether one was a Puritan or not, it would have been difficult to escape the sights and sounds of Scripture—they were everywhere. The Word of God was the rule that gave direction on how to glorify and enjoy God forever. It was read and heard with reverence as a gift of God's grace. Its authority was evident in the manner by which its hearers sought after, retained, and practiced its truths.

Fast-forward to the twenty-first century. Biblical resources abound as no other previous generation could ever imagine. Yet, the twofold problem still exists: how to get into the Bible and how to get the Bible into us. A high view of Scripture and its authority appears to have had broad implications for increasing the breadth and depth of biblical literacy in the Puritan era. Perhaps we can echo the words and wisdom of Samuel Crossman (1624?–1684) as he describes the character of a virtuous Christ-follower as "one that loves and delights indeed in his Bible" and "that he might never lose his Bible, he laies it up safely in his best Cabinet, his very heart."[73]

As Puritan literature is explored and the exercise of holy conference is uncovered, the process requires the creation of a systematic categorizing that will enable the reader to appreciate the shared characteristics and clear differences found with the employment of this means of grace. Highlighting these features will bring clarity to any application for contemporary times.

---

73. Crossman, *Young Mans Monitor*, 131, 133.

CHAPTER FIVE

Holy Conference: "A Kinde of Paradise"

Negative connotations associated with the word "piety" emanate from a history of people who tended to scoff at the lack of religious devotion in others while exalting their own form of religiosity. The hypocrisy that is often associated with piety has influenced the present day understanding of this word, narrowing its language to a more pejorative sense. In Puritan vocabulary, however, the word "piety" was used primarily in a positive sense; it involved the manners of putting faith into practice.

John Turner (seventeenth century) defines sanctification as, "A changing of the mind from delighting in the things of this world, to delight in heavenly things."[1] This involves means God uses to "manifest unto us that we have faith."[2] The Puritan practices of piety, referred to as "means" or "means of grace," were understood as practices through which God communicated Himself; they were tools that assisted the Puritan believer toward conversion and growth in godliness. In response to faith, by and through these means, God would supply the believer with grace sufficient for growth in godly living, or sanctification, strengthening the inward man or woman.

---

1. Turner, *A Heavenly Conference*, 18.
2. Turner, *A Heavenly Conference*, 21.

Means of Grace

The means of grace were given in the gift of the Holy Spirit. The saint was to guard against depending on the means without God, and on God without the means. Careless and unconscious employment of them yielded shallow souls, "dwarfes in grace and holinesse."[3] It was clear to the Puritan divines that in order to live the Christian life (beginning with the pre-conversion experience, then growing in spiritual maturity while having an impact on its community), the means were essential. The Puritan minister Richard Rogers (1551–1618), in *Seven Treatises*, argues for the importance of means:

> Now seeing this Christian life is upholden and continued by meanes, and every one which shall set upon it, will be desirous to know them, as he hath good cause, and how to use them aright, because the hindrances and discouragements from the same are many and great;…seeing that God hath promised by the right and reverent use of them, and the same constantly continued to give such grace, even to weake ones, whereby they shall bee able in truth (as hard as it seemeth) to lead this godly life, and sensibly to discerne that they doe so. For as it was not begunne without meanes, so neither can it grow without them.[4]

Means were not without obstacles, but neither were they without necessity.

Isaac Ambrose (1604–1664) delineates the various means, "duties," or "ordinances," into three categories: "secret," "public," and "private."[5] Secret duties are exercised by the individual and include such practices as meditation and "experiences." Practices that are exercised in small groups or gatherings are labeled "private," whereas those exercised in larger groups, as in worship services, are identified as "public." Richard Rogers lists three public

---

3. John Preston, *Remaines of that Reverend and Learned Divine John Preston* (London: Printed by R[ichard] B[adger] [and John Legate]), 112.

4. Rogers, *Seven Treatises*, 280–81.

5. Ambrose, *Media*, 39.

means: ministry of the Word read, preached, and heard; the administration and receiving of the holy sacraments; and the exercise of prayer, with thanksgiving and singing of psalms. In order to complement the use of these public means, which cannot be "daily had and enjoyed, (and yet we need daily releefe and helpe)," he recommends seven private exercises that God commands His people to use: watchfulness, meditation, "armour of God," conference, family exercise, prayer, and reading.[6] Conference is listed here among private means, perhaps because of the depth of interaction between participants. In other instances, conference was listed among public duties because of its communal character.[7] So important was the exercise of these means that Rogers asserts the potential for impact in one's life beyond the means: "The necessity of these private helpes is so great, that if they be not knowne and used rightly and in good sort, the publike will prove but unprofitable, and the whole life out of square."[8]

Church of England clergyman and author Edward Reyner (1600–1660) reminds his readers that both public and private means are instituted and purposed of God for the believer:

> Whether you seeke and waite for Christ, (out of the sense of your spirituall want and penury) in every ordinance publike and private, Word, Sacraments, Prayer, Meditation, Conference; not as they are your owne works of sanctification, but as they are Gods Ordinances appointed of purpose for the manifestation and communication of Christ to the soule.[9]

The means of grace were gifts of God given with the intention to further the Christlikeness in and of the believer, to be made ready and sensitive to growth in faithfulness as God leads. Soul-deep impact

---

6. Rogers, *Seven Treatises*, 281.
7. Bunyan, *The Pilgrim's Progress*, 126.
8. Rogers, *Seven Treatises*, 281.
9. Edward Reyner, *Precepts for Christian Practice* (London: Printed for Rich. Cotes, 1645), 5.

and spiritual transformation via these means were God-ordained objectives. Richard Baxter holds to this:

> All the means of Grace, and all the working of the spirit upon the soul, and all the gracious actions of the Saints, are so many evident Mediums to prove, that there remaineth a Rest to the people of God.... All these means and motions, implie some End to which they tend, or else they cannot be called means, nor are they the motions of Wisdom or Reason.... God would never have commanded his people to repent and beleeve, to fast and pray, to knock and seek, and that continually, to read and study, to conferr and meditate, to strive and labor, to run and fight, and all this to no purpose.[10]

The ensuing piety was one that demonstrated clearly and accurately the expression of Christ in and through each follower.

Conference as a Means of Grace

When the practices of piety are explored, one finds the Puritans faithfully engaged in the exercise of these private means of grace. Scholarly attention to these means has tended to gravitate toward the individual practices of Puritan piety, whereas research dedicated to the communal practice of conference appears eclipsed. Yet, this communally practiced private means appears widely supported and promoted by the Puritans.

John Turner compiled a list of ordinary means that included afflictions, reading, conference, prayer, preaching, and meditation.[11] A possible contemporary describes conference as being exercised among various people:

> a Select Number of Holy Experience'd Souls, full of Zeal for God's Glory, and Love to each other; being under the Sacred Influences of the Same Spirit, Exciting and Stirring them up, to sequester themselves from the World, and from Sinners; that

---

10. Baxter, *Saints' Everlasting Rest,* 171.
11. Turner, *A Heavenly Conference,* 21.

they might the more freely and mutually discourse of Divine Matters, to each others Edification, and sweet Satisfaction.[12]

In conference, participants regularly engaged with one another in discussions on biblical texts in conjunction with more intimate conversations over the spiritual state of their souls. The use of Scripture, obtained by way of the minister, his sermons, the auditor's sermon notes, or private Bible reading, played an essential role in conference. Scripture is perspicuous; the wisdom and knowledge it offers is all that every Christian would need to know for living a life of godliness. Nevertheless, the idea of a Christian interpreting and applying principles from Scripture in isolation was rejected. Puritans were persuaded to gather in smaller communities for the purpose of investigating and studying the Word.

Richard Greenham (early 1540s–1594), a leading Puritan divine, includes conference in his list of eight properties required for a faithful reading and hearing of the Word: diligence, wisdom, preparation, meditation, conference, faith, practice, and prayer.[13] No doubt Greenham exercised and encouraged conference while well aware of problems that stemmed from neglecting the reading and hearing of the Word. He understood that, just as with matters of the natural order where people needed assistance, people should investigate and explore spiritual matters in community. This community may or may not include the clergy. When a minister was not present, Greenham advisesd that congregants go about conference in this way:

> This rule must be kept, that conference with our equals must be of those things which we heard of our Ministers, as it must be kept also in meditation, which is conference with our selves. We must for a time like babes hang at the mouthes of the Min-

---

12. Anonymous, *Stated Christian Conference*, 14. Although this work does not designate its author, it is signed by a T. B. If this is Thomas Beverley (d. 1702), he was an independent minister and contemporary of Richard Baxter. Inconclusive data warrants the assignment of authorship as anonymous.
13. Greenham, *Workes*, 382.

isters, because we cannot runne before we goe: nay we cannot goe without a leader. No man may presume to understand above that which is meet to understand, but labour to understand according to the measure of sobrietie, as God hath dealt to every one the measure of faith: and when they have laid the foundation, then build the walles and pillars. The Eunuch would not interpret the word without a guide, but he laid it up in his heart, as the virgin Mary did.[14]

Not only was conference to be based on the discoveries and newfound insights from the biblical text, but it was to be exercised by procuring "things honest before men, that it may be done wisely, without confusion and destruction: & not by too great a multitude, that wee may affoorde our doings before men."[15] The created environment was conducive to the exchange of thoughts and ideas of practices and habits of the participants, as these may be judged against the newly discerned biblical truths.

Rogers, too, recognized the lack of attention given to the preached Word and the duplicity that followed:

> What is more manifest than this, that almost all in a congregation doe by and by forget that which they have heard, and make little use of it in their lives? And what greater cause can be rendred hereof than this, that they never looke after matters concerning their soules, when they are about their private dealings, and (as we say) out of the Church doores.[16]

To resolve this state of affairs, Rogers placed a particular emphasis on a number of means of grace that supported continued growth in godliness. Of the seven private means mentioned above, he devoted significantly more space to the discussion of meditation than to any other. He argued that meditation was a "stranger to

---

14. Greenham, *Workes*, 369–70. An error in pagination in the original document results in a misnumbering of pages. These pages should read 385–86.
15. Greenham, *Workes*, 370.
16. Rogers, *Seven Treatises*, 298.

many"[17] and stated his concern: "Because I am too sure, that few are acquainted with it, though it be an helpe most profitable to godliness," and hopes "that the practise of it may be more common."[18] It can be deduced that the other aforementioned means, including conference, may have been practiced with greater familiarity and regularity. He added that along with the reading of sound interpreters, the opportunities taken to confer "with the learned" is "like to finde much fruit and profit by his reading."[19]

Conference proved a great help for many Puritans. Church of England clergyman and leading Puritan theologian Richard Sibbes (1577?–1635) found great profit in conference:

> Here is the benefit of holy conference and good speeches, one thing drawes on another, and that drawes on another, till at length the soule be warmed and kindled with the consideration and meditation of heavenly things…so that talking about heavenly things is good for others and ourselves also… they are stirred up to be inquisitive after Christ.[20]

The profitability of conference was clear: enhanced biblical understanding, the warming of the soul, and even a greater desire for the Word. Sibbes noted an extended profitability in the community fostered:

> We see the poor disciples, when they were in a damp loss of Christ, after he comes, meets them, and talks of holy things. In that very conference their hearts were warmed and kindled, Luke xxiv.32. For, next to heaven itself, our meeting together here, is a kinde of Paradise, the greatest pleasure of the world is, to meet with those here, whom we shall ever live with in Heaven. Those who are good should not spend such opportunities fruitlessly.[21]

---

17. Rogers, *Seven Treatises*, 316.
18. Rogers, *Seven Treatises*, 313.
19. Rogers, *Seven Treatises*, 385.
20. Richard Sibbes, *Bowels Opened* (London: Printed by R. Cotes, 1648), 295–96.
21. Sibbes, *Bowels Opened*, 297.

These discussions fostered a level of discourse that reached deep into the life of persons engaged in this practice. Church of England clergyman and religious writer, Nicolas Bownd (d. 1613), summarized in a margin notation on this form of corporate learning and discourse, "We ought privatly to conferre and talke of Gods word one with another." He encouraged:

> the conferring and talking with others of that which we have in the word read or heard: especially seeing both it is commended unto us in the Scripture, & also by experience we shall finde the profit of it to be so great, to our selves and others

and considers Conference as "a most excellent helpe in our infirmities."[22]

The communal nature of conference facilitated the application of the Word, which was found relevant for all of life's challenges and trials. Exercised in a godly community that fostered biblical literacy and growth in godliness, conference stood as a fundamental means for Puritan sanctification.

The Objective of Conference

It was common for the pious to meet at one another's homes to discuss the Bible or sermons that were heard. These private meetings served as venues where parishioners discussed their sermon notes, prayed, fasted, and conferred over the state of their souls. Their discourse on the subject of God and His glory was seen not only as a duty but also a privilege for the Christian. The mutual freedom and liberty exercised in speaking to one another in conference created a safe atmosphere in which growth in godliness could be most unreservedly nurtured. Conference includes the daily reading of the Word and catechism, hearing the Word publicly read and preached (followed by meditation on what was read), and continual praying and practicing. In a brief description, Richard Bernard offered a clear synopsis of this spiritual discipline: "Conference by asking

---

22. Bownd, *Sabbathum Veteris*, 391.

of superiors and Ministers, by reasoning with equals, and teaching inferiours, all in reverence and humility, to understand that I know not, to be resolved in that I doubt of, and to call to memorie what I have forgotten."[23]

One writer affirms both the academic and experiential aspects of conference:

> The proper Scope, and Subject of which is the Improvement of the Tongue, and Speech, according to the Understanding, we have in Scripture, and the Sense we have of it upon our Hearts for the mutual Enlightning of one another, and the Inflaming our Hearts mutually in Things pertaining to the Kingdom of God. For this is the Great Advantage we have in All Things from this Conferential Faculty; That we can by it mutually Instruct, and Inform, as also Perswade, Affect, and work upon one another.[24]

The common sharing of learned truths and principles fostered a knowledge enhancement not found elsewhere in any other form or by any other means. Although there would be an understanding that the participants in conference be those who profess a saving knowledge of God, there would be no prerequisite of advanced knowledge of the faith for engagement of conference. It mattered not if one lacked the funds to purchase books or the time to read them; those with little understanding of the Scriptures were encouraged to join in discussions in order to further their understanding. Even those with a rudimentary grasp of the Bible were encouraged to participate in conference:

> So those that have but a small Stock of Knowledge, may improve by the help of him that hath more, for the Wise God *hath given nothing in Vain*. Now Christian Conference (in the very Nature of the thing) is an apt means, Conducing both to Knowledge and Experience. Therefore it is a Christian Duty.[25]

---

23. Bernard, *Josuahs Resolution*, 51.
24. Anonymous, *Stated Christian Conference*, 7.
25. Anonymous, *Stated Christian Conference*, 20.

Conference was instructive and enlightening as both knowledge and experience were promoted. There existed a complementarity of the two with one primarily preceding the other but requiring the other for greatest effect. The writer noted above witnessed to this: "'Tis a common Observation, That those Discourses, that Savour most of inward Experience, are more Influential and Warming, Than Those that are more Scholastick, wanting that Experience; For what comes from the Heart, reaches it."[26]

One might be inclined to think that the experience referred to would be those life lessons offered by an attending pastor. Indeed, ministers were highly revered, and their words carried much weight when it came to spiritual matters. There were, however, others in a given community who were highly qualified to tender wisdom from their own pilgrimages:

> And it is further granted by Ministers, and others, that some private Christians have a richer Stock of Experiences, then Ministers generally have: For oft-times a private Christian hath the Thing treated of, whilst the other hath it only in theory. Now Christian Conference is a proper Season for such as are stored with Experiences, to communicate them to their Fellow-Christians. And therefore such Conference is the more a Duty.[27]

The experiences of those on the Christian pilgrimage were invaluable to the caring of souls and the understanding of living out the Word in everyday life. Joseph Alleine commented on this convergence of soul care and knowledge of God's Word:

> Brethren beloved, how fares it with your souls? are they in health? do they prosper? I wish your temporal prosperity. It is a joy to me to hear when your trade doth florish: but these are but very little things if we look into Eternity. Brethren, my ambition for you is, that you should be Cedars among the Shrubs, that from you should sound out the Word of the

---

26. Anonymous, *Stated Christian Conference*, 23.
27. Anonymous, *Stated Christian Conference*, 23.

Lord, and that in every place your Faith to God-ward should be spread abroad.[28]

In conjunction with one's growth in biblical knowledge was the sharing of that knowledge in discourse: what was on the heart was expressed in words, in life, and in community.

Biblical Support for Godly Conference

So committed were the Puritans to ground their life and activities in the Bible, that scriptural bases for all activities, including conference, were essential. Its proponents affirmed biblical support for godly conference throughout the Old and New Testaments, from the writings of the prophets to the epistles of Paul, and in specific examples found in the life of Jesus.

Thomas Watson asserted conference as a duty of religion and offered Psalm 37:30 as a support for godly discourse: "A gracious person hath not only Religion in his heart, but in his tongue. *The Law of God is in his heart, and his tongue talketh of Judgement*: he drops holy words as Pearls."[29] Nicholas Bownd added support from Psalm 119:13: "With my lippes have I declared all the judgements of thy mouth." The Christian was to speak the Word of God to others, "Showing in his own person what should be the exercise of all the faithfull."[30]

Isaac Ambrose (1604–1664) drew support for conference from the prophet Malachi in 3:16:

> In holy Conference: This indeed is it that might much improve the meeting of Christians. In the Prophets time, when proud scorners, and prophane spirited men talked vainly, and did even what they lift, then *they that feared the Lord met, and spake often one to another*; no doubt they spake of God, and his councels, of his works and ways, of his providence and

---

28. Joseph Alleine, *Christian Letters* (London: Printed for and sold by Nevil Simmons and Dorman Newman, 1673), 71.

29. Watson, *Heaven Taken by Storm*, 71.

30. Nicholas Bownd, *The Doctrine of the Sabbath Plainely Layde Forth* (London: Printed by the Widow Orwin, 1595), 211–12.

goodness, of the baseness of Atheistical thoughts concerning God: would Christians thus meet and exchange words and notions, they might build up one another, they might heat and inflame one another, they might strengthen and encourage one another, as the brethren did Paul: and have we not an express Command for this Duty of Conference?[31]

Both Watson and Bownd cited the prophet Malachi in confirming this means. Watson observed the disregard for conference and added, "Indeed we are backward enough to it, therefore had need herein provoke our selves (Mal. 3:17).[32] From the same verse, Bownd expounded, "Malachy noteth out the godly in his time, by this marke, that they conferred one with another of the Scripture, which they heard, when he thus writeth, Then spake they that feared the Lord every one to his neighbor." He then asserted, "Afterwardes he declareth what was wrought in the godly, namely, that they conferred of those things diligently among themselves: both of the judgements… that they may avoid them: and of the promises," so that "they might be comforted over them, & incourage themselves to wait upon God for the accomplishment of them."[33] Conference was a distinguishing mark of a believer. The added benefit of God involving Himself in conference as He hears and "takes special notice of every good word we speak when we meet,[34] led Bownd to summarize in a statement based on Malachi 2:7, "The people ought to conferre with the Minister, and he with them, and they with one another."[35]

The Gospels give evidence of Jesus personally exercising conference with His disciples. He is found to be conferring with His disciples and the rest of His hearers, "opening" many parables to them (Mark 4:10). Richard Baxter added, "You will find that most of the preaching recorded in the New Testament, was by confer-

---

31. Ambrose, *Media*, 296.
32. Watson, *Heaven Taken by Storm*, 71.
33. Bownd, *Doctrine of the Sabbath*, 212; Bownd, *Sabbathum Veteris Et Noui Testamenti*, 392.
34. Bownd, *Sabbathum Veteris Et Noui Testamenti*, 393.
35. Bownd, *Doctrine of the Sabbath*, 220.

ence, and frequently interlocutory, and that with one or two, fewer or more, as opportunity served. Thus Christ himself did most commonly preach."[36] In addition, further support is derived from Jesus' appearance to the two disciples as they walked along the road to Emmaus and communed over the death and sufferings of Christ (Luke 24:15). This encounter served as evidence that by holy discourse, Jesus drew near and accompanied them.

Watson understood that as believers "have holy and gracious conference, Jesus draws near, and where-ever he comes, he brings a blessing along with him."[37] Holy discourse brought Christ into one's company, which in turn enabled believers to resemble Christ more closely. Furthermore, "Christ never came into any company, but set good discourse on foot. Levi made his a feast, Luke 5:29, and Christ feasted him with holy discourse.... The more holy our speeches are, the more we are like Christ."[38]

In his most famous work, *Christian Warfare,* John Downame (1571–1652) described the advantages of inclusion in conference. This Church of England clergyman and author found grounds for conference in Romans 14:1:

> Holy conference with our godly brethren; for hereby those which are falling are confirmed, and the wearie hands and weake knees strengthened, as Eliphas speaketh, Job 43:4 And those who are weake in faith are comforted and established with the godly instructions, profitable exhortations and sweet consolations of those who are more strong. And therefore the Apostle Paul exhorts those who had attained unto a great measure of faith, that they admit such as were weake into their company to be made partakers of their Christian conferences, to the end that hereby they might be more and more strengthened and confirmed.[39]

---

36. Richard Baxter, *The Reformed Pastor,* ed. William Brown (Edinburgh: Banner of Truth, 1974), 228.
37. Watson, *Heaven Taken by Storm,* 74.
38. Watson, *Heaven Taken by Storm,* 73.
39. John Downame, *The Christian Warfare* (London: Printed by William Standsby, 1634), 259.

Indeed, such advantages of empathy, encouragement, and direction were inherent for those engaged in conference. Again, from the Pauline Epistles, Bownd asserted Paul's desire for the church to engage in conference by his understanding of Colossians 3:16: "He willeth them to conferre of the Scriptures, to the profit of one another, so he sheweth them how they shall come unto it."[40] The profit was echoed in Watson's assertion that holy conference is edifying, based on Paul's words:

> The Apostle bids us edifie one another, Eph. 4:29. And how more than this way? Good conference enlightens the mind when it is ignorant; warms it when it is frozen; settles it when it is wavering. A good life adorns Religion; good discourse propagates it.[41]

Conference afforded its participants to grow in biblical knowledge and to have an impact that would reach beyond their sessions. Conversations were seasoned with thoughts enlarged by the gathered time in Scripture. The Word-infused speech of a pilgrim on his or her journey produced a particular verbiage characteristic of the Puritans, the "language of Canaan." Watson described this audible marker from his interpretation of Hebrews 11:16:

> What should our words dilate and expatiate upon but Heaven? The world is a great Inne; we are guests in this Inne. Travellers, when they are met in their Inne, do not spend all their time in speaking about their Inne; they are to lodge there but a few hours, and they are gone; but they are speaking of their home, and the Country whither they are travelling. So when we meet together, we should not be talking only about the world; we are to leave this presently; but we should talk of our heavenly Country.[42]

---

40. Bownd, *Doctrine of the Sabbath*, 214.
41. Watson, *Heaven Taken by Storm*, 72–73.
42. Watson, *Heaven Taken by Storm*, 72.

One's speech mirrored the stirrings of the heart. Echoing Proverbs 27:19, Watson used two metaphors to illustrate that speech reveals the content of the heart:

> The discourse demonstrates what the heart is. As the Glass shews what the face is, whether it be fair or foul: so the words shew what the heart is. Vain speeches discover a light feathery heart: gracious speeches are the birth of a gracious heart. The water of the Conduit shews what the Spring is.[43]

The biblical rationale for employing this means of grace substantiated the wide use of this discipline. Conference was encouraged and practiced as a means of establishing a biblical foundation for living out the Word in speech as well as practice.

Neglect of Conference

Biblical support for conference did not always ensure the practice of it. The lack of spiritual growth in professing Christians was attributed to many things, one of which was the inattention to conference. A company of fifteen ministers of Wight and Southampton "seriously and sadly" assessed the ignorance of many in their congregations:

> But, how little, or no acquaintance many of our people have with the things of God, how unhappy a qualification this is for any thing that is evil, and what unavoidable advantages the Devil hath against those poor souls, whom he is sure to set upon in the dark.[44]

These concerned pastors were sure of the benefits of conference; a congregation that knew their Bibles was more apt to apply the Word:

---

43. Watson, *Heaven Taken by Storm*, 72.
44. Anonymous, *The Address of Some Ministers of Christ in the Isle of Wight & County of Southampton to the People of Their Respective Charges* (London: Printed by J. H., 1658), 4–5. The identities of these ministers remain largely unknown with the exception of Robert Dingley, who, in 1648, was presented to the rectory of Brighstone near Newport on the Isle of Wight where he published three works.

> Your selves, Brethren, are our witnesses, that in the course of our Ministry, we have made it much of our business to informe mens judgments, being very sure of this, that unless we could have a knowing people, we should never have a gratious people.[45]

As a collective response, the concerned pastors drafted an address exhorting their parishioners to allow them the opportunities to meet for conference with them in "this service of your soules."[46] They were confident of the positive outcomes of such a venture and willingly invested their time and attention to promoting conference.

Watson, too, observed the same neglect of conference, refraining from heavenly discourse while preoccupied with the verbiage of and about the world:

> 'Tis the fault of Christians, that they do not in company words provoke themselves to set good discourse on foot: it is a sinfull modesty: there is much visiting, but they do not give one anothers souls a visit. In worldly things their tongue is *as a Pen of a ready Writer*; but in matters of Religion, they are as if their tongue *did cleave to the roof of their mouth*. As we must answer to God for *idle words*; so for *sinfull silence*.[47]

Engagement in dialogue about God and His ways and manners were supplanted by empty conversation on worldly subjects. Bownd scrutinized,

> We shall find that our nature is so wholly corrupt in this thing, that wee had rather speake of, and listen unto the things of the world many hours, than unto heavenly things the least moment of time, yea even upon the Lords day.[48]

The content of one's speech, engrossed with worldly matters and concerns, gave evidence to the mind's propensity toward earthly versus heavenly affairs.

---

45. Anonymous, *Addresse*, 5.
46. Anonymous, *Addresse*, 27.
47. Watson, *Heaven Taken by Storm*, 71.
48. Bownd, *Sabbathum Veteris Et Noui Testamenti*, 394.

Holy Conference: "A Kinde of Paradise"

John Bunyan (1628-1688) understood that a change in mind produced change in behavior. Through his characters Christian and Hopeful, he furthered the discussion on the plight of Christians who backslide from faith in his closing of part 1 of *Pilgrim's Progress*. Having successfully come to their journey's end, Hopeful asked Christian of the manner by which this backsliding occured. Christian's response included the lack of conference as a cause of such spiritual decline. Of the nine points given, Bunyan listed these as third and fourth: "They shun the company of lively and warm Christians," and "After that they grow cold to public duty, as hearing, reading, godly conference, and the like."[49] Listed here as a public duty, likely because of its communal aspect, conference was identified as a profitable discipline whose neglect could mean a compromise in spiritual wellness.

The siege of temptations, persecutions, and infirmities beckoned the Christian soul. Francis Rous (1580/81-1659), a religious writer and politician, saw the world as "a strange Countrie" through which Christian pilgrims and their brethren were joined as fellow travelers. He understood the need for one to be with another in close conversation over the perplexities of life. Rous's imperative targeted this need:

> Let us not bind our selves to our own infirmities, falls and wants for lack of opening and communicating our estates; for many have falen and never risen againe, because they have gone alone, neglecting the companie of such who could have given them the hand, to raise them from their falls.[50]

The crushing weight of confusion caused many in spiritual seclusion to succumb to weakened faith. How great the need to confer with one another's souls on spiritual matters!

---

49. Bunyan, *The Pilgrim's Progress*, 126.
50. Francis Rous, *The Arte of Happines* (London: Printed by W. Stansby, 1619), 399-400.

Benefits of Conference

The benefits gleaned by the Puritans as they engaged in conference were far-reaching. Evidence shows that the advantages of gathering in small groups to discuss biblical passages as they relate to life experiences were extensive and were not limited to any one particular group of people. There was no gender, literacy, or class distinction. In conference there would be no discrimination.

1. Ministerial care. Richard Baxter was well aware of the benefits of appropriating ample care to the souls of his congregants. He wrote of conference in *Reformed Pastor*:

> By means of it, we shall come to be better acquainted with each person's spiritual state, and so the better know how to watch over them.... We shall know better how to preach to them.... We shall know better how to lament for them, and to rejoice for them, and to pray for them.[51]

He found the ministry of preaching alone was insufficient for setting "all home for the conscience and the heart." Conference may be more time intensive, but its benefits are undeniable. Baxter argued, "I have found by experience, that some ignorant persons, who have been so long unprofitable hearers, have got more knowledge and remorse of conscience in half an hours close discourse, than they did from ten years public preaching."[52]

In a later work addressing the pastoral ministry, Baxter added this:

> You know we cannot speak so familiarly, and come so close to every ones case, in a common Sermon, as we may do by conference: And in conference it is not a little rambling discourse upon the by that is fit for so great a business; and therefore I intreated you to allow me now and then an hours set and

---

51. Baxter, *The Reformed Pastor*, 178.
52. Baxter, *The Reformed Pastor*, 196.

sober talk with you, when all other matters might for that time be laid by.[53]

This one-on-one time gave opportunity to plumb the depths of one's piety with the hope that a pastor could better individualize the care given to members of his congregation.

The group of ministers previously mentioned from Wight and Southampton, England, were contemporaries of Baxter. They, too, were certain of the profit from conference. These pastors were confident of the benefit in their congregations, "If they knew more, they would live better, if they did not see so little, they would not sin so much; they would not so constantly go out of their way, did they not go in the dark."[54] Corporately they voiced their commitment to "revive and constantly to practise the too long neglected duties of Private Conference and Catechizing."[55] They were convinced of the advantages conference with their parishioners would offer. Congregants would grow in their "proficiency in grace and knowledge," redeeming the time that would typically be spent on "what will doe your soules no good, and some of you what doth them harme."[56] Conference allowed for the type of interaction between clergy and laity that furthered the ability for ministers to know the members of their congregations. Nothing replaced the face-to-face interaction in developing and deepening the relationships necessary to tailor their efforts in communicating to, praying for, and overall ministering to their flock.

2. *Memorization aid.* Conference assisted the memory. Richard Bernard affirmed, "If thou hast forgot, the memories of other may help thine, as also thine understanding, in that thou thy selfe knowest not."[57] Memory was intrinsically linked with the growth in under-

---

53. Richard Baxter, *The Poor Man's Family Book* (London: Printed for Nevill Simmons, 1675), 1–2.
54. Anonymous, *Addresse*, 5.
55. Anonymous, *Addresse*, 6.
56. Anonymous, *Addresse*, 29.
57. Richard Bernard, *A Weekes Worke Containing Rules and Directions*

standing of Scripture. If the Word of God was to be the constant guide on which one relied for direction in the conduct of life, then the understanding of it was not only basic but also crucial. John Udall (ca. 1560–1592/3) described the method whereby conference was used for helping to ensure one's recording of their sermon notes as well as to augment the remembrance of said notes, to their mutual edification:

> After that the sermon is done, we ought at our coming home, to meete together, & say one to another: come, we have al bene where we have heard Gods word taught, let us confer about it, that we may not onely call to remembrance those things that every one of us have caried away, but also that one may have (any) benefit of the labors of others: & surely it must needes prove a very profitable way: for if one have missed any observation of this or that point, another hath marked it, so that among them they may bring away a whole, and so be edified one by another.[58]

Conference ensured that nothing of importance was lost in transmission or translation. The risk of missing a principle or misinterpreting it was possible, and the mutual edification was too great not to warrant conference with one another.

Complaints of inability to memorize were not regarded as adequate grounds of excuse and were countered with a swift commentary:

> Whereas many complaine of ill memorie in good things, thinking thereby to cover many wants, this is found the onely remedie, that they must first reforme their hearts, and bring them to affect such heavenly doctrines, and then valuing them as they be, they would as well remember, as a worldly man hearing of a good bargaine, whereby hee is assured he may have great gaine, will hardly forget the same, yet hereto let this be added, an hiding of Gods Word, and treasuring of it up in

---

how to Walke in the Wayes of Godliness both to God and Man (London: By Felix Kingston, 1650), 155.

58. John Udall, *Obedience to the Gospell* (London: Imprinted [by J. Windet?], 1584), image 17 of 55, n.p.

our hearts, which oft recounting with our selves and others, the same shall not be forgotten.[59]

Stimulated recollection of God's Word was the avenue for expanding knowledge.

3. *Biblical literacy.* In conference, the process of this growth in knowledge was not to attract those who could articulate biblical truths or who were well versed in Scripture. The appeal of conference was that it attracted those from every point on the biblical literacy spectrum. To those who were literate, it gave them opportunities to come alongside in sharing their knowledge as well as experience in the Christian journey. It was not an arena to show one's spiritual prowess but to invest in others' lives and offer counsel for their pilgrimage. For those whose biblical literacy was low, conference was an opportunity to glean from those more spiritually knowledgeable and experienced. It was a gathering of those of humble desire for growth and community. Bownd explained:

> for though it be a sinne in us indeede, that the worde of Christ doth not dwell in us more plenteouslie, and that we be no more filled with the Spirit, and so cannot speake so profitable as we should; yet none that is desirous to learne can be so ignorant, but hee may ask a question concerning some thing that hath been taught, and say, what is the meaning of this? or how do you understand that? or how was such a thing prooved? and so begin the conference, and glue occasion to other to prosecute it: which if he doe in the feare of God, he shall find his blessing to bee such, that though hee conferre with others that have as little knowledge as himselfe, hee shall not depart from them altogether unprofitable. For that which every man severally cannot doe, all of them together (as it were joyning their strengths) shal be able to bring to passe; and as in a common gathering, though every one give but a little, yet the summe

---

59. Ezekiel Culverwell, *Time Well Spent in Sacred Meditations* (London: Printed by T. Cotes, 1635), 218–19.

amounteth to a great deal: so the knowledge of many being put together, shall increase that, which was in every man before.⁶⁰

Surely the learning of biblical truths together as a small community and experiencing accountability afforded great benefits. Bownd recognized the dynamics of spiritual camaraderie found in conference:

> Wherunto agreeth that Proverbe of Solomon: Even as *iron sharpeneth iron, so doth the face of a man sharpen his friend*: That is, even as a knife that is blunt being rubbed upon the whetstone (though it bee more blunt then it selfe) receiveth thereby a sharpnes, which it had not before: so one man by the presence and *conference of another receiveth instruction*, and getteth that which hee had not before.⁶¹

Participants of conference had much to gain when exercising this communal discipline. Minds were challenged by the truths found in the Scriptures. Sibbes pens this metaphor, "Good conference, then, is good for ourselves; for we see a little seed brings forth at length a great tree, a little fire kindleth much fuel, and great things many times rise out of small beginnings."⁶² It was right that believers gleaned from their Bible reading or sermon notes and then intentionally drew together for the purpose of seeking clarity and relevance. After all, as Isaac Ambrose argued, it was so modeled in Acts 17:11:

> This is it for which the noble *Bereans* are commended to us, *They searched the Scriptures daily, concerning the things that were delivered by Paul*: A man that comes into a pleasant garden, will not content himself with the present scent onely, but will carry some of the flowers away with him: So after we have been in the Garden of Spices and have felt the savour of Christs ointments in Church-Assemblies, let us take some of the flowers away with us, and smell them again and again. *Repeating,*

---

60. Bownd, *Sabbathum Veteris Et Noui Testamenti*, 399.
61. Bownd, *Sabbathum Veteris Et Noui Testamenti*, 400.
62. Sibbes, *Bowels Opened*, 296.

conferring, examining the word, is as pounding of spices, that will make them smell more.[63]

One's recall of the sermon, beyond the "heads" of the message, which was the exercise of repeating the sermon, was central to conference. Brilliana Harley (d. 1643) was a staunch Puritan known for the over two hundred preserved letters to her husband and eldest son, Edward. Her letters were rich with religious overtones. One written in 1639 to Edward (1624–1700) as he matriculated from the Puritan Magdalen Hall, Oxford, urged her son to heed her counsel to pursue conference:

> My deare Ned, omite not privet dutyes, and stire up your self to exercise yourself in holy conference, begg of God to give you a delight in speaking and thinkeing of thos thinges which are your eternall treasure. I many times thinke Godly conference is as much neglected by Gods chillderen, as any duty. I am confident you will noways neglect the opertunity of profeting in the ways of lerning, and I pray God prosper your endevors.[64]

Harley is conscious of the depth of knowledge obtained through conference and attentive to Edward's need of it. Her concerns echo the importance and essential nature of conference. No one should be without it, least of all her beloved son.

4. *State of the soul.* Time and attention were given in conference to the advancement of biblical knowledge as well as to explore the states of souls. Downame reveals some of what was involved when we examine the state of our souls: we are to "seriously examine our estate in the Audit of conscience, and as in God's presence, how it standeth betweene him and us, and whether it thriveth and groweth better, or decayeth and waxeth worse in spiritual graces, and in

---

63. Ambrose, *Media*, 341.

64. Brilliana Harley, *Letters of the Lady Brilliana Harley, Wife of Sir Robert Harley, of Brampton Bryan, Knight of the Bath*, ed. Thomas Taylor Lewis, Camden Society Publications, vol. 58 (London: Printed for the Camden Soc., 1854), 65.

the practice of Christian and holy duties."[65] The intersection of life experiences with the biblical truths that were intended to inform those experiences came to the fore in conference.

The consolation in conference could be provided by ministers; however, they were not the sole source. Nonclerical laypersons also provided great solace and support. John Rogers stated:

> Society and conference with our fellow-brethren; especially some experienced Christian or faithfull Minister, and revealing unto them our doubts, is a notable meanes. For they may confirme us, by their counsels and consolations fetched out of the Word, and by their owne experience laid before us; for it availes much to our comfort to heare that others have beene in our case, and yet are now.[66]

Again, one is impressed by the intersection of biblical knowledge with soul care.

The divine element of conference cannot be ignored. God may ordain an apparent spiritual weakness or void for the very purpose of seeking out another pilgrim to meet and fill that need. His intent may be for the uniting of one with another for the benefit of more—those gathered and God Himself. Sibbes suggested:

> When a question is moved, it will not be quiet till it have satisfaction. Therefore doubting at the first, breeds resolution at the last. It is good therefore to raise questions of the practice of all necessary points; and to improve the good parts and gifts of others that we converse with, to give satisfaction. What an excellent improvement is this of communion and company, when nothing troubles our spirit, but we have satisfaction from others upon our proposing it. Perhaps God hath laid up in parts of others, satisfaction to our souls; and hath determined that we shall be perplexed and vexed with scruples, till

---

65. John Downame, *A Guide to Godlynesse* (London: By Felix Kingstone and William Stansby, 1622), 76.

66. John Rogers, *The Doctrine of Faith* (London: Printed for Nathanael Newbery and Henry Overton, 1632), 262. Because of an error in pagination, the correct page number should be 216.

we have recourse to some whom he hath appointed to be helpful to us in this kind. Many go mourning a great part of their days in a kind of sullenness this way, because that they do not open their estate to others.[67]

Conference was a means of grace, a spiritual discipline that afforded opportunities to ask questions and to converse with the spiritually mature. In this way, Puritans would have the greatest potential for personal spiritual recalibration that would have a direct impact on their immediate community, culture, and society. Promoted and exercised by both clergy and laity, conference was a widely accepted means of grace among the godly, a form of enabling that was encouraged and enjoyed.

Format

As an ordinary means that was to be exercised commonly, conference served as an intimate forum in which people at various stages in their spiritual pilgrimages came together for the purpose of sharing the mountain heights, valley depths, and ordinary plains of their pilgrimage. Questions and confusions over God's Word were honestly presented. Doubts and fears were intimately disclosed. Joys and victories were pleasurably shared.

1. Logistics. Depending on the participants involved, the regularity of conference could vary. Isaac Ambrose described the frequency of conference as weekly. He proposed "that every Wednesday (especially during winter) we will meet for Conference about soul affairs."[68] Others frequented conference "as often as conveniency will permit, to stir up, and exhort each other…and to give each other a Lift Heaven-ward."[69] The group of pastors of Wight and Southampton offered this familiar way of personal instruction by conference: "A greater number of you together at such Times and places, as wee

---

67. Sibbes, *Bowels Opened*, 298.
68. Ambrose, *Media*, 297.
69. Anonymous, *Stated Christian Conference*, 13.

shall appoint for that purpose, or if any inconvenience be found in what we shall offer, you would be pleased to propound a better methode your selves, and wee shall readily comply with you in it."[70]

They further asked this: "That when you are come together, you would not necessitate us to be the onely *speakers*, but be ready to ask when you doe not *know*, and to express your selves (according to the matter in hand) so farre as you doe *know*, that we may by this meanes informe our selves what acquaintance you have with the things of God, and be the better inabled to apply ourselves to your respective conditions and necessities, as well in this as in other duties of our Ministry."[71]

Samuel Clarke arranged for an entire day of conference every three weeks:

> Both Men and Women out of all the Country; and this Meeting was held by turns at all the richer mens Houses: in the Morning when they first met, the Master of the Family began with Prayer, then was the question to be conferred of read, and the younger Christians first gave in their answers, together with their proofs of Scripture for them; and then the more experienced Christians gathered up the other answers which were omitted by the former; and thus they continued till Dinner time, when having good provision made for them by the Master of the Family, they dined together with much cheerfulness; after Dinner, having sung a Psalm, they returned to their Conference upon the other questions (which were three in all) till towards the Evening; at which time, as the Master of the Family began, so he concluded with Prayer, and I gave them three new questions against their next Meeting; which being appointed for time and place, every one repaired to his own home: the benefits which came by these days of Conference, were many and great.[72]

---

70. Anonymous, *Addresse*, 27.
71. Anonymous, *Addresse*, 28.
72. Samuel Clarke, *The Lives of Sundry Eminent Persons* (London: Printed for Thomas Simmons, 1683), 4.

Frequency, times, and venues could be determined by a pastor or by the participants themselves. It appeared that whenever these professors of the Christian faith regularly met, it afforded them significant opportunities to cultivate their faith and nurture the bonds connecting them, thus creating a cohesive community.

2. *Content.* An investigation into the elements of discussion that made up dialogue of conference can help inform an understanding of this spiritual discipline. One author described the dynamics of conference:

> Tis a mutual conferring about the things of God, things of the greatest moment, things of Eternal Consequence, the subject matter of which generally is, Viz. How may I Glorifie God in my Generation? Or, how may I know my self to be Spiritually alive? How may I distinguish between common grace, and saving grace? Or, when may I be said to Act Faith?
>
> Or, how shall I discern between raging Corruption, and Reigning? Or, what are the most proper means, to mortify a special Sin?
>
> With many other Questions of like import, which are frequently Discours'd of in Conferences.[73]

Ambrose asserted from his interpretation of Jeremiah 23:35 that as an obligation to confer with one another, the seed of conversation is provided: "*Thus shall ye say every one to his brother, and every one to his neighbour, What hath the Lord answered? and what hath he spoken?*" A moderator was assigned to each of these conference groups, whose responsibility it was to "propound the question and matter of our Discourse the week before it be discussed; and at every meeting begin with Prayer and end with Thanksgiving."[74] He continued in the following sections of *Media*, to "lay down some experiments and proceedings of some Christians as willingly joyned themselves in a Christian Society, and by Gods blessing thereby sweetly improved

---

73. Anonymous, *Stated Christian Conference,* 19.
74. Ambrose, *Media,* 297.

themselves."[75] Confidentiality was the rule from the outset as was the need to spell out the process of confronting the sin of a fellow society member.

Of particular interest were the details and insights revealed by Ambrose in his recording of some questions asked in conference proposed by Puritans, each with a corresponding answer. Only the questions are presented here. The questions propounded were of several sorts:

I. Choyce heads of Practical divinity
    A. What was the happiness of Mans condition in the state of Innocency?
    B. What are the Miseries of Man in State of Nature?
    C. What means hath God appointed to come out of this miserable state?
    D. What are the signs of a sound and sincere Humiliation?
    E. What [means] hath God appointed for brokenness of heart?
    F. What are the means both for the obtaining and increasing of Faith?
    G. What are the signs of a true justifying Faith?
    H. What motives to Evangelical Repentance?
    I. What are the signs of true Evangelical Repentance?
    J. How may a believer Redeemed by Christ, acknowledge his thankfulness to Christ?
    K. What are the signs of a sincere love to Christ?
    L. What are the causes in us of Christ withdrawing from us?
    M. What are the causes for which Christ on his part withdraws himself from us?
    N. What means for the recovery of Christ's comfortable presence?
    O. Of what use is Christ to a believer already justified?

II. Wholesome Cases of Conscience
    A. Whether a believer may profit more, or be more intent in publique, or secret Prayer?

---

75. Ambrose, *Media*, 296.

B. Whether a Christian in his own apprehension decaying in Grace, may not yet grow in Grace? and if so, What are the reasons of his wrong apprehensions?
C. What signes of true grace, though for the present but small or weak grace?
D. Whether is a Christian always bound to reprehend an offender? or in what cases may he forbear?
E. How may we know whether we profit by afflictions?
F. How should a Christian fortifie himself against the reproaches of wicked men?
G. Whether a true Believer may not sometimes doubt? and what are the several causes of doubting?
H. What are the cures or remedies of doubtings incident to Believers?
I. What are those Remora's that hinder the growth of Christianity, or the spreading of the Kingdom of Christ?
J. What means to preserve Unity and Amity amongst Christians?

III. Some Controverted Points
A. Whether doth God see sin in Believers, so as to be offended at it? and how may it appear?
B. Whether are Believers to repent for their sins? And upon what grounds?
C. Whether are Believers to pray for pardon of sin? And what are the reasons?
D. Whether it is the duty of Christians to observe the Lords-day (now being the first day of the week) as a Christian Sabbath? And what grounds for it?
E. Whether may not Christians lawfully sing David's or Moses psalms? And how may it appear?
F. Whether admitting or of joining with scandalous persons in the Sacrament of the Lords Supper, and not endeavoring to keep them back (whiles such) be not sin in the admitters and joiners? And how may it appear?

> G. In such case, what is the duty of admitters and joiners, to keep themselves blameless, and the Ordinance undefiled?[76]

Responses to these posed questions revealed a type of spirituality that required a strong and developing faith grounded on a solid biblical foundation. They also demonstrated that biblical literacy and soul care were not mutually exclusive. Attendees would not be satisfied with their own or others' simple, easy, effortless answers. These questions required thoughtful and clear discernment and, given the opportunity for discussion over these matters, conferees could derive principles for life application. This was clear evidence of a piety that sought to be biblical, intensely personal, and practical.

3. *Conference in absentia.* Conference refers to the face-to-face interaction between members; however, conference via letters was not uncommon. The concern of mutual care and growth in godliness was not restricted to the care received in the interface between spiritual pilgrims. Richard Alleine (d. 1668), an ejected minister and devotional writer, communicated this type of concern in his *Christian Letters*, written while jailed for preaching:

> Brethren beloved, How fares it with your Souls? Are they in Health? Do they prosper? I wish your Temporal prosperity. It is a joy to hear when your Trade doth flourish: But these are but very little things if we look into Eternity. Brethren, my ambition for you is, that you should be Cedars among the Shrubs, that from you should sound out the Word of the Lord, and that in every place your Faith to God-ward should be spread abroad.[77]

Neither the lack of physical presence nor the distance that separated many Puritans from each other diminished the longing for conference. This was demonstrated by correspondences from Jonathan Mitchel (1624–1668), an English-born minister in America:

---

76. Ambrose, *Media*, 298–327.
77. As cited in Wallace Jr., *Spirituality of the Later*, 185.

Holy Conference: "A Kinde of Paradise" 121

> But yet considering some passages in your last and former Letters concerning your Spiritual Condition, and knowing by experience in my self the reality of such Complaints, I would not be so graceless as to neglect you wholly therein: And though I can say or do very little, yet a word or two might be of some use; nor do I know what guilt might lye upon me, if I should be silent or slight in this Case! And therefore [Dear —] if my barren heart would suffer me, I would present you with a few words, as if you and I were alone in a Corner in the presence of God.[78]

Mitchel was particularly intent on ensuring the depth of mutual care and attention required of spiritual health. He understood and expressed the common need and benefits of conference:

> And truly when I am most near God, I have no greater request then this for my self and you, that God would use any means to make us see things really as they are, and pound our hearts all to pieces, and make indeed sin most bitter, and Christ most sweet; that we might be both humbled and comforted to purpose![79]

Not dependent on letters that out of necessity were irregular at best and could not substitute for the interaction that personal, one-on-another conference proffered, Mitchel was sure to add this:

> Do not think it much to have some speciall seasons of seeking God, besides those I have named. If you have a friend with whom you might now and then spend a little time, in conferring together, in opening your hearts, and presenting your unutterable groanings before God, it would be of excellent use: Such an one would greatly strengthen, bestead, and further you in your way to Heaven. Spend now and then [as occasions will permit] an hour [or so] with such a friend more then ordinary. [sometimes a piece of a day, sometimes a whole

---

78. Jonathan Mitchel, *A Discourse of the Glory* (London: Printed for Nathaniel Ponder, 1677), 1–2.
79. Mitchel, *A Discourse of the Glory*, 3.

day of extraordinary fast, in striving and wrestling with God for everlasting mercy.][80]

Mitchel's directive was based on the verity of proven conference in the life of believers. The regular support and guidance obtained through conference was exceptional and unrivaled as a means for the community to foster their interest after Christ. He charged his reader:

> Be much in quickning conference, giving and taking mutuall encouragements and directions in the matters of heaven! Oh! The life of God that falls into the hearts of the Godly, in and by gracious Heavenly conference. Be open-hearted one to another, and stand one for another against the Devil and all his Angels. Make it thus your business in these and such like wayes, to provide for Eternity while it is called today, looking to Jesus the Author and finisher of your Faith.[81]

Mitchel's reader was encouraged to pursue a type of spiritual friend who understood the substance and value of conference.

Conclusion

In conference, Puritans and Puritan pastors provided opportunities to seek advice and learn from the spiritually mature. Imparting biblical knowledge and discerning the spiritual condition of their parishioners were necessary elements of a productive ministry, professional or lay. Biblical truths that were ushered into their souls would then be translated into the affairs of life. This was practical divinity. Whether done with pastors or with laypersons, in one-on-one encounters or in groups of godly persons, the strength and effectiveness of such spiritual counsel was that it connected biblical knowledge with actual life experience. These were times and places where the experiences of souls with their troubles, temptations, disillusionments, joys, celebrations, and victories came together. Living the Christian life often meant facing the counterintuitive challenges

---

80. Mitchel, *A Discourse of the Glory*, 15.
81. Mitchel, *A Discourse of the Glory*, 16.

it presented. Conference afforded its participants to be attuned to God, His Word, and His community, thus helping many along their spiritual pilgrimage.

The variegated forms of conference pose problems of nomenclature. It has been difficult to devise a system that clearly extrapolates the distinctiveness of this means of grace while maintaining the integrity of its form. The following chapter proposes a working rubric for the organization of conference followed by a sampling of historical figures that exercised this means of grace.

CHAPTER SIX

Holy Conference: Categorized and Exercised

The English Puritans understood that growth in one's spiritual life and ministry was accomplished by well-intentioned effort. This effort was manifested in their exercise of the means of grace, or spiritual disciplines. A spiritual discipline is an activity that enables one to accomplish what he or she cannot do by direct effort: an activity to bring a believer into more effective cooperation with Christ and His kingdom.[1] This definition supports the identification of conference as a spiritual discipline because it contributes to the process of spiritual transformation.

As a spiritual discipline, or means of grace, employed by the English Puritans, conference was a spiritual activity exercised by small groups of believers whose goal was to explore biblical truths and determine their practical application in conjunction with the estate of the soul. It was found in a number of different venues and exercised among a variety of participants. Due to the multiplicity of these elements, clarification and explication proved problematic without a method to assist in arranging the various types of conference.

Few scholars have identified conference. Fewer yet have endeavored to practically systematize the diversities, and none have developed the practicalities of this means of grace, particularly as it can apply to the contemporary church. The objective of this chapter

---

1. Dallas Willard, *The Divine Conspiracy: Rediscovering Our Hidden Life in God* (San Francisco: Harper, 1997), 353; Dallas Willard, *The Spirit of the Disciplines* (San Francisco: Harper & Row Publishers, 1988), 156.

is to provide a working rubric that encompasses the various nuances of this means of grace, in the hope that it will facilitate further research of this discipline and application of its relevant implications for contemporary use.

A Rubric for Puritan Conference

The forms of conference exercised by the Puritans were many and varied. A systematic classification of the categories and sub-categories of conference will assist in defining the various purposes, participants, outcomes, and implications of this discipline. Utilizing a rubric of identifiable types will foster a more clear and efficient study of this means as practiced by its sixteenth- and seventeenth-century English contemporaries and assist in the potential use of this means for contemporary application.

Two primary categories of conference can be established: ministerial and lay. Ministerial conference involves clergy in a setting either among peers or with members of their congregations. Thus, ministerial conference can be further delineated into two subcategories: professional and pastoral.[2]

Ministerial Conference
Originally practiced among clergy in the Elizabethan church after the exercise of prophesying, conference served to foster discussions of varying personal and corporate interest and importance. This practice had two expressions: ministers gathering with one another and pastors meeting with members of their congregations. As a practice commonly found among ministers, conference assisted in maintaining and nurturing the spiritual brotherhood. As the practice of conference continued, it evolved into an integral part of

---

2. J. William Black, *Reformation Pastors: Richard Baxter and the Ideal of the Reformed Pastor*, Studies in Evangelical History and Thought (Carlisle, England: Paternoster, 2004), 297. Black distinguishes two forms of conference in his index: ministerial and personal. The examples of personal conference fall within the ministerial duties performed by the clergy. Thus, this conference is classified as pastoral—one of two subcategories of ministerial conference.

church ministry: an expectation for the pastor to be available for conference with members of his congregation, as well as an expectation on the part of the pastor that his congregants would desire conference with him.

1. *Professional.* Professional conference[3] provided for the exchange of ideas with colleagues and was critical in the supplemental education of godly clergy.[4] Times of conference were generally held after regular weekly combination lectures designed to provide good preaching in strategic places and times through preaching exercises, discussion, and fellowship.[5] Pastors drew their inspiration from these sermons and conferences to sharpen their own homiletic skills and to cultivate a strong sense of belonging to their fellow preachers. As ministers turned to their godly brethren for advice and support, the needs for fellowship and sociability were met,[6] and the spiritual brotherhood was maintained.[7]

Professional conference oftentimes manifested cross-generational aspects, portrayed through the investment of an elder minister's time and attention into the lives of younger ministers. An example of this is pictured in the life of Richard Baxter. At age twenty, on his way to becoming an ordained deacon and curate, Baxter was influenced by several godly pastors and "became acquainted with Mr. Simmonds, Mr. Cradock, and the other very zealous godly Nonconformists in Shrewbury, and the adjoyning parts, whose fervent Prayers, and savoury *Conferences* and holy Lives did profit me much."[8] In a work written for those entering into the ministry, Baxter charged his read-

---

3. Webster, *Godly Clergy*, part 1. Webster refers to the conference exercised among the clergy as clerical conference, which is identified here as "professional."

4. Black, *Reformation Pastors*, 233.

5. Black, *Reformation Pastors*, 148; Patrick Collinson, *Godly People: Essays on English Protestantism and Puritanism*, History Series, vol. 23 (London: Hambledon Press, 1983), 477–98.

6. Webster, *Godly Clergy*, 46.

7. Collinson, *The Elizabethan Puritan Movement*, 129.

8. Baxter, *Reliquiae Baxterianae*, 13.

ers to "study, and pray, and confer, and practise; for in these four ways your abilities must be increased."[9] His conviction was evident in his establishing regular meetings of likeminded clergy, where opportunities for conference, fellowship, and mutual encouragement through shared meals were offered. A forum was made available where local clergy could address contentious issues and circumstances while still maintaining unity in the basics.[10]

Thomas Hooker (1586?–1647), an English-born minister who emigrated to New England in 1633, established a monthly meeting for the nonconformist clergy of Essex[11] and was known for his ability to give direction to other ministers. Cotton Mather (1663–1728), an American minister, venerated Hooker and observed how "the wonders of New England could be beheld in one, Thomas Hooker." He described an aspect of Hooker's ministry and influence:

> The Godly Ministers round about the Country, would have recourse unto him to be directed and resolved in their difficult cases; and it was by his means that those Godly Ministers held their Monthly Meetings, for Fasting and Prayer, and profitable Conferences. 'Twas the Effect of his Consultations also, that such Godly Ministers came to be here and there settled in several parts of the Country; and many others came to be better establish'd in some great Points of Christianity by being in his Neighbourhood and Acquaintance.[12]

On an equally flattering note, John Fuller (b. 1640 or 1641), lecturer of Great Waltham, wrote in the introductory notes of *The Journal*, of his friendship with John Beadle, author of that work:

> We were of an intimate society and vicinity for many years, we took sweet counsell together, and walked unto the house

---

9. Baxter, *The Reformed Pastor*, 71.
10. Black, *Reformation Pastors*, 261.
11. Spurr, *English Puritanism*, 84.
12. Cotton Mather, *Magnalia Christi Americana: Or, the Ecclesiastical History of New-England from its First Planting in the Year 1620 Unto the Year of Our Lord 1698*, Research Library of Colonial Americana, book 3 (New York: Arno Press, 1972), 59–60.

> of God in company. He was my guide, and my acquaintance, as David hath it. We oft breathed and powred out our souls together in Prayer, Fasting and conferences. When walking after the Lord in a wildernesse, we had lesse allowed liberty, but more inward enlargednesse of Spirit. At which time he had the happiness of a younger Elisha (not to powre water on the hand, but) to be watered by the droppings of the great Elijah, that renowned man of God in his generation, Reverend Mr. Thomas Hooker.[13]

Hooker served as a working example of those spiritually mature ministers who invested time in the lives of the next generation of clergy. The experiences of conference with people such as Hooker may have led one Jacobean lecture participant to list nine benefits attesting to the value of such lectures, two of which can be ascribed to conference: increase of love and acquaintance among preachers, and increase of religion and learning by meeting and conference.[14]

Ministers were also found to have enjoyed conference in closer relationships as described by Richard Rogers. A diary entry described the conference he had with neighboring minister and friend Ezekiel Culverwell:

> Of things worth the remembr[ance] in this month, this was one: a most sweet iorney with mr. Cu[lverwel] 2 dayes, and much time bestowed in the way about our christian estat, of godes mercy in our calleing to the felowsh[ip] of the gospel, of the true testemonies of fayth, and of the great comfort which by continuinge herein doth come unto godes people....
> For it is not out of season at any time, to be occupied ether in conference about knowledge atteininge or groweing in godlines.... And this shall be one of the greatest stayes unto myne heavy hart if it may please the lorde to continue this benefit unto us.[15]

---

13. Thomas Fuller, introduction to *The Journal or Diary of a Thankful Christian*, by John Beadle (London: Printed by E. Cotes, 1656), n.p.
14. *Registrum Vagum* I, 97, cited in Collinson, *Godly People*, 498.
15. Richard Rogers and Samuel Ward, *Two Elizabethan Puritan Diaries,*

The conference these two colleagues enjoyed was mutually beneficial, and stood as grounds for its continuation. Rogers also recorded a time when he wrestled with a sense of unwillingness to attend to his work. He sought out his neighbor:

> I set my selfe to goe confer that day with my neighbour and to bring back my mind againe from untowardnes to my book, for, that excepted, there is no great thing of import[ance] which need greatly to cause me to complaine…in few wordes, I found good stirreing up of my minde by our confer[ence], which seldome is, at our particular meetinges, without some sensibl frut and bles[sing], that though we were at that time more then comonly heavy for some unsetlednes, yet, I thanck god, I was well refreshed, recovered my desire to study and willingn[ess] to renue my christian course.[16]

The refreshment and renewed clarity of direction experienced through conference produced gratefulness to God for His mercy and provision, a familiar result from the exercise of this means of grace.

2. *Pastoral.* Pastoral conference involved a minister as he functioned in the role of pastor to his congregation. Classified by the purpose for each form of pastoral conference, three distinct categories can be identified: conversion, pilgrimage, and *mortem obire* (upon meeting one's death).

• *Conference in Conversion.* Attendance at sermons was often mentioned in Puritan biographies as instrumental in the spiritual lives of their subjects when skilled preachers summoned persons to conversion and holiness. The plain and powerful ministry of preaching was understood to be the primary means to prepare a heart for Christ. Puritan preachers understood the goal of preaching not as

---

ed. M. M. Knappen, Studies in Church History, vol. 2 (Chicago: American Society of Church History, 1933), 53.
16. Rogers and Ward, *Two Elizabethan Puritan Diaries*, 99.

theological speculation but conversion—the salvation, or winning, of souls.

The "use" segment of sermons focused on bringing the auditors of that sermon to a decision. Beyond the pulpit was a network of private communications where individuals revealed their spiritual health.[17] Pastoral conference was an integral part of the preconversion and conversion process. This type of conference helped to prepare a seeker for his or her public profession of faith and church membership. From a collection of autobiographical testimonies, or spiritual autobiographies, one J. H. recorded that after hearing a sermon he was left with questions. Meeting with the minister afterward where he "opened some Scriptures," the unbelieving inquirer acknowledged and confessed his own sinfulness.[18] Such intense inmost searching came from hearing sermons, taking and reviewing sermon notes, conferring with pastors, and talking with converted laymen.[19]

Baxter was particularly attentive to the need of a ministry to the unconverted individual. Of all people, the unconverted should not be ignored: "He that seeth a man of a mortal disease, and another only pained with the toothache, will be moved more to compassionate the former, than the latter, and will surely make more haste to help him."[20] The pastor was to make himself available to those whose spiritual doubts and questions came to the fore. He was expected to invite them to conference, whether for conversion, strengthening, or repentance and a renewed start. Baxter informed his readers of this type of pastoral conference:

> [It] will be a most helpful mean of the conversion of souls; for it unites those great things which most further such an end.
>
> (1) As to the matter of it: it is about the most necessary things, the principles or essentials of the Christian faith.

---

17. Cohen, *God's Caress*, 163.
18. Vavasor Powell, *Spirituall Experiences of Sundry Beleevers* (London: Printed by Robert Ibbitson, 1653), 377–78, corrected pagination.
19. Shepard, *Confessions*, 5:2.
20. Baxter, *The Reformed Pastor*, 94–95.

(2) As to the manner of it: it will be by private conference when we have an opportunity to set all home for the conscience and the heart.[21]

He regretted his own neglect of this work in earlier years, and also regretted that as ministers, they had "done so little by personal instruction and conference for the saving of men's souls,"[22] and attempted to influence others in this means of evangelism.

- *Conference in Pilgrimage.* The regenerative process was lengthy and pilgrims were often in need of direction. Oftentimes the new believer required continued spiritual counseling after becoming a member of the church. After spiritual conversion came spiritual guidance. The pilgrimage theme in Puritan spirituality was a favorite metaphor for the Christian life. Inherent in that life was the godly direction needed to face the perils and perplexities of being a Christian. Richard Bernard understood this when he penned these words of a prayer:

> Make us in this our pilgrimage, while we here live from home, mingled among Aliens and strangers from the life of God, so faithfull in beleeving, so conscionable in living, so patient in suffering for wel-doing, as hereby our hearts by thy Spirit may ascertaine us that wee be truely the children of regeneration and grace.[23]

Ministers made themselves accessible for private meetings with those who were experiencing anxieties, having doubts about their faith, or were experiencing any form of spiritual or physical malady.[24]

Sermons certainly aided the first uncertain strides toward conversion. At each step of their spiritual pilgrimage, people welcomed the preacher's assistance. It was common for ministers to meet for

---

21. Baxter, *The Reformed Pastor*, 174.
22. Baxter, *The Reformed Pastor*, 200.
23. Richard Bernard, "A Prayer for a Family at all Times," in *A Good Mans Grace* (London: Printed by Felix Kingston, 1621), n.p.
24. Hambrick-Stowe, *The Practice of Piety*, 153.

conference with members of their congregation for didactic purposes, establishing and fostering biblical knowledge. In conjunction with preaching responsibilities, Baxter found that conference promoted a greater understanding of the Word and exhorted his readers to engage in this activity. Baxter observed this about meeting with one's congregants in private:

> [It] will make our public preaching better understood and regarded.... This prepareth their minds and openeth a way to their hearts; whereas, without this, you may lose the most of your labor; and the more pains you take in accurate preparation, the less good you may do. As you would not, therefore, lose your public labour, see that you be faithful in this private work.[25]

Benefits of this type of conference were undeniable. Baxter affirmed the manifold profit in investing time in conference with members of his congregation. He showed conference in pilgrimage to augment the benefits, or lack of benefits, from sermon messages: "I have found by experience, that some ignorant persons, who have been so long unprofitable hearers, have got more knowledge and remorse of conscience in half an hours close discourse, than they did from ten years public preaching."[26]

Baxter cited an added benefit to this type of conference: the ability to further inquire and assess the spiritual estates of his members. He wrote:

> But in private we can take our work *gradatim*, and take our hearers along with us; and by our questions and their answers, we can see how far they understand us, and what we have to do next. In public, by length and speaking alone we lose their attention; but when they are interlocutors, we can easily cause them to attend. Besides, we can better answer their objections, and engage them by promises before we leave them, which in

---

25. Baxter, *The Reformed Pastor*, 177.
26. Baxter, *The Reformed Pastor*, 196.

public we cannot do. I conclude, therefore, that public preaching will not be sufficient.[27]

This building of strength to strength allowed an engaging pastor to become more acquainted with his parishioners, and also to better know how "to watch over them.... We shall know better how to preach to them.... We shall know better how to lament for them, and to rejoice for them, and to pray for them."[28] Twice every week, Baxter and his assistant traveled and visited fourteen families between them for this purpose:

> Private Catechising and Conference (he going through the Parish, and the Town coming to me)...I spent about an Hour with a Family, and admitted no others to be present, lest Bashfulness should make it burthensom, or any should talk of the Weaknesses of others: So that all the Afternoons on *Mondays* and *Tuesdays* I spent in this (after I had begun it; for it was many Years before I did attempt it); And my Assistant spent the Morning of the same Days in the same Employment. Before that, I only catechized them in Church; and conferred with, now and then, one occasionally.[29]

Occasional conference was insufficient for the goals Baxter had for his congregation. Coordinating both visitation schedules, his and that of his assistant, was quite a feat considering the two were the only ministers in a church that numbered approximately one thousand.[30]

At times, ministers organized groups for the purpose of conferencing together. Clergyman, ejected minister, and biographer Samuel Clarke (1599–1682) organized such a group, which met regularly every three weeks. He observed six benefits manifested in those who gathered for conference as strong bonds of spiritual friendship were created, maintained, and nurtured:

---

27. Baxter, *The Reformed Pastor*, 197, 212.
28. Baxter, *The Reformed Pastor*, 178.
29. Baxter, *Reliquiae Baxterianae*, 83.
30. Martin, *Puritanism and Richard Baxter*, 151.

First, Hereby knowledge was wonderfully increased, so that I was never acquainted with more understanding Christians in all my Life, though the best of them went but in Russet Coats[31] and followed Husbandry. Secondly, Holy affections by this mutual whetting of them each in other were exceedingly kindled, and kept alive in them. Thirdly, Love, by frequent Society, was nourished and increased; so that all the Professors, though living ten or twelve miles asunder, were as intimate and familiar, as if they had been all of one household. Fourthly, The necessities of the poorer sort being made known, there was plentiful provision made for them. Fifthly, The weak were strengthned, the mourning comforted, the erring reclaimed, the dejected raised up, and all of them mutually edified in their most holy Faith. Sixthly, Under the pretence of these Meetings, we enjoyed the opportunities, as occasion was offered of private Fasts, and days of Thanksgiving, which otherwise would quickly have been taken notice and suppressed.[32]

Of interest is the order by which Clarke arranged his list. He first recorded the continued growth in biblical knowledge, which may predicate the attitudes and actions that follow. The mutual edification was evidenced in the transformation into wholehearted followers of Christ. The interactive relationship of truly knowing each other was evidenced in the familiarity they shared between them. The relationship had positive consequences: no acknowledged need was unmet; faith was strengthened; other occasions for meeting were more meaningful. This appeared to have shadows of an Acts 2 church community. The impact of conference, with its focus on biblical literacy and "practical divinity" within and without the drawn community, was obvious.

---

31. A coat of russet, homespun woolen, or coarse cloth of reddish-brown color typical of a humble or rustic condition and formerly used for the dress of peasants and country folk.

32. Clarke, *Lives of Sundry Eminent Persons*, 4–5.

Mortem Obire. A high infant mortality rate and the brief life expectancy of an adult, which was thirty-two years,[33] fostered a near-obsession with death in the Puritans. The inordinate amount of premature deaths furthered the unquestioned duty of every right-thinking Puritan to keep the thought of death ever on his mind. As the counselors of their souls, ministers had a clear obligation to visit those who were facing imminent death. The religious writer Richard Younge's (d. 1673) imperative is clear: "Yea, let a Minister come to them upon their death bed, and question with them about their estates, or ask them how their souls fare, and what peace they have; what will be their manner of answering, (especially if they have not been notorious offenders?)"[34]

Pastoral visits to the dying began well before death approached.[35] A pastor was to be mindful of death when meeting with members of his congregation, whether they were enjoying good health or were in the throes of illness. Baxter urged pastors to "admonish them in time of health to prepare for death." For this reason, congregants were encouraged to frequently "confer with their minister about the estate of their souls."[36] Thomas Tregoss (d. 1670) was known for his tenderness and regard in his ministerial visitation of the sick. While he often waited for an available opportunity and refrained from intruding, he did not fail to season his visits with "such spiritual advise and counsel as he judged most proper for the state of their Souls,"[37] imparting his own spiritual, as well as temporal, gifts and offering prayer before his time with them came to a close.

The *Mortem Obire* conference that pastors held with congregants who were on their deathbed was the third type of conference

---

33. Lawrence Stone, *Family, Sex and Marriage in England, 1500–1800* (New York: Harper & Rowe, 1979), 55.

34. Richard Younge, *A Short and Sure Way to Grace and Salvation* (London, 1674), 2.

35. John Thomas McNeill, *A History of the Cure of Souls*, ed. John T. McNeill (London: SCM Press, 1952), 266–67.

36. Baxter, *The Reformed Pastor*, 44.

37. Clarke, *The Lives of Sundry Eminent Persons*, 122.

ministers were expected to offer. Ministers were called to be attentive in the spectrum of the life experiences of their members, including impending death. As death approached, the clergy would be found frequenting the dying and engaging in conference. James Janeway (1636?–1674) reflected on a series of such visits to his dying brother:

> A Reverend, Judicious and holy *Minister* came often to visit him, and discoursed with him of the excellency of Christ, and the glory of the invisible World. *Sir,* said he, *I feel something of it; my heart is as full as it can hold in this lower state; I can hold no more here. O that I could but let you know what I feel!*
>
> This Holy Minister praying with him his soul was ravished with the abundant incomes of light, life and love; so that he could scarce bear it, nor the thought of staying any longer in the world, but longed to be in such a condition, wherein he should have yet more grace and more comfort, and be better able to bear that weight of glory.[38]

As death drew near for the Puritan, men and women faced the realities of life and death alone with God. Similarly, Edmund Calamy (1600–1666), in a funeral sermon for Lady Anne Walker, recorded this of her closing moments of life on earth:

> A Reverend Minister coming to visit her, she entertained him with a cheerful Aspect, and desired him, to search and examine her heart, what way of wickedness he could find in it, and pressed him to deal freely and plainly with her, and not to spare her. (I deliver her own expressions) His discourse was comfortable to her. She complained of the sinfulness of her Nature, and the wickedness of her heart, but still with a Confidence in the Merits of her Saviour, upon whom alone she rolled her self. After that, she desired him to pray by her; which he did, and she heard him with an unmoveable Stilness and Attention, giving him thanks when he had done.[39]

---

38. James Janeway, *Invisible Realities* (London: Printed for Tho. Parkhurst, 1684), 103.

39. Calamy, *Happinesse*, 32.

Holy Conference: Categorized and Exercised 137

Conference with ministers offered a welcomed salve. It was with these times in mind that Younge counseled his readers:

> Converse chiefly with those that shall be your Companions for ever: A Stranger Rejoyces when he meets with his own Countrey men. In your Pilgrimage enjoy as much as you can of *Heaven*, which begins Here: let your Treasure, your Heart, your Conversation be in *it*.[40]

In this way, the beliefs of the departing, the surrounding community as well as those of the attending minister were strengthened and confirmed.

Lay Conference

Conference was a practice not exclusively performed by clergy. Family, friends, and acquaintances of saints and prospective saints also engaged in this discipline. The form of conference that did not necessarily involve ministers is identified as lay conference. Two types of lay conference can be distinguished: household and community.

1. Household. Puritans regarded every household as a religious community. William Gouge described the family as "a seminary of the Church," for people are brought up in families and then sent into the Church.[41] William Perkins (1558–1602) described the family as "little Churches, yea, even a kinde of Paradise upon earth,"[42] with the father considered the pastor to his flock. A great responsibility for spiritual growth lay within the home wherein the "chiefe of the house, the Father, the Mother, the Master and Governour is to teach their children and houshold in the waies of God."[43] Baxter, a bachelor at the time, strongly endorsed the promotion of religious

---

40. Richard Younge, *The Whole Duty of a Christian* (London: Printed for Tho. Sawbridge, 1681), 224.
41. William Gouge, *Workes* (London: Printed by John Beale, 1627), 10.
42. William Perkins, *Workes* (London: Printed by John Haviland, 1631), 3:670.
43. Bernard, *Josuahs Resolution*, 18.

training and discipline in the family: "You are not like to see any general reformation, till you procure family reformation."[44]

The goal of household conference with family members was to set the truth deep in the soul of loved ones. Both sons and daughters were to be the object of such godly counseling. The household service to God was comprised of two parts: "Conference upon the Word of God, for the edification of all the members thereof to eternall life and Invocation, which was the giving of thanks for his benefits."[45] In household conference, godly parents played a significant role. Perkins offered this counsel for the family:

> Between the publike exercises, as also when both of them are finished, use meditation and *conference* about heavenly things; assemble thy Family together, conferre with them what they have learned at the Sermon; instruct and catechize them, read, or cause to be read somewhat of the Bible, or some other godly booke unto them.[46]

Mothers and fathers were held responsible for leading the discussion on the sermons. The minister's message customarily provided fodder for discussion at meals, especially in the evenings in the presence of children and servants who were catechized on what they remembered.

Pilgrim's Progress characterized the importance of catechism and conference of the family that is provided primarily by parents, yet sometimes offered by others. Along the journey of Christiana, the wife of Bunyan's protagonist, she encountered Prudence, who spends time questioning Christiana's three sons. Prudence charged:

> You must still hearken to your mother; for she can teach you more. You must also diligently give ear to what good talk you hear from others: for your sakes do they speak good things. Observe also, and that with carefulness, what the heavens and the earth do teach you; but especially in the meditation of that

---

44. Baxter, *The Reformed Pastor*, 102.
45. Perkins, *Workes*, 3:669–70.
46. Perkins, *A Garden of Spirituall Flowers*, 119.

Book which was the cause of your father's becoming a pilgrim. I, for my part, my children, will teach you what I can while you are here, and shall be glad if you will ask me questions that tend to godly edifying.[47]

Both sons and daughters were the objects of such godly counseling, but clearly others without biological ties and beyond the nuclear family constituted the Puritan household.

The title of "father" was extended to mean "fathers to their servants." Exercising fatherly care over them included "causing them to be *instructed* in the way to Heaven."[48] Perceived not as chattel but as members of the family, servants received the same regard with respect to biblical instruction. It was the duty of the heads of households to bring those in their households to Christ and to the knowledge of truth. Furthermore, it was a defining characteristic of a true believer who "reformes his family, and sets up Gods Worship therein, performing duties of Prayer, reading, repeating, &c, and instructing his children and servants."[49]

Joseph Alleine (bap. 1634, d. 1668), an ejected minister and devotional writer, referred the expectation of care over the souls of those in one's household: "Beloved you have no dread of the Almighties Charge, That you should teach these things diligently to your Children, and talk of them as you sit in your houses…and train them up in the way they should go, Prov. 22: 6." Abraham had servants and instructed them—so too the head of a household carries that same responsibility:

> Say not, they are careless, and will not learn. What have you your Authority for, if not to use it for God, and the good of their Souls? You will call them up, and force them to do your work; and should you not, at least be as zealous in putting them

---

47. Bunyan, *The Pilgrim's Progress*, 192.
48. Anonymous, *Addresse*, 20.
49. Richard Younge, *A Touch-Stone to try (by Our Knowledge, Belief, and Life) whether we be Christians in Name Onely, or Christians in Deed* (London: sold by Andrew Crooke, 1648), 7.

upon Gods work? Say not, they are dull and are not capable. If they be dull, God requires of you the more pains and patience, but so dull as they are, you will make them learn how to work; and can they not learn as well how to live![50]

A contemporary of Alleine, Isaac Ambrose (1604–1664) exhorted his readers that as masters over their homes it was a duty to provide physical and spiritual nourishment for the bodies and souls of servants:

> The duty of Masters to the Souls of their Servants, consists in these particulars" viz. In teaching them the Principles of Religion, and all the duties of Piety: In causing them to go to the publike Ministery of the Word & Worship of God: In taking account of their profiting by the publike and private means of Edification: In praying for them: and as they observe an grace wrought in them, praising God for it, and praying for the encrease of it: Nothing so much wins a Servants heart, or the affections of any gracious heart, as the edifying of it in grace.[51]

Many took this level of care and concern for a person's spiritual welfare seriously.

Diary reflections of Puritan lawyer Robert Woodford (d. 1654) provide evidence of his great concern for the souls of all the members of his household. The regularity with which he exercised various means of grace can be seen as he consistently repeated sermons with his wife and read the Bible with his children and servants. After a stirring conversation with one of his servants, he noted in his diary the "great Comfort and Satissfaccon in speakinge with hatton [his servant] tonight I trust the Lord hath begunne the good work of grace in his soule."[52]

---

50. Alleine, *Christian Letters*, 107.
51. Ambrose, *Media*, 275.
52. As cited in John Fielding, "Opposition to the Personal Rule of Charles I: The Diary of Robert Woodford, 1637–1641," *The Historical Journal* 31, no. 4 (December 1988): 774.

Samuel Clarke authored the spiritual biography of his wife, Katherine. The account stressed the piety of the ideal Puritan woman and wife. Not only did he recount the manner and intent of her instruction to their children, but also her extended concerns for those also under her care as a "Mistress to her Maids":

> And having occasion to be much in their Company, she would take all occasions, and opportunities to manifest her love and care of their Souls, by frequent dropping in good Counsel, and wholesome Instructions; By Catechizing; Enquiring what they remembered of the Sermons they heard; Reading her Notes to them.[53]

The Bible was to be the primary source of instruction, with the responsibility and privilege of conferencing with family members resting with the heads of households. Mothers and fathers facilitated this exercise with others in the home, and also with each other.

Not to be overlooked was the conference that took place between spouses. Paul Seaver's *Wallington's World* assimilated the remnants of Nehemiah Wallington's writings to recreate his family life and social milieu of this seventeenth-century artisan. Of the various means of grace he exercised, prayer in his closet was then followed by meditations and conference with his wife.[54] Diarist Lady Margaret Hoby (d. 1633) recorded frequent times of conferencing with her husband on a variety of issues.[55] Lady Brilliana Harley discussed spiritual issues on a regular basis with her husband and shouldered much of the responsibility for the religious education of their children.[56] Indeed, as Culverwell summed up, "There are no stronger meanes to make man and wife, or two brethren or sisters living

---

53. Clarke, *Looking-Glass for Good Women*, 22–23.
54. Paul S. Seaver, *Wallington's World: A Puritan Artisan in Seventeenth-Century London* (Stanford: Stanford Univ. Press, 1985), 40.
55. Margaret Dakins Hoby, *Diary of Lady Margaret Hoby, 1599–1605*, ed. Dorothy M. Meads (London: G. Routledge & Sons, 1930), 89, 93, 94, 100.
56. Durston and Eales, *Culture of English Puritanism*, 28.

together, in peace and love, than to joyne together often in prayer and christian conference."[57]

The shared responsibility within the household entailed assessing and caring for the state of the souls of all who resided in the home. In cyclical fashion, the minister's words gave rise to conference discussion, and household conference, with its good counsel and instruction, gave rise to a greater receptivity to what ministers said in public. The common goal was to see Christ formed in their souls as each grew in godliness.

2. *Community.* The saints had an obligation to have a care for each other's spiritual health. By exercising conference together, the common goal of growth in godliness would be more rightly achieved. Community conference was exercised in the wider godly community where saints were encouraged to meet together whether or not a minister was present. The primary element of community conference was the Word. Because of the great mysteries found in the Scriptures, John White (1575–1648)—an important figure in the transatlantic network of ministers—encouraged his readers to add to their meditation "much conference, especially with Ministers, and other experienced Christians, much use of learned mens writings, which give great light to the understanding of darke places in Scripture, which wee shall often meet withal."[58]

Parishioners commonly came together in private meetings to discuss the Word, which was received and recorded in their sermon notes. Greenham advised that conference in community "with our equals must be of those things which we heard of our Ministers."[59] Nicholas Bownd echoed the challenge to interact with Scripture through conference:

---

57. Culverwell, *Time Well Spent*, 208.
58. John White, *A Way to the Tree of Life* (London: Printed by M. F., 1647), 7–8.
59. Greenham, *Workes*, 227.

Holy Conference: Categorized and Exercised

> A most excellent help in our infirmities...the conferring and talking with others of that which we have in the word read or heard: especially seeing both it is commended unto us in the Scripture, & also by experience we shall finde the profit of it to be so great, to our selves and others.[60]

Conference involved the poring over of biblical texts in association with conferring over the state of souls. Church of England clergyman John Rogers (ca. 1570–1636) commented on the communion of the saints:

> [They] be the most usefully and can doe us good, by their counsell, example, prayers, when we be present with them, yea absent from them: *Hee that walkes with the wise, shall be the wiser*; much good may we learne, and comfort may we get, by conversing with them that be truely godly.[61]

There was a clear connection between Scripture as it related to the state or estate of one's soul. Submission to Scripture was the litmus test; it was against Scripture that one could correctly determine whether grace was received. The light of Scripture determined and judged the estate of the soul. Conference provided the safe environment for such disclosure.

Conference clearly impacted those who participated in these gatherings. Even when facing death, believers were exhorted to maintain both public and private exercises, which, no doubt, included conference. Within the sphere of intimacy and confidentiality, godly instruction, divine consolation, brotherly admonition, and charitable reprehensions were more tenderly received. A believer of the faith grew in belief, knowledge, and care for one another. It was considered by others to be an indication of a true follower when he "delights in the Saints company above all others, as finding an

---

60. Bownd, *Sabbathum Veteris Et Noui Testamenti*, 391.
61. John Rogers, *A Treatise of Love* (London: Printed by H. Lownes and R. Young, 1629), 149–50.

heavenly sweetnesse in their *conference* and society, where every ones words doe savor of grace and wisedome."[62]

Conference Exercised

Extant diaries, spiritual autobiographies, and funeral sermons are fruitful resources that furnish abundant insights into the accounts of individual lives and practices of the English Puritans. Many provide the reader with the notable achievements, particular habits, ordinary traits, or distinguishing character qualities of well-known divines and lesser-known commoners. These sources continue to reveal much about the Puritans: their times, practices, and culture.

Biographical Evidences of Those Known for Conference
In Samuel Clarke's well-known collection of biographies of eminent English divines, holy conference is found as an entry in "A Table of the Principal things contained in these Lives." This particular discipline was highlighted in the lives of two men: Mr. Thomas Tregoss and Dr. Edmund Staunton. Tregoss (d. 1670) was described as "one of the divine Lights and Heats for God" who spent his spare hours in walking, meditating, praying, and conversing with Christians about their soul-affairs.[63] His religious care of instructing souls in his own family and beyond gave cause for him to be described thus:

> [He was] endowed and invested with a singular Gift of personal conference, which talent he carefully imployed for the good of many Souls; Being ready to take, yea to seek all convenient opportunities to treat with them about their Eternal estate. He was much in pressing Men unto Holiness. He was wont to propose questions to those whom he conversed, and desired the like of them, which course the Lord made successful. He esteemed it no finall burden to be cast into any Company, where his time was spent in unprofitable Discourse, and when he was, by Providence, cast upon such, his manner

---

62. Younge, *A Touch-Stone to try*, 6–7.
63. Clarke, *The Lives of Sundry Eminent Persons*, 123.

was to put a stop to such unedifying conference, by Spiritual Divertisments, or turning it to some Holy Discourse.[64]

This tribute to Tregoss exemplifies the level of care for souls that could be given.

Arthur Hildersham (1563–1632) was one of the patriarchs of spiritual brotherhood of Puritan preachers and one of the dominant spirits of the English Puritan movement. In an earlier collection of Clarke's, Hildersham was remembered for expounding the Scriptures, aiding in the repetition of sermons, and "being also willing by private conference to instruct the ignorant, to satisfie the doubtfull, to settle the wavering, to comfort the dejected, and to encourage all sorts in the exercises of Religion."[65]

Notable accolades were bestowed on Staunton (1600–1671), an ejected minister and college head, who was known to find opportunities to "speak of some Scripture that he had read that Morning, from which he would raise some useful observations, or propose some Practical Questions to the Edification of the hearer."[66] Whether it be a spiritual discourse by way of letter-writing or in personal visitation, Staunton kept mindful of the ever-appropriateness of Scripture. In conferencing by letters, "He seldom wrote any Letter but he added three, or four, or more Scriptures for a Post-script, and those very pertinent, either to the present occasion of his writing, or to the condition of the Person to whom he wrote."[67] In personal visitations, Staunton took advantage of the opportunity to "leave some Scripture or other with him. Pray you (he would say) let me leave one Text of Scripture with you, and think of it when I am gone."[68] Clarke recorded the quality of care and concern, along with the manner of conference that was demonstrated by Staunton:

---

64. Clarke, *The Lives of Sundry Eminent Persons*, 122.
65. Clarke, *Lives of Thirty-Two English Divines*, 122.
66. Clarke, *The Lives of Sundry Eminent Persons*, 168.
67. Clarke, *The Lives of Sundry Eminent Persons*, 168.
68. Clarke, *The Lives of Sundry Eminent Persons*, 168.

> He took much delight in, and excelled in Christian Conference, for which he deserves to be Recorded to all Posterity. If he came behind some for Learning, Elocution, etc. Yet he went before them in this Grace and gift. As Men have their perticular sins, so they have perticular Graces and Excellencies: Abraham excelled in Faith; *Moses* in Meekness; *Job* in Patience, and our worthy Doctor in Holy and Godly *Conference*. Whoever conversed with him, and was not a gainer by his Heavenly discourse? His speech was *always with Grace*, which as it argued grace in the speaker, so it was apt to work, or stir up Grace in the hearers, it was ever *savoury, seasoned with salt*, and good to the *use of Edifying, Ephs.4.29*. His heart was alwayes *inditing a good matter*, and therefore his tongue was as the *Pen of a ready Writer, Psa.* 45.1, 2. *His Lips fed many, Prov* 10.21. They always *dropped as the Hony comb (Cant.* 4. 11.) *Grace was poured into them*, and it flowed plentifully from them. He had a good flock, and Rich Treasure in his heart, and from thence (upon every occasion) he brought forth *things both New and Old*.... He delighted in conversing with such (Ignorant), and instructing of them; and would say, their Souls are as precious as the Souls of Nobles.[69]

Staunton's ability to see and serve the soul of a person reaffirms the spiritual nurture and care given in conference.

Women Who Conferenced

Much of any discussion on the Puritans focuses on the key characters and events that shaped, fueled, or directed the movement. The significant characters of the movement are most notably male, but female participation is not without mention. Because figures for membership suggest that women predominated, John Spurr makes a plausible claim that the majority of Puritans were women and notes that hostile observers often jeered at the "she-puritans."[70] Patrick Collinson refers to observations made by contemporary

---

69. Clarke, *The Lives of Sundry Eminent Persons*, 171.
70. Spurr, *English Puritanism*, 195.

observers, including Richard Hooker, that the largest and most enthusiastic following of Puritan preachers were often women. These female followers were predominently London merchants' wives, famous and godly matrons, and gentlewomen.[71] They were neither given considerable power or equality nor a role in public prayer, but sat apart from men at meetings. In John Goodwin's gathered church, women were allowed to be members and to contribute to discussions, but they were not permitted to vote, hold office, or publicly represent the church.[72]

In seventeenth-century England, and in every walk of life, women shouldered responsibilities and burdens equal to those borne by men. They had to be capable of managing a large number of servants and supervising the working estates of which they were often left in charge. Their responsibilities included ensuring a store of food and clothing sufficient for the needs of a household. In spite of the somewhat restricted sphere of action, a woman's sphere of influence included the development of every capacity: mental, moral, and physical, and, with the incorporation of conference, one might add religious.

Participants in conference included both men and women. A seventeenth-century writer asserted that women should not be disallowed from this Christian right:

> (To me it) is very unreasonable; For, Have they not Souls as well as Men? Have they not Doubts and Fears, yea, generally more (because of their Weakness)? And though they are prohibited from speaking, yet I hope they may learn something from what is spoken.[73]

He continued with the equal charge to both genders to employ this means, "Surely if it be the Duty in Men, 'tis consequently, as much a Duty in Women." As was typical, Scriptural support for this assertion was supplied. In this argument, Malachi 3:16 provided the

---

71. Collinson, *Godly People: Essays on English Protestantism and Puritanism*, 316.
72. Spurr, *English Puritanism*, 195–96.
73. Anonymous, *Stated Christian Conference*, 30.

rationale for the inclusion of women with men: "*They that feared the Lord, spake often one to another,* Mal. 3. He doth not say, there were no Women among them." Additional support was garnered from Acts: "We find the Holy Women, among the Apostles, and Primitive Christians, in their daily Conventions; See Acts 1:14. So that to prohibit Women from such Meetings, is entirely *Non*-Scriptural."[74]

Women's involvement as participants is easily demonstrated. Jane Ratcliffe (d. 1638) provided a colorful illustration. After her death, the Chester minister, John Ley, in a funeral sermon published in 1640, memorialized her spiritual life. Though the details of her life are few, she remains an example of the Puritan style of godliness and godly conviction. Jane Ratcliffe's spiritual advisor and biographer praised her proficiency:

> [In] the most sound and the most useful points of religion [achieved] by her continual and attentive hearing of sermons and reading good books, the bible especially...and by moving questions to such of her acquaintance as she thought best able to answer: And truly (I can speak it upon mine own certain knowledge and frequent experience) many of her questions to me upon her reading of scripture were very solid and substantial instructions, as such as argued a deep insight into the sacred text, and an especial acquaintance with the spirit that indited it.[75]

For Ratcliffe and Ley, and for the Puritans in general, the Bible was more than an instructional manual; it was the devotional book that served as a focus for meditation and prayer that could benefit men and women alike. In the Puritan spiritual autobiography of M. K., the writer recognized the person with whom conference was shared, be it male or female, as one "who tooke great delight to instruct me, to heare me read, and ask questions. She alloted me a portion of

---

74. Anonymous, *Stated Christian Conference*, 30.
75. John Ley, *A Patterne of Pietie* (London: Printed by Felix Kingston, 1640), 26.

Scripture every day, as likewise a part of Eramus Rotterdamus upon the foure Evangelists."[76]

Discussions over the Bible aided in their interpretation of a Puritan's spiritual life as well as the world around him or her. Peter Lake suggests that such lives may have become "repositories of the Holy Spirit, active in the world, almost holy objects themselves."[77] Lady Hoby (d. 1633) learned the Puritan habits of self-examination and regular religious exercises while in the household of Henry Hastings, third Earl of Huntingdon. She continued to practice these in her own household. Her diary is the earliest known by an Englishwoman and is notable for its depiction of the domestic disciplines of Elizabethan Puritanism. She described the religious exercises and prayers for the whole household, as well as the private prayers and readings that occupied a large part of each day. Conference was featured throughout her diary:

> *Saterday the 22*...wher I had Conferrance with a religious gintelwoman....[78]
>
> *The Lordes day 30*...after I had hard Catcizising and sarmon, I returned home and wret notes in my bible, and talked of the sarmon and good thingse with Mrs Ormston:....[79]
>
> *Saterday the 27*...then I took leave, with some Conferance, of some that Came to se me....[80]
>
> After Catezising and sermone, I walked abroad: then I medetated of the sarmons, and raed and spoke to Mrs Ormstone of the chapter that was read in the morning, and so went to privat praier.[81]

---

76. Powell, *Spirituall Experiences*, 161.
77. Peter Lake, "Feminine Piety and Personal Potency: The Emancipation of Mrs. Jane Radcliffe," *The Seventeenth Century* 2, no. 2 (October 1987): 145.
78. Margaret Hoby, *The Private Life of an Elizabethan Lady: The Diary of Lady Margaret Hoby, 1599–1605*, ed. Joanna Moody (Stroud: Sutton, 1998), 21.
79. Hoby, *The Private Life of an Elizabethan Lady*, 24.
80. Hoby, *The Private Life of an Elizabethan Lady*, 31.
81. Hoby, *The Private Life of an Elizabethan Lady*, 32.

Frequent discussions of a spiritual nature stemming from sermon messages appeared to have been a main concern for her. Conference served as an important avenue for the growth in spiritual understanding, especially when counsel on theological doctrine was imparted:

> In the after none A freind of mine Came to me with a godly preacher, Mr wilson, of whom I learned this, among other Conferences—that religion consisted of 2 princepall heades, which, who so ever did denie, Could not be saved: the one was Justefecation by and in christes Righteousnes: the other, of life touchinge the true worssheppe of god, so that, who so ever were ether Idolaters, or grounded their Justefecation on workes, did denie so farr the truth in the foundation of christian religion.[82]

Conference furthered the understanding of doctrinal principles and grounded the truthfulness of Scripture and faith in the lives of believers.

The spiritual counsel and guidance that women received through conference with their ministers was a common trait in the Puritan movement. What remains a topic for further research is the involvement of women in the role of offering spiritual counseling or guidance, although there is an indication that Lady Hoby offered such direction. She records, "After privat praers I did eate and was busie about dyinge of stuffe tell diner time, saving I had some Conference with John browne unto whom I gave the best advise I Could."[83] Discovering the depth and regularity of such encounters would foster a greater appreciation for women's involvement in this exercise.

Other cases illustrate the model of women providing spiritual guidance in conference and the role women played as they exercised conference, as mothers with their children or as overseers of the home. The influence of mothers was undeniable. Cotton Mather (1663–1728) recognized that as he expounded on family instruction,

---

82. Hoby, *The Private Life of an Elizabethan Lady*, 75.
83. Hoby, *The Private Life of an Elizabethan Lady*, 70.

"You that are *Mothers* have a special Advantage to instil the Fear of God into the souls of them that sit upon your knees."[84]

Though not as well-known as her sons, Charles and John, who are recognized for founding Methodism, Susanna Wesley was a highly influential figure in their lives. Susanna's family heritage was staunchly Puritan. Her father, Samuel Annesley, was a nonconformist minister who helped facilitate the Puritan movement alongside notable contemporaries Richard Baxter and John Owen. Susanna was highly educated and exercised independent thinking and an autonomous spirit. As a young woman, she methodically enumerated the points of nonconformity as well as those of the Church of England, the latter with which she determined to be associated. She followed her husband into the rustic setting of the Lincolnshire parishes but did not abandon the conscience nurtured in Puritan London. She bore eighteen or nineteen children with only ten surviving. She may have taken to heart the words of Timothy Rogers (1658–1728), as he spoke these words at her sister Elizabeth's funeral: "Mothers may do great Service to Religion, by leaving good Advise to their Children." In developing this point, he stated:

> If good Women would apply themselves to reading and study, as the Men do, or had equal Advantage for Knowledge in their Education, no doubt we should have more of their excellent Composures, many of them have an *happy Genius*, and a smooth Expression, and might write as well as work, and the Pen might have as good success as the Needle; especially, they may make Observations, or draw up Rules for the good order of their own Families, and when they see fit, communicate them for the Good of others.[85]

When each child turned five, a discipline in her parenting practice was the inclusion of a household schedule initiated with a daylong first

---

84. Cotton Mather, *The Resolved Christian Pursuing the Designs of Holiness and Happiness* (Boston: To be sold by Nicholas Boone, 1700), 44.

85. Timothy Rogers, *The Character of a Good Woman* (London: Printed for J. Harris, 1697), 48–49.

reading lesson, using the book of Genesis as a primer. She believed in the education of her children—sons as well as daughters. In a letter written to her son on the education of children, she asserted:

> No girl be taught to work till she can read very well...for the putting children to learn sewing before they can read perfectly is the very reason why so few women can read fit to be heard, and never to be well understood.[86]

As the children grew, she arranged a weekly session devoted to each individual child. Her weekly one-on-one conference, where she gave personal instruction in the faith with each of her children, incorporated a mélange of age-appropriate spiritual activities in the family. Her pedagogical skills affirmed the importance she held in the theological training of her children. Susanna's dedication to her children's education and the format she employed was undeniable, and her use of conference was clear. John Wesley would capitalize on this means of grace as he incorporated this into the use of small groups, or "bands," to nurture the spiritual growth of his followers. It is plausible to identify this correlation as his bands met on Thursdays, the same day his mother held weekly conference with him as a young child. John Wesley favored corporate direction whose common purposes were mutual encouragement, examination, and service within the context of Christian conference as a means of grace.

Whether within the sphere of their homes or outside of it, gracious women who employed godly conference likely played some informal role in private visits. If they lived in the country where the village was still largely self-contained, they could, and often did, take an active part in the formation of public opinion and the life of the little community.[87]

Perhaps it was serendipitous community conference that John Bunyan happened upon that proved to be a spiritual marker in his life. He had repented of sin and had begun to live a life according to

---

86. Charles Wallace, *Susanna Wesley: The Complete Writings* (Oxford: Oxford Univ. Press, 1997), 373.

87. Hoby, *Diary of Lady Margaret Hoby*, 8.

God's commandments when he encountered something that jolted him out of complacency. He recalled a group of women sitting in a sunny doorway talking of things:

> I heard, but I understood not...for their talk was about a new birth, the work of God on their hearts, also how they were convinced of their miserable state by nature: they talked how God had visited their souls with his love in the Lord Jesus, and with what words and promises they had been refreshed, comforted, and supported against the temptations of the Devil.[88]

Bunyan found something new and confessed, "They were to me as if they had found a new world."[89]

The spiritual journey was not without episodes of need as Bunyan's allegorical classic, *Pilgrim's Progress*, revealed. It was lived in fellowship with other Christians, whether in times of peace, conflict, fellowship, learning, temptation, depression, or despair. Comfort in the throes of death and courage mustered in the face of obstacles were evidence of the camaraderie and community fostered by conference, but so was the simple encouragement in renewing one's "Christian course." Conference was crucial to the lives of these pilgrims because it "made the way easy."[90]

Conference reflected the edifying talk that the apostle Paul described in his letter to the Ephesians. Edifying talk is that which builds others up according to their needs that it may benefit those who listen. The ubiquitous nature of conference makes it difficult to know the full extent and effect of this exercise. What is clear from extant material is that men and women were encouraged to be or were full-fledged participants of this means of grace.

---

88. John Bunyan, *Grace Abounding to the Chief of Sinners* (London: Printed by George Larkin, 1666), 10.
89. Bunyan, *Grace Abounding to the Chief of Sinners*, 11.
90. Bunyan, *Pilgrim's Progress*, 72.

Conclusion

The communal nature of conference provided the arena for integrating scriptural truths with spiritual growth in godliness. One's pilgrimage was not a process of mere isolation, as is popularly understood. On the contrary, it would involve a community that was engaged in conference for the purposes of mutual encouragement and instruction. Christian fellowship was a walking together in the presence of God.

The sense of common purpose to grow in grace together encouraged the participants of conference to explore biblical truths and discuss their deeply personal experiences. The depth of relationship and intimacy supplied the believing community with the vehicle for growth in godliness. Whether its participants were clergy or laity, men, women, or children, those who served as heads of households or those who served within those households, two underlying elements consistently appeared in conference: biblical truths, and the incorporation of biblical truths in a genuine care for the souls of others. The godly provided each other with tangible comfort and spiritual aid, which, in turn, bound them together in a dynamic community.

Continued research into the rediscovery of Puritan conference will confirm this practice as pervasive throughout the Puritan movement, where members of a believing community gathered for mutual edification. A further understanding of the practice of conference, with its various methods, styles, and elements, may offer a correlation with the communal aspects of contemporary spiritual formation. Piety's forgotten discipline may help inform the evangelical perspective on community and its place in spiritual formation, especially with its similarities in format and function to its twenty-first-century distant cousin: the small group, employed in and by many churches.

Each of the classifications of conference has implications that serve to foster the depth of spiritual formation in various small group settings. Continued exploration of the extant materials of the Puritan era will no doubt offer illumination to the historical experience as well as ecclesiastical practice.

Exploring the Puritan practice of conference, steeped in Protestant tradition, affords the contemporary evangelical community a vibrant and timely perspective of Christian spiritual formation. The next chapter discusses the implications of the findings in each of these categories, with particular emphasis placed on the community conference as it relates to the current small group movement.

CHAPTER SEVEN

Puritan Conference for the Contemporary Church

As a means of grace, conference served its sixteenth- and seventeenth-century English communities well in promoting growth in biblical literacy and care for one another's souls. Puritan conference was neither a mystical nor secretive means of spiritual formation, but was a subject in many devotional guides and a common practice among clergy and laity. A certain distrust and misgiving arises when practices of meditation and spiritual direction are discussed for fear that these resonate too closely with Roman Catholic tradition or New Age practices. Revival of the Puritan practice of conference can serve to alleviate the jitters many modern-day evangelicals have over spiritual formation while providing a vehicle for soul care that is found within their own Protestant tradition. The various natures and nuances, types, and practices of conference have been explored, categorized, and labeled in previous chapters. In this concluding chapter, following a current assessment of the American small group movement, category-specific suggestions are made for the application of conference for contemporary spiritual formation. The evangelical public will benefit from the rediscovery and re-incorporation of this Protestant practice that has been dormant for too long.

The Puritans sought spirituality deep within their own souls, but they were also a communal people who met regularly in corporate acts of worship[1] and holy conference. Incorporating the

---

1. Robert Wuthnow, *Sharing the Journey: Support Groups and America's New Quest for Community* (New York: Simon & Schuster, 1994), 31.

exercise of conference in small groups can help meet the challenges facing the contemporary small group movement.

Because it is a familiar word in the English language, the term "conference," with its newly recovered potency, can be easily adapted. In conference, participants can expect to hear and interact with biblical truths. These truths inform the perplexities, victories, and normal activities of everyday life in an effort to achieve a sustainable pace in the Christian journey.

The environment nurtured in conference is one of mutual relationship, commitment, and attentiveness. It is based on the understanding that living the Christian life requires community.

The Challenge Facing the Small Group Movement in American Culture

Isolation was never intended to be the mode of operation for the Christian pilgrimage, yet the fragmentation that characterizes American society counters the efforts toward spiritual growth in community. We succumb to our overcrowded, conflicting, and unrelenting schedules in this information-seeking, entertainment-soaked, image-driven culture that wrestles with boredom, thrills, and materialism. Our addiction to information technology, with its online connections, news and Internet communication, websites, blogs, and streaming (to name a few), exacerbates the pre-existing flood of intruding must-haves and must-dos that demand our time and attention. There is cause for concern.

According to Lynn Smith-Lovin and Miller McPherson, sociologists at Duke University and the University of Arizona, significant changes have come about in the social isolation of America over the past twenty years. Americans' circles of confidants have waned dramatically; the number of people who talk to no one about matters they consider important has almost tripled since 1985.[2] Their find-

---

2. Miller McPherson and Lynn Smith-Lovin, "Social Isolation in America: Change in Core Discussion Networks over Two Decades," *American Sociological Review* 71, no. 3 (June 2006): 353–54.

ings show many more Americans are completely isolated from those with whom they would discuss important matters.[3] These same researchers, over a decade earlier, found that those with whom we have stronger ties influence us directly as we observe their actions, which indirectly shapes the kinds of people we become.[4]

Couple this isolationism with the pervasive individualism that has permeated American culture, and it is no wonder that authentic spiritual transformation fostered in community is threatened. Our society has been described as being composed of individualists, taught from early childhood to be independent. Americans are told not to let anyone get too close. Any disclosure of hurts, doubts, or weaknesses should be reserved for a select few, if any at all. Any lack of strength or determination would certainly reflect a flaw in character and render a person unhealthy and unable to live out a full and prosperous life. People are expected to "go it alone," making them become relationally challenged.

The human soul was created for, thrives on, and is nurtured by face-to-face interaction and communication. It is in a Christian's DNA to interface with others for spiritual sustenance, for his identity in Christ, and for the development of his own faith. Christian fellowship is a means of spiritual growth. Spiritual autonomy is not an option. The small group movement has sought to address this problem by contending with the effects of fragmentation and anonymity in American society.

The Small Group Movement: An Assessment

Small groups have been utilized as a means to combat the fragmentation of today's society and feed the hunger for community that

---

3. McPherson and Smith-Lovin, "Social Isolation in America," 372.

4. Lynn Smith-Lovin and Miller McPherson, "You Are Who You Know: A Network Perspective on Gender," in *Theory on Gender/Feminism on Theory, Social Institutions and Social Change*, ed. Paula England (New York: A. de Gruyter, 1993), 223–51.

is rooted in the displacement and disconnection of society.[5] Their rapid proliferation is partially attributed to the increasingly fractured, anonymous, hurried nature of American life.[6] Their current popularity is historically unprecedented. Though clearly not a new phenomenon, small groups have been comfortably woven into the fabric of American religion. Christian small groups meet for purposes of discipleship, Bible study, and evangelism.

The Good News

The experience of the church throughout history and in many places around the world today attests to the fact that people follow Christ not only as individuals but also as members of a family, clan, or tribe.[7] Thus, churches have employed the small group model to create opportunities for a greater range and depth of pastoral care and spiritual support in community.

Princeton sociologist Robert Wuthnow describes the small group movement as affecting a quiet revolution in American society. Its growth has been incremental, resulting in a profound reorientation in life, yet gradual, so that those involved see it less as a revolution, and more like a journey.[8] Small group membership is a phenomenon that shows no lines of demarcation; it embraces people from all walks of life, in every region of the country, and in communities of every size. Numerically speaking, more people of faith meet today in small groups than ever. Church attenders and members participate in small groups with greater frequency than the general population (62 and 52 percent respectively).[9] Quantitatively speaking, the small group movement shows no signs of waning. As

---

5. Jacqueline Olds, Richard Schwartz, and Harriet Webster, *Overcoming Loneliness in Everyday Life* (New York: Carol Pub. Group, 1996), 90.
6. Olds, Schwartz, and Webster, *Overcoming Loneliness*, 90.
7. William Hendricks, *Exit Interviews* (Chicago: Moody Press, 1993), 80–81.
8. Wuthnow, *Sharing the Journey*, 2.
9. George Gallup and Michael Lindsay, *Surveying the Religious Landscape: Trends in U.S. Beliefs* (Harrisburg, Penn.: Morehouse, 1999), 90.

encouraging as the figures may be, however, its qualitative aspect may leave something to be desired.

The Not-So-Good News

Americans are learning that one cannot accomplish spirituality in isolation, but their involvement in small groups is producing some rather subtle effects on the ways people relate to each other and how one conceives of the sacred.[10] Important weaknesses lie in the small group's inability to strongly resist the mounting fragmenting forces in our society and to forge the level of enduring bonds that many still covet.

1. Too polite. In an attempt to attract members to a small group, it would appear that accommodating their perceived needs has backfired. Two Boston psychiatrists, Jacqueline Olds and Richard Schwartz, suggest that because of the episodic nature, groups "fail to replicate the sense of belonging we have lost. Attending weekly meetings, dropping in and out as one pleases, shopping around for a more satisfactory or appealing group—all these factors work against the growth of true community."[11] A culture of niceness is adopted where commitment-challenged attenders are constantly on the move. The search for short-term solutions and satisfaction has proven less productive.

Small groups can help people adapt to societal demands and pressures, but they do not fundamentally enable them to lead their lives in a significantly different way. Challenges, especially where genuine transformation is concerned, are either not considered at all or left abandoned, especially if personal sacrifice or discomfort is involved. They may not be encouraged to seek and explore higher goals, such as a healthy sense of the transcendent that infiltrates and influences how one can live differently. The individual becomes the gauge of all things. Wuthnow states:

---

10. Wuthnow, *Sharing the Journey*, 3.
11. Olds, Schwartz, and Webster, *Overcoming Loneliness*, 90.

At one time, theologians argued that the chief purpose of humankind was to glorify God. Now it would seem that the logic has been reversed: the chief purpose of God is to glorify humankind. Spirituality no longer is true or good because it meets absolute standards of truth and goodness but because it helps us get along.[12]

With more attention being focused on the temporal, material, and human side of spiritual experiences, the invisible, divine side is marginalized.

2. Too small. God has become small—too small. He is less an external authority and more an internal presence. A more intuitive spirituality is being fostered today than one grounded in biblical traditions. For many, God now exhibits a limited capacity to work and fits better into our boxes. He has become more manageable and serviceable to us in meeting our needs. God exists more to mollify difficult life situations. This picture of God results in a kind of faith and teaching that focuses more on feelings and getting along in life than worshipful obedience to or reverence toward a transcendent God.[13] One must reconcile these effects with the finding that a majority of small groups include Bible study among their activities.[14]

3. Too illiterate. A third effect is the pervasive biblical illiteracy found not only among Christians but also, as studies show, among those whose involvement in small groups included time studying the Word. Involvement in a small group *does* heighten a member's interest in the Bible, yet, as Gallup observes, "A close look at where people are in their spiritual lives and the level of their knowledge would shock most clergy: We read the Bible, but we are a nation of biblical illiterates."[15] David Gibson asserts that in a society where

---

12. Wuthnow, *Sharing the Journey*, 18.
13. Wuthnow, *Sharing the Journey*, 18–19.
14. Wuthnow, *Sharing the Journey*, 278.
15. George Gallup and D. Michael Lindsay, *The Gallup Guide: Real-*

the Bible continues to be a best seller, it remains essentially unread.[16] The number of college diplomas awarded over the last seventy years has tripled, whereas the level of biblical knowledge appears to have nearly flatlined.[17] Knowledge of Scripture has failed to be commensurate with growth in education. Wuthnow found small group members whose spirituality had been deepened by their participation, yet were no more likely than other members to give the correct answer to a factual question. One must question the kind of biblical understanding being fostered in small groups.

In a typical two-hour small group Bible study, Wuthnow found only fifteen minutes were devoted to the study of the Bible. The usual verse-by-verse examination kept participants from understanding the larger metanarratives of the Bible, and instead promoted a more individualistic interpretation of a passage. Placing a greater emphasis on seeking personal significance gleaned from a passage, rather than actual meaning, reduced the dialogue into a more prominent discussion of members' personal interpretations or experiences.[18]

In 1994, Wuthnow, in an almost prophetic sense, asserted this challenge:

> The [small group] movement stands at an important crossroads in its history. It can continue on its present course. Or it can attempt to move to a higher level of interpersonal and spiritual quality. Given its success over the past two decades, it can easily maintain the same course. It can draw millions of participants by making them feel good about themselves and by encouraging them to develop a domesticated, pragmatic form of spirituality. By helping people feel comfortable, it can perhaps even expand its numbers. The other option will

---

ity Check for 21st Century Churches (Loveland, Colo.: Gallup Organization Group, 2002), 14.

16. David Gibson, "America's Favorite Unopened Text," *Beliefnet*, (December 2000), http://www.beliefnet.com/Faiths/Christianity/2000/12/Americas-Favorite-Unopened-Text.aspx, accessed 1 April 2010.

17. George Gallup, *Emerging Trends* 19, no 2 (Feb 1997), 1.

18. Wuthnow, *Sharing the Journey*, 243.

require it to focus less on numerical success and more on the quality of its offerings.[19]

Bible study participants can have an adequate understanding of the biblical text without being confronted by what the text has to do with them.[20] One can have Bible knowledge without transformation, but there is no transformation without knowledge of the Word of God. Biblical knowledge in itself is not a panacea or guarantee of Christian living, but it remains central. We need to understand the salient facts about God's Word for spiritual transformation to take place because the casualties of biblical illiteracy are many: families, church communities, the disillusioned post-churched, interested seekers, and the lost.

4. *Too little transformation.* As critical as biblical knowledge is to the process of spiritual transformation, it does not guarantee its actualization. A purely academic approach to small group Bible study seeks to master the text and to articulate its truths and principles. This technique often results in a formulaic system of living where a behavior is prescribed and the grappling with one's true self in community is disregarded. There exists a serious limitation of Bible knowledge when it does not translate into a transformed life. This disparity was symptomatic of the lack of and need for engagement with the Word in conjunction with the care for one another's souls. Knowledge must be incorporated into the core of our beings. Gallup presents this challenge:

> We need to work toward closing the gap between belief and practice—we need to turn professed faith into lived-out faith. What is called for is not new communities, new strategies or position papers; we need nothing less than changed hearts.[21]

---

19. Wuthnow, *Sharing the Journey,* 27.
20. Howard L. Rice, *Reformed Spirituality: An Introduction for Believers* (Louisville: Westminster, 1991), 110.
21. Gallup and Lindsay, *The Gallup Guide,* 14.

As long as scriptural accuracy and strict application supplant the need to engage that knowledge at the heart level in community, genuine Christian spiritual transformation will remain meager. Observed as "occasions for individuals to focus on themselves in the presence of others,"[22] or where fellowship is no more than "well-calculated distance,"[23] where pious platitudes traverse its airwaves, the small group movement appears to have reached a point of need for re-evaluation and course correction.

Applying Conference for Contemporary Spiritual Formation

The above findings on small groups can be applied to any number of groups, whether composed of participants drawn together by life stage, life roles, ministry functions, or family. The spiritual strength a small group community is able to achieve and maintain is in direct relationship to the depth of intimacy realized. The following implications for groups fall into the two primary categories of conference described in the previous chapter: ministerial and lay.

Implications from Ministerial Conference

Though the greater part of the recommendations for the application of conference will focus on small groups as we know them, implications for conference at a number of different levels are warranted, especially as one understands pastoral staff, staff with congregants and families as small groups, and the need for improved biblical literacy and furthered spiritual transformation within these groups. The two subcategories of ministerial conference, professional and pastoral, will help direct and illumine relevant applications for our times.

1. Professional conference. Conference was for the godly preacher what spiritual direction was for the Roman Catholic.[24] A wide spec-

---

22. Wuthnow, *Sharing the Journey*, 6.
23. Dallas Willard, "The Reality of the Spiritual Life," Christian Spirituality and Soul Care Lecture Series, Talbot School of Theology, Biola University, (La Mirada, Calif.,) Fall 2006.
24. Morgan, *The Godly Preachers of the Elizabethan Church*, 169.

trum of matters and issues were discussed in professional conference among pastors: exegetical, homiletical, theological, ministerial, and personal. It was understood that a pastor's spiritual life must be nurtured for growth. The mutual attentiveness to one another's souls became the platform for cultivating the same spiritual sensitivity for members of their congregations. The significant reason for a church's well being, then, was centered on spiritual guidance as experienced in conference.

Gathering the pastoral staff of a given community for the purpose of conference can yield great benefits. This type of gathering moves beyond the typical staff meeting and actually serves to foster care to a group of those leading the church. A climate must be cultivated where pastors are given opportunity to focus on the stirrings, blockages, and questions of the heart, honestly responding to the question, "How stands it between God and your soul now?" Depending on the size of any pastoral staff, time and venues need to be available for the mutual exchange of ministry and life issues that crowd pastors' hearts, minds, and calendars.

The roles, responsibilities, joys, and challenges inherent in the calling of a pastor require intentional engagement with others of like heart and passion and further maturity. Even amid the external rush of ministry, the disquiet of a heart in even the most gifted of pastors can remain unattended and ignored. The growth in character development, spiritual depth, and soul attentiveness achieved through conference addresses these concerns. Both formal and informal settings can be useful for this practice. Critical components for effective conference are frequency, consistency, trust, and commitment. Each party must bring to these gatherings a spirit of humility and care. The level of spiritual health and refreshment will be proportional to the level of trust and engagement shared. Times together will become the spiritual oasis where, amid the external and internal demands of leadership of a church or Christian organization, one receives comfort, guidance, and spiritual recalibration.

2. Pastoral conference. Involvement in this second of two types of ministerial conference finds pastors better able to minister well, as they are favorably inclined to confer with their congregations. Richard Rogers recognized this precondition for pastors, that there "must bee in them affabilitie & readinesse to satisfie their doubts by private conference."[25] These doubts may be stirred by their concern for the level of spiritual education they are receiving and the spiritual condition of their souls.

One of the most accurate ways of assessing and building the biblical literacy of a congregation is found in the private conversations between pastors and their church attendees. These conversations can focus on the various ways people choose to grow in their knowledge of God. Whether it is from personal Scripture reading, small group Bible studies, class discussions, sermons, or any combination of these, pastors can ascertain the present level of Bible knowledge and the desire to grow in this knowledge through simple dialogue. A caring and skillful pastor can address spiritual doubts, any lack of understanding, or truths needing clarification. Biblical truth, explained as clearly as possible and in a trusted relationship, will foster the expression of that truth in life.

Additionally, as pastors engage in conference with members of their congregations, they gain a deeper understanding of the spectrum of their members' life stages and circumstances. The time given to inquire of the spiritual states of their members' souls affords pastors the opportunities to know their congregations more personally. Invaluable information gleaned from these encounters can impact a pastor's service both directly and indirectly. Direct one-on-one encounters allow a pastor the personal contact that paves the way for the exercise of the parishoner's Spirit-given shepherding gifts. One is able to observe and experience firsthand the learning and growth in those under the pastor's care, especially as the accompanying Word of God sheds light on life situations. Questions that

---

25. Richard Rogers, *The Practice of Christianitie* (London: Printed by B. Alsop, 1623), 33.

arise from a congregant's personal Bible reading, study, sermon notes, or application of the truth of Scripture to real life can be asked and answered in a nonthreatening environment that furthers the Christian walk. The opportunities to see the Word lived out in a pastor who seeks to reflect the compassion and commitment of Christ serve as a tangible help for pilgrims on the pilgrimage.

Indirectly, these encounters help facilitate the minister in sermon preparation and delivery. The resulting messages become less detached from society and more in touch with the pain, challenges, distresses, joys, and celebrations of the world. John R. W. Stott offers sound advice on this type of engagement:

> The best preachers are always diligent pastors, who know the people of their district and congregation, and understand the human scene in all its pain and pleasure, glory and tragedy. And the quickest way to gain such an understanding is to shut our mouth (a hard task for compulsive preachers) and open our eyes and ears.... We need, then, to ask people questions and get them talking. We ought to know more about the Bible than they do, but they are likely to know more about the real world than we do. So we should encourage them to tell us about their home and family life, their job, their expertise and their spare-time interests. We also need to penetrate beyond their doing to their thinking.[26]

The impact this can have on sermon messages for the congregation as a whole stems largely from the conference shared with the congregation in its smallest parts. The pastoral care and guidance given in conference to another's soul is grounded in the knowledge of the Holy Spirit's desire and commitment to one's growth in authenticity and His dissatisfaction with the complacency and fraud of a counterfeit or impotent faith. This should be no less a value for those who hold the position of pastor.

---

26. John R. W. Stott, *Between Two Worlds: The Art of Preaching in the Twentieth Century* (Grand Rapids: Eerdmans, 1982), 192.

Ministerial conference has been shown to have impact in the lives of those participating in these types of small groups. This discussion furthers the impact conference can have in and with those engaged in small groups. First comes the challenge, then the hope.

Implications from Lay Conference

Two subcategories of lay conference assist in drawing recommendations to foster biblical literacy and spiritual transformation: household and community. The descriptions above can be applied to a variety of small group venues whether within or outside of a home.

1. Household conference. The benefits of conference are not dependent upon the presence of a pastor. Household conference finds the members of a family engaged in caring for souls of varying ages. This type of conference upholds the integrity and value of the family in its role of fostering biblical literacy and spiritual formation. Parents and other significant adults are involved, taking the responsibility for instilling biblical truths in the lives of their children.

According to Leonard Sweet, a Christian historian and futurist, "The best way into the postmodern home is through the family."[27] He describes further the idea of "cocooning," which is the cultural phenomenon "where a postmodern desires to seek refuge in the inner circle of the home for relief from the harsh nightmarish outside world."[28] As critical as relief found in the home is, something is still missing. Noting the trends of 2005, George Barna reported, "American Christians are biblically illiterate.... And the trend line is frightening: the younger a person is, the less they understand about the Christian faith."[29] Barna's most recent assessment of the church has found "universally-known truths about Christianity are now

---

27. Leonard I. Sweet, *Faithquakes* (Nashville: Abingdon, 1994), 29.
28. Sweet, *Faithquakes*, 21.
29. Barna Group, "The Barna Update," 20 December 2005, accessed 28 June 2006, www.barna.org. Used by permission.

unknown mysteries to a large and growing share of Americans—especially young adults."[30] This trend has continued.

David Nienhuis says that the involvement of the family to address biblical literacy will have to involve more than encouraging children to memorize a select set of Bible verses. He asserts the need to be able to "address the text," moving beyond knowing snippets of the Bible to being able to read and interpret Scripture in light of who He is and whose story is related in the Bible and celebrated by the church.[31] This is not only the responsibility of Christian higher education, but also of the Christian home. Among the reasons Jo Lewis gives for the religiously illiterate is the deprivation of some essentials by their elders. What appears to be missing is the incorporation of godly principles into their daily living.[32]

Spiritually growing and mature adults occupy a critical position and fill an important role in the spiritual transformation process. Although Christian parents and other adults of a believing community share the responsibility for the training of children, the first line of spiritual engagement with children is the parents. A need exists to expand the idea and conviction of parents to the spiritual nature of their children and the privilege that exists to invest and speak into their souls. The nurturing of the souls of their children takes seriously the need to expose them to the Bible while demonstrating how these truths can be lived out.

Regarding a study on the correlation between spiritual activity at an early age and spiritual activity of adults, president of Barna Research David Kinnaman states:

> The study shows that most American adults recall frequent faith activity when they were growing up. Moreover, it provides clarity that the odds of one sticking with faith over a

---

30. Barna Group, "Six Megathemes Emerge from Barna Group Research in 2010," 13 December 2010, accessed 15 February 2010, www.barna.org.
31. David R. Nienhuis, "The Problem of Evangelical Biblical Illiteracy," *Modern Reformation* 19, no. 1 (Jan–Feb 2010): 10–13, 17.
32. Jo H. Lewis and Gordon A. Palmer, *What Every Christian Should Know* (Wheaton, Ill.: Victor Books, 1989), 84–85.

lifetime are enhanced in a positive direction by spiritual activity under the age of 18. And it raises the intriguing possibility that being involved at least a few times a month is correlated with nearly the same sticking power as weekly involvement—especially among teenagers.[33]

Breadth of exposure to spiritual training as children and teenagers appears to have some correlation to adult religious commitment. Further research could explore the impact regular spiritual conversations in early childhood might have had and could have on this population.

Conference encourages the regular and intentional dialogue between family members. In conference, parents become more alert to their children having souls in need of nurturing and can begin to understand the child's responses to God, even in their formative years. A critical link between a growing knowledge of God and His Word with the biblical impact it is making can be reinforced. Not surprisingly, this kind of conference can have continuing effects and impact well beyond the teenage years.

2. Community conference. In community conference, the depth of a soul's journey with the inward teaching of the Holy Spirit is brought to consciousness. The gift of mutual attentiveness and the courage to listen with intent openness to soul-deep transformation then results. Understood as one of "Gods ordinances appointed of purpose for the manifestation and communication of Christ to the soule,"[34] conference was the vehicle for significant renovation of the soul.

To be sure, there is always the tension of living out what we say we believe. Soul-shaping spiritual transformation is foundational for closing the gap between what we know and what we do. Even when knowledge is not the Christ-follower's problem, responding

---

33. Barna Group, "New Research Explores the Long-Term Effect of Spiritual Activity among Children and Teens," accessed 3 April, 2010, www.barna.org/barna-update/article-familykids/321.

34. Edward Reyner, *Precepts for Christian Practice* (London: Printed for Rich. Cotes, 1645), 5.

to and acting on godly convictions remains a challenge. Disparities exist between intellect and character, between knowing, doing, and being. The process of moving from knowing to becoming is a journey not easily mapped and can often be frustrating and bewildering.

Conference can be effective in reducing the general spiritual ennui that exists and replacing it with a greater commitment and passion for thriving in the Christian life. It can provide a sustainable pace in the long-term endeavor of one's pilgrimage. Conference can spell the difference in one's spiritual pilgrimage as greater responsibility is taken for the condition of one's own as well as others' souls. Providing a spiritual think tank for the soul, conference can be incorporated into a number of potential venues. Four areas of recommendations are proposed for incorporating conference as a means of grace for spiritual transformation in small groups.

Bible reading and study materials. Utilizing skillful hermeneutics is foundational to the growth in biblical knowledge necessary for understanding biblical revelation of God's purposes and plans. The common use of Bible study materials to foster biblical knowledge can be easily modified to incorporate the type of conference questions and discussions that seek to engage the soul. These questions can be extracted from the recorded treatises on Puritan conferencing and reformatted with present-day phraseology to offer specific tools to cultivate and augment an intimacy that seeks to address and deepen the approach to and response of the soul. The following is a sample of redesigned questions that might be used in conjunction with the study of a particular Bible passage:

- What are the words or actions that demonstrate your soul's love for Christ?
- What is your soul afraid of God knowing?
- For what is your soul thankful?
- How does God seem to be stepping away from you?
- What does He want you to know about Him? About yourself?
- What are your soul-doubts?
- Does your soul desire unity?

- To what extent is your soul willing to go to preserve unity in your community?
- What will your soul need to depend on God for the sake of unity?
- What keeps your soul from believing a particular truth?

The inclusion of the word "soul" allows a person to ponder more deeply for a truthful and candid response. Questions such as these may even uncover the reality of souls that have been void of much needed care and attention. These and similar questions can be incorporated into the dialogue of those who desire a deeper, more connected and committed experience of community via Bible study materials. Engagement with such thought-provoking, soul-level questions in conversation allows for greater interpersonal interaction within a small group. Greater biblical insights, learned with the intent to connect the soul with truth, create an affirming cycle. As greater truths are learned and adopted, there is a greater desire to know and experience more truth.

The small group member's knowledge of Scripture, regardless of level, in harmony with a desire to attend to soul-issues, fosters mutual care and growth. Not only is the Bible read and studied for informational purposes, but also for its desired transformational effects. "Trans[in]formational" reading and studying furthers one's knowledge of Scripture and enables one to see more of the Spirit's work in one's life. As the word "trans[in]formational" implies, the Bible is to be read for information—information that God has sought to communicate to the human race. The skill of correct reading and interpretation of God's Word can add depth to one's knowledge of the work of God in this world for kingdom purposes, and will naturally impact the practical aspects of living that Word. Words were not meant to stay on a page but to affect personal change. Again, as the word "trans[in]formational" implies, the goal is transformation. Character is developed when it is informed by Scripture. Our soul is more than a repository for what we permit to enter; at its deepest part it is who we are.

Conference amplifies the necessity to study Scripture, to be a lifelong learner and partner in God's ways and the outworking of His plan. It is exercised in a safe and nurturing environment as one learns to sense and share the stirrings, convictions, and movements of the Holy Spirit in his life.

Spiritual attentiveness and direction. A strong foundation of knowing God through His Word allows for the growth in sensitivity to the presence of Christ and the workings of His Spirit since one has the potential for contradicting the other, and all must be consistent with Scripture. As one becomes better equipped in knowing and discerning the character and ways of God, the wisdom brought and shared in godly conversation can be used by God to foster change and transformation in others.

One of the distinguishing characteristics of a church's small group is the type of conversation that takes place within it. Richard Peace summarizes this small group characteristic: "Life-changing group conversation around important issues of a spiritual nature is the genius of small groups."[35] Critical to these types of conversations is the attentiveness to one another's hearts. A careful observing of our hearts and a diligent looking to our ways requires a growing sensitivity to the Holy Spirit's work. Trained Christian spiritual directors can offer sound spiritual direction, yet it should also be recognized and exercised among small group members as an important part of any healthy growth environment for Christian relationships.

Richard Foster understands the ministry of many small groups as a form of spiritual direction.[36] Healthy, life-changing conversation stems from the understanding and expectation of the Holy Spirit's work in a small group. Spiritual direction is concerned with the whole person and the interrelationship of all of life. It takes up the concrete daily experiences of our lives and gives them spiritual significance.

---

35. Richard Peace, "The Genius of a Small Group, Part 1: The Design of Small Groups," course syllabus for Spiritual Formation in a Postmodern World, CF 705, Fuller Seminary, Fall 2004, 17.

36. Richard J. Foster, *Celebration of Discipline: The Path to Spiritual Growth*, rev. ed. (San Francisco: Harper, 1988), 187.

The ordinary kinds of caring and sharing that belong to the Christian community are the starting points for spiritual direction.[37]

Dallas Willard offers this insight on the historical survey of spiritual direction: It was "understood by Jesus, taught by Paul, obeyed by the early church, followed with excesses in the medieval church, narrowed by the Reformers, *recaptured by the Puritans,* virtually lost in the modern church."[38] Spiritual direction is the "help given by one Christian to another which enables that person to pay attention to God's personal communication to him or her, to respond to this personally communicating God, to grow in intimacy with this God, and to live out the consequences of the relationship."[39] Puritan conference restored the art of spiritual attentiveness and direction as evidenced by its use by and with pastors and members of a congregation.

Knowledge of Scripture was essential in conference; being spiritual attentive to one another was expected. They were two sides of the same coin. When life-changing conversation takes place in a group, the need for soul care can be more fully realized and met and the goal of spiritual formation can be realized in authentic transformation. Small groups in American churches provide an excellent venue for the spiritual direction that occurs in conference. Indeed, many of the ideals of small groups resonate with those objectives of conference. Groups that thrive are centered on a worthwhile topic, use a certain process by which to explore that topic, engage in in-depth relationships between people who are focused on conversation around that topic, and possess a spiritual vantage point that brings about change in their lives.[40] Conference echoes these objectives, with the aim for participants of not only getting into the Word but also allowing the Word to get into them, into their hearts and souls, which then gives visible expression in their lives.

---

37. Foster, *Celebration of Discipline*, 186.

38. Dallas Willard, in discussion with the author, January 2008. Emphasis added.

39. William A. Barry and William J. Connolly, *The Practice of Spiritual Direction* (San Francisco: Harper & Row, 1982), 8.

40. Peace, "Genius of Small Group," 3.

It is necessary to note that this kind of spiritual attentiveness differs from accountability. Often when accountability is desired or discussed, the focus is kept on external behaviors. A mentor or trusted friend helps monitor a particular behavior or moral commitment that addresses family relationships, money, or personal struggles, or even the exercise of spiritual disciplines used in their relationship with God. This person can help motivate another to stay focused on a specific change.

The spiritual attentiveness associated with conference focuses more on matters of the soul. These are the stirrings in the heart that cover a wide spectrum, from wrestling with God to being content in God. The condition of the heart or soul will be expressed in external behaviors. Conference allows for the truth of God, through His Word and by His Spirit, to shed light on the soul-deep matters of a life. It is the heart that matters so deeply to God, as from it flows the thoughts, words, and choices of life (Prov. 4:23).

Conference, with its accompanying spiritual attentiveness, presupposes that God acts in our world in such a way that we can experience His actions. The God of Christians is the God who desires to be known as He has revealed Himself in Jesus Christ and in His Word. His mysterious presence draws the believer into community with the Trinity and thus with one another. Yet, we have become less sensitive to the gentle presence of the Holy One in our midst. Perhaps in considering the exercise of conference, a discipline found within the Protestant tradition, spiritual attentiveness can be more broadly exercised by more in evangelical circles.

Training small group leaders. Training classes for small group leaders often have more to do with techniques of leadership, handling conflict, and drawing quiet people into the discussion than with spiritual dependence, spiritual character, and spiritual wisdom.[41] Even less attention is given to personal growth in biblical knowledge. Small group leadership training can include ways to

---

41. Larry Crabb, *The Safest Place on Earth: Where People Connect and Are Forever Changed* (Nashville: Word, 1999), 126.

assist leaders in developing growth in both biblical literacy and caring for the souls of others.

The advantages of incorporating the elements of conference into a new or preexisting small group structure are clear. A key piece to its incorporation is the leading and training of leaders, including small group leaders, in the church. With the backing of the pastoral staff and church leadership, support must be offered to small group leaders in the training necessary to assimilate the use of this discipline. Continuing education can be offered for the utilization and refinement of good hermeneutical skills for the accurate reading and interpretation of Scripture.

A number of excellent resources are available that address understanding God's Word, intellectually making sense of it, and the practical application of and obedience to it. As the word "trans[in]formational" implies, the Bible can be read for information, information that God has sought to communicate to the human race. Correctly reading and interpreting God's Word can add depth, understanding, and knowledge of His work in this world for kingdom purposes. This knowledge can impact the practical aspects of living that Word as God's Spirit demonstrates His commitment to transform believers, each in unique and sometimes similar ways. These skills can enhance one's own personal growth in these areas as well as be instrumental in the hope of extending this kind of biblically informed care to members of a small group.

Words were not meant to stay as printed ink on a page but to affect personal change. Again, as the word "trans[in]formational" implies, the goal is transformation. Christians develop character as they allow Scripture to inform them. We are what we permit to enter the deepest parts of our souls. The need here is for leaders to be trained with increased intentional exposure to ministering and caring for one another's souls, and in growing familiar with the work, purpose, and ways of the Holy Spirit. Larry Crabb affirms the same necessity for studying and applying the Word of God:

> Study the text not only as a good scholar, but also as an honest struggler.

First, ask what questions God has bothered to answer in the Word. Only He is wise enough to know which questions need answering. Then study his answers for the rest of your life.

Second, as study continues, bring to what you're learning the questions that honest living requires you to ask. And assume (this is important) that in the community of faith where the Bible is trusted, you will find all you need to know to live as you were re-created to live. The result will be neither prescriptive counseling nor therapeutic counseling but rather communitarian counseling—an approach rooted in deep respect for the power of God's Spirit to change lives through spiritual community.[42]

What Crabb describes as "communitarian counseling" has strong parallels with conference without the psychological inferences.

Small group leaders who genuinely care for the members they are called to shepherd will benefit from the investment church leadership provides in growing in biblical knowledge and soul care, critical elements for conference.

Well-formatted questions. Conference was a widespread practice that was found not only among the participants as they gathered for their regular meetings to review truths from a sermon message or private Bible reading and open their lives to one another, but it was also found in the rather serendipitous conversations in homes and the marketplace. A key element found in all of the above is the well-formatted question aimed at growth in godliness. The potential found in these types of questions can be powerful. Consider how the types of questions Jesus asked were always intended to reach the heart of a matter. The context surrounding a recorded gospel account advances the opportunity to elicit a response to Jesus' questions. Similarly, questions asked in conference sought to integrate the cerebral with the spiritual, knowledge with experience, the Bible with the soul.

---

42. Crabb, *Safest Place on Earth*, 9.

Influenced by some of the original questions posed by Puritans in conference, a list of updated, intentionally formatted inquiries that seek to connect conversation partners in a deeper way is offered:

- What is God saying to your soul?
- What is He asking you to trust Him for?
- What truth is He revealing about Himself? If you believed that truth, what change would there be in your soul?
- What truth about Himself does He desire to instill in your soul?

One line of questioning perhaps stands at the root of deep concern for another, "How fares it with your soul?" and "How stands it between God and your soul?" The Puritans' common vernacular expressed a deep level of concern for one another. They were accustomed to ask, accustomed to care. A twenty-first-century version, "How's it with your soul?" is a conversation starter that expresses the same concern for "soul-concerning affairs," for deep, spiritual matters. Our preoccupation with the busyness of our times should not preclude us from expressing care for one another's souls in the way we inquire and, equally critical, remain attentive to the responses.

The Puritans can enlighten our expression of community. They understood that community starts with one, grows to two, and becomes a catalyst for meaningful dynamics in a small group. It was more than hanging out; it was hanging tough. Growth in community for them meant being centered on the Word, not the world. Obstacles were often necessitated to further that growth. Authentic community was not instant. It was not found; it was developed, expressed, and gradually reached each other's protected soul. They understood that though human beings were designed for deep and vulnerable community, sin distorted that design and people shunned those relationships. They seized opportunities to ask difficult questions and await the answers because the risk of impoverished souls was too great.

Conclusion

Conference allows for a safe environment in which one is free to ask questions, not for the sake of asking questions but for the purpose of finding answers. This type of dialogue is critical for transformation. The teachable spirit and desire for transformation in the conferee can be evident in the relationships offered in conference.

It has been charged, "Evangelicalism has done well in areas of knowing and doing but poorly in being or in the spiritual nurture of the inner life."[43] Evangelicals can remain faithful to the authoritative nature of Scripture, to orthodox Christian faith, and to growth in biblical literacy while appropriating life-giving resources offered by the spiritual formation movement. A viable avenue for this can be found in the exercise of conference, where knowledge engages the soul and the mind, where intelligence and introspection come together. Distinctly Puritan, characteristically communal, mutually beneficial, and manifestly practical, conference may offer the kind of optimal care needed for life-transforming communities of spiritual transformation.

The time is ripe to explore the untapped mine of Puritan contributions to spiritual transformation. A recovery of the discipline of conference would serve as a welcomed catalyst for spiritual formation, strengthening the spiritual pulse of community. In so doing, a greater appreciation for the Puritan movement and piety may be fostered, and unforeseen benefits would abound for strengthening the momentum of the spiritual formation movement.

Those who long for the deeper understanding and expression of God's Word in their lives will resonate with the discipline of conference in fostering biblical community. God may have sent a famine in our present days, "Not a famine of bread, nor a thirst for water, but of hearing the words of the LORD" (Amos 8:11). As His people hunger and thirst for His Word, may He be pleased to restore the ancient practice of the Puritans as we confer together to receive His Word in concert with attending to one another's souls.

---

43. Bruce Demarest, "An Inside Look: An Evangelical Theologian Evaluates the Spiritual Formation Movement," paper presented at Evangelical Theological Society, Atlanta, 15 November 2003.

Bibliography

Primary Sources

Alleine, Joseph. *Christian Letters.* London: Printed for and sold by Nevil Simmons and Dorman Newman, 1673.

Ambrose, Isaac. *Media.* London: Printed by T. R. and E. M., 1652.

Ames, William. *Disputatio Theologica, De Perfectione.* Cantabrigia: Ex officina Rogeri Danielis, 1646.

———. *The Marrow of Theology.* 1629. Edited and translated by John D. Eusden. Reprint, Grand Rapids: Baker, 1997.

Anonymous. *The Addresse of Some Ministers of Christ in the Isle of Wight & County of Southampton to the People of Their Respective Charges.* London: Printed by J. H., 1658.

———. *Stated Christian Conference Asserted to be a Christian Duty.* London: Printed for and sold by Will. Marshal, 1697.

Baxter, Richard. *A Christian Directory.* London: Printed by Robert White, 1673.

———. *The Poor Man's Family Book.* London: Printed for Nevill Simmons, 1675.

———. *The Reformed Pastor.* Edited by William Brown. Edinburgh: Banner of Truth, 1974.

———. *Reliquiae Baxterianae.* London: Printed for T. Parkhurst, 1696.

———. *The Saints' Everlasting Rest.* London: Printed by Rob White for Thomas Underhill and Francis Tyton, 1650.

Bayly, Lewis. *The Practice of Piety Directing a Christian how to Walk that He may please God*. Delf, Great Britaine: Printed by Abraham Iacobs, 1660.

Bernard, Richard. *The Faithfull Shepheard*. London: Printed by Arnold Hatfield, 1607.

———. *Josuahs Resolution for the Well Ordering of His Household*. London: Printed for John Legatt, 1629.

———. "A Prayer for a Family at all Times." In *A Good Mans Grace*. London: Printed by Felix Kingston, 1621.

———. *A Weekes Worke Containing Rules and Directions how to Walke in the Wayes of Godliness both to God and Man*. London: By Felix Kingston, 1650.

Bownd, Nicholas. *The Doctrine of the Sabbath Plainely Layde Forth*. London: Printed by the Widow Orwin, 1595.

———. *Sabbathum Veteris Et Noui Testamenti: Or the True Doctrine of the Sabbath*. London: By Felix Kyngston, 1606.

Bradshaw, William. *English Puritanisme*. London: W. Jones's secret press, 1605.

Bunyan, John. *Grace Abounding to the Chief of Sinners*. London: Printed by George Larkin, 1666.

———. *The Pilgrim's Progress: From this World to that which is to come, Delivered Under the Similitude of a Dream*. Peabody, Mass.: Hendrickson, 2004.

Calamy, Edward. *The Godly Man's Ark*. London: Printed for John Hancock, 1672.

———. *The Happinesse of Those Who Sleep in Jesus*. London: Printed by J. H. for Nathanael Webb, 1662.

Calvin, John. *The Acts of the Apostles*. Edited by David W. Torrance and Thomas Forsyth Torrance. Translated by W. Fraser John. Grand Rapids: Eerdmans, 1966.

———. *The Institutes of the Christian Religion*. Edited by John T. McNeill. Louisville: Westminster, 1960.

Clarke, Samuel. *The Lives of Sundry Eminent Persons*. London: Printed for Thomas Simmons, 1683.

———. *The Lives of Thirty-Two English Divines*. London: Printed for William Birch, 1677.

———. *A Looking-Glass for Good Women to Dress Themselves By*. London: Printed for William Miller, 1677.

Crossman, Samuel. *The Young Mans Monitor*. London: Printed by J. H., 1664.

Culverwell, Ezekiel. *Time Well Spent in Sacred Meditations*. London: Printed by T. Cotes, 1635.

Dent, Arthur. *The Plain Mans Path-Way to Heaven*. London: Printed for M. Wotton and G. Conyers, 1684.

Doe, Charles. *A Collection of Experience of the Work of Grace*. London: Printed for Chas. Doe, 1700.

Downame, John. *The Christian Warfare*. London: Printed by William Standsby, 1634.

———. *A Guide to Godlynesse*. London: Printed by Felix Kingstone and William Stansby, 1622.

Fuller, Thomas. *The Church History of Britain: from the Birth of Jesus Christ until the Year 1648*. 3 vols. London: T. Tegg, 1837.

———. Introduction to *The Journal or Diary of a Thankful Christian*, by John Beadle. London: Printed by E. Cotes, 1656.

Geree, John. *The character of an Old English-Puritan or Non-Conformist*. London, 1659.

Gouge, William. *Workes*. London: Printed by John Beale, 1627.

Greenham, Richard. "A Profitable Treatise. Concerning a direction for the reading and understanding of the holy Scriptures," in *Workes*. London: Imprinted by Felix Kingston, 1599.

———. *The Workes of the Reverend and Faithfull Servant of Jesus Christ M Richard Greenham*. London: Imprinted by Felix Kingston, 1599.

Grindal, Edmund. *The Remains of Edmund Grindal: Successively Bishop of London and Archbishop of York and Canterbury*. Edited by William Nicholson and Great Britain Ecclesiastical Commissioners for England. Cambridge: University Press, 1843.

Harley, Brilliana. *Letters of the Lady Brilliana Harley, Wife of Sir Robert Harley, of Brampton Bryan, Knight of the Bath*. Edited by Thomas Taylor Lewis. Camden Society Publications, vol. 58. London: Printed for the Camden Soc., 1854.

Hoby, Margaret Dakins. *Diary of Lady Margaret Hoby, 1599–1605*. Edited by Dorothy M. Meads. London: G. Routledge & Sons, 1930.

———. *The Private Life of an Elizabethan Lady: The Diary of Lady Margaret Hoby, 1599–1605*. Edited by Joanna Moody. Stroud: Sutton, 1998.

Hooker, Thomas. *The Poor Doubting Christian Drawn to Christ*. London: Printed by J. D. for Nath. Ranew, 1684.

Janeway, James. *Invisible Realities*. London: Printed for Tho. Parkhurst, 1684.

Ley, John. *A Patterne of Pietie*. London: Printed by Felix Kingston, 1640.

Manningham, John. *The Diary of John Manningham of the Middle Temple, 1602–1603*. Edited by Robert P. Sorlien. Hanover, N.H.: University Press of New England, 1976.

Mather, Cotton. *Magnalia Christi Americana: or, the Ecclesiastical History of New-England from its First Planting in the Year 1620 unto the Year of Our Lord 1698*. Research Library of Colonial Americana, book 3. New York: Arno Press, 1972.

———. *The Resolved Christian Pursuing the Designs of Holiness and Happiness*. Boston: To be sold by Nicholas Boone, 1700.

Mitchel, Jonathan. *A Discourse of the Glory*. London: Printed for Nathaniel Ponder, 1677.

———. "Letter to a Friend." Appended to *A Discourse of the Glory*. London: Printed for Nathaniel Ponder, 1677.

Owen, John. *Phronema Tou Pneumatou, or, the Grace and Duty of Being Spiritually-Minded Declared and Practically Improved.* London: Printed by J. G. for Nathaniel Ponder, 1681.

Perkins, William. *The Arte of Prophesying.* London: By Felix Kyngston, 1607.

———. *A Garden of Spirituall Flowers.* London: Printed by R. B[adger], 1638.

———. *The Work of William Perkins.* Edited by Ian Breward. Abingdon, England: Sutton Courtenay Press, 1970.

———. *Workes.* 3 vols. London: Printed by John Haviland, 1631.

Powell, Vavasor. *Spirituall Experiences of Sundry Beleevers.* London: Printed by Robert Ibbitson, 1653.

Preston, John. *Remaines of that Reverend and Learned Divine John Preston.* London: Printed by R[ichard] B[adger] [and John Legate], 1637.

———. *Riches of Mercy to Men in Misery.* London: Printed by J. T., 1658.

———. *Saints' Spiritual Strength.* London, 1637.

Reyner, Edward. *Precepts for Christian Practice.* London: Printed for Rich. Cotes, 1645.

Rogers, John. *The Doctrine of Faith.* London: Printed for Nathanael Newbery and Henry Overton, 1632.

———. *A Treatise of Love.* London: Printed by H. Lownes and R. Young, 1629.

Rogers, Richard. *The Practice of Christianitie.* London: Printed by B. Alsop, 1623.

———. *Seven Treatises.* London: Printed by the assignes of Thomas Man, 1630.

Rogers, Richard, and Samuel Ward. *Two Elizabethan Puritan Diaries.* Edited by M. M. Knappen. Studies in Church History, vol. 2. Chicago: American Society of Church History, 1933.

Rogers, Timothy. *The Character of a Good Woman*. London: Printed for J. Harris, 1697.

Rous, Francis. *The Arte of Happines*. London: Printed by W. Stansby, 1619.

Shepard, Thomas. *Subjection to Christ in All His Ordinances*. London: Printed for John Rothwell, 1652.

———. *Thomas Shepard's Confessions*. Edited by George Selement and Bruce C. Woolley. Collections, vol. 58. Boston: Colonial Society of Massachusetts, 1981.

Sibbes, Richard. *Bowels Opened*. London: Printed by R. Cotes, 1648.

———. *The Complete Works of Richard Sibbes*. Edinburgh: James Nichol, 1862.

Smith, Henry. *The Works of Henry Smith: Including Sermons, Treatises, Prayers, and Poems with Life of the Author*. Edited by Thomas Fuller. Edinburgh: James Nichol, 1866.

Turner, John. *A Heavenly Conference for Sions Saints*. London, 1645.

Udall, John. *Obedience to the Gospell*. London: Imprinted [by J. Windet?], 1584.

Watson, Thomas. *A Body of Practical Divinity*. London: Printed for Thomas Parkhurst, 1692.

———. *Heaven Taken by Storm*. London: Printed by R. W., 1670.

———. *Religion Our True Interest, or, Practical Notes upon the Third Chapter of Malachy the Sixteen, Seventeen and Eighteen Verses*. London: Printed by J. Astwood, 1682.

White, John. *A Way to the Tree of Life*. London: Printed by M. F., 1647.

Younge, Richard. *A Short and Sure Way to Grace and Salvation*. London, 1674.

———. *A Touch-Stone to try (by Our Knowledge, Belief, and Life) whether We be Christians in Name Onely, or Christians in Deed*. London: sold by Andrew Crooke, 1648.

———. *The Whole Duty of a Christian*. London: Printed for Tho. Sawbridge, 1681.

Bibliography

Books and Articles

Armstrong, Brian G. "Puritan Spirituality: The Tension of Bible and Experience." In *The Spirituality of Western Christendom, II: The Roots of the Modern Christian Tradition*. Edited by E. Rozanne Elder. Cisterian Studies Series 55. Kalamazoo, Mich.: Cisterian, 1984.

Barna Group. "The Barna Update," 12/20/05, accessed 28 June 2006, www.barna.org. Used by permission.

———. "New Research Explores the Long-Term Effect of Spiritual Activity among Children and Teens," accessed 3 April, 2010, www.barna.org/barna-update/article-familykids/321.

———. "Six Megathemes Emerge from Barna Group Research in 2010," accessed 15 February 2011, www.barna.org/culture-articles/six-megathemes-emerge-from-2010.

Barry, William A., and William J. Connolly. *The Practice of Spiritual Direction*. San Francisco: Harper & Row, 1982.

Beeke, Joel R. *Puritan Reformed Spirituality*. Grand Rapids: Reformation Heritage Books, 2004.

Beeke, Joel R., and Randall J. Pederson. *Meet the Puritans: With a Guide to Modern Reprints*. Grand Rapids: Reformation Heritage Books, 2006.

Bettenson, Henry Scowcroft. *Documents of the Christian Church*. 2nd ed. London: Oxford, 1963.

Black, J. William. *Reformation Pastors: Richard Baxter and the Ideal of the Reformed Pastor*. Studies in Evangelical History and Thought. Carlisle, England: Paternoster, 2004.

Bray, Gerald Lewis, ed. *Documents of the English Reformation*. Minneapolis: Fortress, 1994.

Bremer, Francis J., ed. *Puritanism: Transatlantic Perspectives on a Seventeenth-Century Anglo-American Faith*. Boston: Massachusetts Historical Society, 1993.

Bremer, Francis J., and Tom Webster, eds., *Puritans and Puritanism in Europe and America: A Comprehensive Encyclopedia.* Santa Barbara: ABC-CLIO, 2006.

Brooks, Peter Newman. "The Principle and Practice of Primitive Protestantism in Tudor England: Cranmer, Parker and Grindal as Chief Pastors, 1535–1577." In *Reformation Principle and Practice.* Edited by Peter Newman Brooks. London: Scolar Press, 1980.

Cohen, Charles Lloyd. *God's Caress: The Psychology of Puritan Religious Experience.* New York: Oxford, 1986.

Collins, Kenneth J., ed. *Exploring Christian Spirituality: An Ecumenical Reader.* Grand Rapids: Baker, 2000.

Collinson, Patrick. *Archbishop Grindal, 1519–1583: The Struggle for a Reformed Church.* Berkeley: University of California, 1979.

———. *The Elizabethan Puritan Movement.* London: Cape, 1967.

———. *Godly People: Essays on English Protestantism and Puritanism.* History Series, vol. 23. London: Hambledon Press, 1983.

———. "Prophesyings." In *Puritans and Puritanism in Europe and America: A Comprehensive Encyclopedia.* Edited by Francis J. Bremer and Tom Webster. Santa Barbara, Calif.: ABC-CLIO, 2006.

———. "Reformer and the Archbishop: Martin Bucer and an English Bucerian." *Journal of Religious History* 6 (December 1971): 327.

———. Review of C. Hill, *The English Bible and the Seventeenth-Century Revolution.* Times Literary Supplement 4697, 9 April 1993.

Collinson, Patrick, John Craig, and Brett Usher. *Conferences and Combination Lectures in the Elizabethan Church: Dedham and Bury St Edmunds, 1582–1590.* Church of England Record Society. Woodbridge: Boydell, 2003.

Crabb, Larry. *The Safest Place on Earth: Where People Connect and are Forever Changed.* Nashville: Word, 1999.

Cross, Claire. *Church and People, 1450–1660: The Triumph of the Laity in the English Church.* Atlantic Highlands, N.J.: Humanities Press, 1976.

Daniell, David. *William Tyndale: A Biography.* New Haven: Yale, 1994.

Davidson, Edward. "John Cotton's Biblical Exegesis: Method and Purpose." *Early American Literature* 17, no. 2 (Fall 1982): 119.

Davies, Horton. *The Worship of the English Puritans.* Morgan, Penn.: Soli Deo Gloria, 1997.

Demarest, Bruce. "An Inside Look: An Evangelical Theologian Evaluates the Spiritual Formation Movement." Paper presented at Evangelical Theological Society, Atlanta, 15 November 2003.

———. *Satisfy Your Soul: Restoring the Heart of Christian Spirituality.* Colorado Springs: NavPress, 1999.

Dickens, A. G. *The English Reformation.* 2nd ed. University Park, Penn.: Pennsylvania State, 1991.

———. *Reformation and Society in Sixteenth-Century Europe.* London: Thames & Hudson, 1966.

Doerksen, Daniel W., and Christopher Hodgkins. *Centered on the Word: Literature, Scripture, and the Tudor-Stuart Middle Way.* Newark: University of Delaware, 2004.

Dugmore, C. W. *The Mass and the English Reformers.* London: Macmillan, 1958.

Durston, Christopher, and Jacqueline Eales. *The Culture of English Puritanism: 1560–1700.* Themes in Focus. New York: St. Martin's Press, 1996.

Elton, G. R. *Reform and Reformation-England, 1509–1558.* Cambridge: Harvard, 1977.

Emerson, Everett H. *English Puritanism from John Hooper to John Milton.* Durham, N.C.: Duke, 1968.

Eusden, John Dykstra. Introduction to *The Marrow of Theology,* by William Ames. Grand Rapids: Baker, 1968.

Ferry, Patrick. "Preaching, Preachers, and the English Reformation under Edward VI: 1547–1553. *Concordia Journal* 18 (October 1992): 361–375.

Fielding, John. "Opposition to the Personal Rule of Charles I: The Diary of Robert Woodford, 1637–1641." *The Historical Journal* 31, no. 4 (December 1988): 774.

Foster, Richard J. *Celebration of Discipline: The Path to Spiritual Growth.* Rev. ed. San Francisco: HarperSanFrancisco, 1988.

Gallup, George. *Emerging Trends* 19, no. 2 (Feb 1997): 1.

Gallup, George, and D. Michael Lindsay. *The Gallup Guide: Reality Check for 21st Century Churches.* Loveland, Colo.: Gallup Organization Group, 2002.

———. *Surveying the Religious Landscape: Trends in U.S. Beliefs.* Harrisburg, Penn.: Morehouse Publishing, 1999.

Gaustad, Edwin S. "Quest for Pure Christianity." *Church History* 12, no. 41 (1994): 9.

George, Timothy. "The Reformation Roots of the Baptist Tradition." *Review & Expositor* 86 (Winter 1989): 9.

Gibson, David. "America's Favorite Unopened Text." *Beliefnet* (December 2000). http://www.beliefnet.com/Faiths/Christianity/2000/12/Americas-Favorite-Unopened-Text.aspx.

Gordis, Lisa M. *Opening Scripture: Bible Reading and Interpretive Authority in Puritan New England.* Chicago: University of Chicago, 2003.

Green, Ian. *Print and Protestantism in Early Modern England.* Oxford: Oxford, 2000.

Guelzo, Allen C. "When the Sermon Reigned." *Church History* 13, no. 1 (1994): 24.

Haller, William. *The Rise of Puritanism: Or, the Way to the New Jerusalem as Set Forth in Pulpit and Press from Thomas Cartwright to John Lilburne and John Milton, 1570–1643.* New York: Harper, 1957.

Hambrick-Stowe, Charles E. *The Practice of Piety: Puritan Devotional Disciplines in Seventeenth-Century New England.* Chapel Hill: University of North Carolina, 1982.

———. "Puritan Spirituality in America." In *Christian Spirituality: Post-Reformation and Modern.* Edited by Louis K. Duprâe and Don E. Saliers. World Spirituality. Vol. 18. New York: Crossroad, 1989.

Healey, Charles J. *Christian Spirituality: An Introduction to the Heritage.* New York: Alba House, 1999.

Hendricks, William. *Exit Interviews.* Chicago: Moody Press, 1993.

Herr, Alan Fager. *The Elizabethan Sermon: A Survey and a Bibliography.* New York: Octagon Books, 1969.

Hill, Christopher. *The English Bible and the Seventeenth-Century Revolution.* London: Penguin, 1994.

———. *Intellectual Origins of the English Revolution—Revisited.* Oxford: Clarendon Press, 2001.

Hinson, E. Glenn. "Puritan Spirituality." In *Protestant Spiritual Traditions.* Edited by Frank C. Senn. New York: Paulist Press, 1986.

Holt, Bradley P. *Thirsty for God: A Brief History of Christian Spirituality.* Minneapolis: Augsburg, 1993.

Howard, Evan B. *The Brazos Introduction to Christian Spirituality.* Grand Rapids: Brazos Press, 2008.

Howard, Leon. *Essays on Puritans and Puritanism.* Edited by James Barbour and Thomas Quirk. Albuquerque: University of New Mexico, 1986.

Hughes, Philip. *The Reformation in England.* rev. ed. London: Burns and Oates, 1963.

Icenogle, Gareth Weldon. *Biblical Foundations for Small Group Ministry: An Integrative Approach.* Downers Grove, Ill.: InterVarsity, 1994.

Johnston, O. R. "The Means of Grace in Puritan Theology." *Evangelical Quarterly* 25 (October 1953): 217.

Jones, W. Paul. *The Art of Spiritual Direction: Giving and Receiving Spiritual Guidance*. Nashville: Upper Room Books, 2002.

Kantzer, Kenneth. Foreword to *What Every Christian Should Know*, by Jo H. Lewis and Gordon A. Palmer. Wheaton, Ill.: Victor Books, 1989.

Kapic, Kelly M. *Communion with God: The Divine and the Human in the Theology of John Owen*. Grand Rapids: Baker, 2007.

Kapic, Kelly M. and Justin Taylor, eds. *Overcoming Sin and Temptation*. Wheaton, Ill.: Good News/Crossway Books, 2006.

Kapic, Kelly M. and Randall Gleason, eds. *The Devoted Life*. Downers Grove, Ill.: InterVarsity, 2004.

Knappen, M. M. *Tudor Puritanism: A Chapter in the History of Idealism*. Gloucester, Mass.: P. Smith, 1963.

Knott, John Ray. *The Sword of the Spirit: Puritan Responses to the Bible*. Chicago: University of Chicago, 1980.

Lake, Peter. "Feminine Piety and Personal Potency: The Emancipation of Mrs. Jane Radcliffe." *The Seventeenth Century* 2, no. 2 (October 1987): 145.

———. Introduction to *The Holy Spirit in Puritan Faith and Experience* by Geoffrey Nuttall. Chicago: University of Chicago, 1992.

Lehmberg, Stanford E. "Archbishop Grindal and the Prophesyings." *Historical Magazine of the Protestant Episcopal Church* 34 (June 1965): 89.

Levy, Babette May. *Preaching in the First Half Century of New England History*. Edited by Matthew Spinka and Robert Hastings Nichols. Studies in Church History, vol. 6. New York: Russell & Russell, 1967.

Lewis, Jo H., and Gordon A. Palmer. *What Every Christian Should Know*. Wheaton, Ill.: Victor Books, 1989.

Lloyd-Jones, David Martyn. *The Puritans: Their Origins and Successors*. Edinburgh: Banner of Truth, 1987.

Lovelace, Richard C. "The Anatomy of Puritan Piety: English Puritan Devotional Literature, 1600–1640." In *Christian Spirituality: Post-Reformation and Modern*. Edited by Louis Dupré and Don E. Saliers. New York: Crossroad, 1989.

———. "Evangelical Spirituality: A Church Historian's Perspective," In *Exploring Christian Spirituality*. Edited by Kenneth J. Collins. Grand Rapids: Baker, 2000.

Luther, Martin, and Kurt Aland. *Kirche Und Gemeinde*. 2. erw. und neubearbeitete Aufl. Edited by Luther Deutsch, 6. Stuttgart: E. Klotz, 1966.

Maas, Robin, and Gabriel O'Donnell, eds. *Spiritual Traditions for the Contemporary Church*. Nashville: Abingdon Press, 1990.

Martin, Hugh. *Puritanism and Richard Baxter*. London: SCM Press, 1954.

McGrath, Alister E. *Christian Spirituality: An Introduction*. Oxford: Blackwell Publishers, 1999.

———. "Loving God with Heart and Mind." In *For All the Saints: Evangelical Theology and Christian Spirituality*. Edited by Timothy George and Alister McGrath. Louisville: Westminster, 2003.

McNeill, John Thomas. *A History of the Cure of Souls*. Edited by John T. McNeill. London: SCM Press, 1952.

McPherson, Miller, and Lynn Smith-Lovin. "Social Isolation in America: Change in Core Discussion Networks over Two Decades." *American Sociological Review* 71, no. 3 (June 2006): 353–354.

Miller, Perry. *The New England Mind: The Seventeenth Century*. Cambridge: Harvard, 1963.

Mitchell, W. Fraser. *English Pulpit Oratory from Andrewes to Tillotson: A Study of Its Literary Aspects*. New York: Russell & Russell, 1962.

Moorman, John R. H. *A History of the Church in England*. London: A. and C. Black, 1961.

Morgan, Irvonwy. *The Godly Preachers of the Elizabethan Church*. London: Epworth Press, 1965.

———. *Puritan Spirituality: Illustrated from the Life and Times of the Rev. Dr. John Preston*. London: Epworth Press, 1973.

Morgan, John. *Godly Learning: Puritan Attitudes towards Reason, Learning, and Education, 1560–1640*. New York: Cambridge, 1986.

Morison, Samuel Eliot. *The Intellectual Life of Colonial New England*. 3rd ed. New York: New York, 1965.

Neal, Daniel. *The History of the Puritans: Or, Protestant Non-Conformists; from the Reformation in 1517 to the Revolution in 1688; Comprising an Account of their Principles; Their Attempts for a Further Reformation in the Church, Their Sufferings, and the Lives and Characters of their most Considerable Divines*. Vol. 1. London: Thomas Tegg and Son, 1837. Reprint, Minneapolis: Klock & Klock, 1979.

Nienhuis, David R. "The Problem of Evangelical Biblical Illiteracy." *Modern Reformation* 19, no. 1 (Jan–Feb 2010): 10–13, 17.

Noll, Mark A., ed. *Confessions and Catechisms of the Reformation*. Grand Rapids: Baker, 1991.

Nuttall, Geoffrey Fillingham. *The Holy Spirit in Puritan Faith and Experience*. Chicago: University of Chicago, 1992.

Olds, Jacqueline, Richard Schwartz, and Harriet Webster. *Overcoming Loneliness in Everyday Life*. New York: Carol Pub. Group, 1996.

Ortberg, John. "No More Mr. Nice Group." *Leadership Journal* 26, no. 3 (August 2005): 37.

Packer, J. I. *A Quest for Godliness: The Puritan Vision of the Christian Life*. Wheaton, Ill.: Good News/Crossway, 1990.

———. "Theology on Fire." *Christian History* 41, no. 12 (1994): 32.

Peace, Richard. "The Genius of a Small Group, Part 1: The Design of Small Groups." Course syllabus for Spiritual Formation in a Postmodern World, CF 705, Fuller Seminary, Fall, 2004.

Puritans and Puritanism in Europe and America: A Comprehensive Encyclopedia. Edited by Francis J. Bremer and Tom Webster. Santa Barbara: ABC-CLIO, 2006.

Rechtien, John G. "Logic in Puritan Sermons in the Late Sixteenth Century and Plain Style." *Style* 13 (Summer 1979): 249.

Rice, Howard L. *Reformed Spirituality: An Introduction for Believers.* Louisville: Westminster, 1991.

Richardson, Caroline Francis. *English Preachers and Preaching, 1640–1670.* New York: The Macmillan Company, 1928.

Rupp, Gordon. "A Devotion of Rapture in English Puritanism." In *Reformation Conformity and Dissent: Essays in Honour of Geoffrey Nuttall.* Edited by R. Buick Knox. London: Epworth Press, 1977.

Rowe, Lawrence. *Family, Sex and Marriage in England, 1500–1800.* New York: Harper & Rowe, 1979.

Seaver, Paul S. *The Puritan Lectureships: The Politics of Religious Dissent, 1560–1662.* Stanford: Stanford, 1970.

———. *Wallington's World: A Puritan Artisan in Seventeenth-Century London.* Stanford: Stanford, 1985.

Selement, George. "The Meeting of Elite and Popular Minds at Cambridge, New England, 1638–1645." *William and Mary Quarterly* 3, no. 41 (January 1984): 40.

Smith-Lovin, Lynn, and Miller McPherson, "You Are Who You Know: A Network Perspective on Gender." In *Theory on Gender/Feminism on Theory, Social Institutions and Social Change.* Edited by Paula England. New York: A. de Gruyter, 1993.

Sommerville, C. John. "On the Distribution of Religious and Occult Literature in Seventeenth-Century England." *The Library,* fifth series, vol. 29, no. 2 (1974): 221–225.

Spurr, John. *English Puritanism, 1603–1689.* New York: St. Martin's Press, 1998.

Stoeffler, F. Ernest. *The Rise of Evangelical Pietism.* Leiden: E. J. Brill, 1965.

Stone, Lawrence. *Family, Sex and Marriage in England, 1500–1800.* New York: Harper & Rowe, 1979.

Stott, John R. W. *Between Two Worlds: The Art of Preaching in the Twentieth Century.* Grand Rapids: Eerdmans, 1982.

Stout, Harry S. *The New England Soul: Preaching and Religious Culture in Colonial New England*. New York: Oxford, 1986.

Strype, John. *The History of the Life and Acts of the Most Reverend Father in God, Edmund Grindal...to which is Added an Appendix of Original Mss*. Burt Franklin Research and Source Work Series. Philosophy and Religious History Monographs 145. New York: B. Franklin, 1974.

Sweet, Leonard I. *Faithquakes*. Nashville: Abingdon Press, 1994.

———. *Quantum Spirituality: A Postmodern Apologetic*. Dayton, Ohio: Whaleprints, 1991.

Towlson, Clifford W. *Moravian and Methodist: Relationships and Influences in the Eighteenth Century*. London: Epworth Press, 1957.

Tyson, John R., ed. *Invitation to Christian Spirituality: An Ecumenical Anthology*. New York: Oxford, 1999.

Wabuda, Susan. *Preaching during the English Reformation*. Cambridge Studies in Early Modern British History. Cambridge: Cambridge, 2002.

Wakefield, Gordon S. *Puritan Devotion: Its Place in the Development of Christian Piety*. London: Epworth Press, 1957.

———. "The Puritans." In *The Study of Spirituality*. Edited by Cheslyn Jones, Geoffrey Wainwright, and Edward Yarnold, SJ. New York: Oxford, 1986.

Wallace, Charles. *Susanna Wesley: The Complete Writings*. Oxford: Oxford, 1997.

Wallace, Dewey D., Jr., ed. *The Spirituality of the Later English Puritans: An Anthology*. Macon, Ga.: Mercer, 1987.

Watkins, Owen C. *The Puritan Experience: Studies in Spiritual Autobiography*. New York: Schocken Books, 1972.

Watt, Tessa. *Cheap Print and Popular Piety, 1550–1640*. Cambridge Studies in Early Modern British History. Cambridge: Cambridge, 1991.

Webster, Tom. *Godly Clergy in Early Stuart England: The Caroline Puritan Movement, 1620–1643*. Cambridge: Cambridge, 2002.

Westcott, Brooke Foss, and William Aldis Wright. *A General View of the History of the English Bible*. 3rd ed. New York: Macmillan, 1905.

Willard, Dallas. *The Divine Conspiracy: Rediscovering Our Hidden Life in God*. San Francisco: HarperSanFrancisco, 1997.

———. "The Reality of the Spiritual Life." Christian Spirituality and Soul Care Lecture Series, Talbot School of Theology, La Mirada, Calif., Fall 2006.

———. *The Spirit of the Disciplines*. San Francisco: Harper & Row, 1988.

Wright, Louis B. *Religion and Empire: The Alliance between Piety and Commerce in English Expansion, 1558–1625*. Chapel Hill: University of North Carolina, 1943.

Wuthnow, Robert. *Sharing the Journey: Support Groups and America's New Quest for Community*. New York: Simon & Schuster, 1994.

Subject Index

accountability, 175
Act of Supremacy
    of 1534, 22
    of 1559, 27, 40
Act of Uniformity (1559), 27, 29, 40, 41
adiaphora, 28, 41–42
administration of sacraments, 14, 69, 93
Advertisements (Parker), 41–42
allegory, 63
Alleine, Joseph, 100–101, 139–40
Alleine, Richard, 120
alliteration, 83
almanacs, 67
Ambrose, Isaac, 88, 92, 101–2, 112–13, 115, 117, 118–20, 140
Ames, William, 57–58, 67, 71, 79, 83
anagogy, 63
analogy, 63
Annesley, Samuel, 151
application(s) of sermons and Scripture, 14, 78, 79–80, 98, 106
Armstrong, Brian, 5
Art of Prophesying, The (Perkins), 14, 74, 78
asceticism. *See* spirituality
attentiveness, spiritual, 173–75

authority
    of church, 28, 30
    of Parliament, 23
    of Scripture, 13, 30, 52, 54–60, 89
Authorized (King James) Version of the Bible (1611), 61
autobiography, spiritual, 130, 144, 148–49

backsliding, 107
ballads, 67
bands, in Methodism, 151
Barna, George, 168–69
Baxter, Richard, 12, 16, 17, 67–68, 72, 83, 87–88, 89, 94, 102–3, 108, 126–27, 130–33, 137–38, 151
Bayly, Lewis, 9, 62
Beadle, John, 127
Beeke, Joel, 7
Bernard, Richard, 14, 51, 74, 75, 77, 81, 98, 109, 131
Bible, the. *See* Scripture
biblical interpretation, 10, 16, 63–64, 70, 74–76, 95, 163, 169, 176
biblical literacy, 8, 53, 89, 98, 111–13, 120, 166
    lack of, 161–63, 168
    See also knowledge of God

biography, spiritual, 85, 141
Bishops' Bible, 41, 41n73, 61
Boleyn, Anne, 21, 22
Book of Common Prayer, 23, 27, 31
Book of Homilies (Cranmer, 1547), 24, 30
Bownd, Nicholas, 20, 98, 101, 102, 104, 106, 111–12, 142–43
Bradshaw, William, 59, 70
broadsides, 67
brotherhood among ministers, 16, 36, 50, 61, 125, 126, 145
Brazos Introduction to Christian Spirituality (Howard, ed.), 6
Bucer, Martin, 23
Bunyan, John, 11, 12, 107, 151–52
Burghley, Lord (Sir William Cecil), 44

Calamy, Edmund, 85, 136
Calvin, John, 24, 55, 57, 65, 69–70, 75
Calvinism, 5, 22
catechism, catechetical instruction, 16, 72–73, 86, 98, 133, 138, 149
Catharine of Aragon, 21, 22
Catholic Reformation, 25, 26
Chaderton, Laurence, 37–38
children, religious instruction of, 138–39, 141, 168–69
Christ
    conferencing with disciples, 97, 103
    followers of, 89, 93, 94, 103, 111, 122, 134, 158, 170–71, 173; *see also* conference; spiritual formation
    kingdom of, 124
    preaching about (gospel of), 47, 70, 74, 129
    and Scripture, 59, 70
    teaching about, in households, 139, 142
Christian Letters (R. Alleine), 120
Christian Spirituality (McGrath), 6
Christian Warfare (Downame), 103
Christlikeness, 20, 93; *see also* Christ; conference
church
    tradition, 54, 58
    true, preaching as mark of, 69
    well-being of, 165
Church of England, 27, 29
    conformity in, 41, 42–43, 48
    founding of, 21–22
    theology of, 24, 56
Clarke, Katherine, 85, 141
Clarke, Samuel, 84, 85, 116, 133–34, 141, 144
clergy. *See* ministers
"closet" exercises, 18
cocooning, 168
Collins, Kenneth, 4–5
Collinson, Patrick, 73, 146–47
community, 11, 18–19, 37, 97–98, 107, 112, 134, 142–44, 154, 165, 170–71, 177–178
conference
    as means of grace, 89, 93, 94–122
    as way to retain sermon content, 88–89
    benefits of, 20, 98, 108–15
    contemporary definitions of, 9
    cross-generational aspect of, 126–28
    emergence of, as successor to prophesyings, 50–52
    format of
        content, 117–20
        in absentia, 120–22
        logistics, 115–17
    lay
        community, 142–44, 170–78

household, 137–42, 168–70
ministerial
   pastoral, 125n2, 129–37, 166–67
   professional, 125–29, 164–65
   neglect of, 105–7
   objective of, 98–101
   practice of, 12–13, 95, 144–53
   Puritan spiritual discipline of, 7–8, 11–12, 18, 83
   scriptural support for, 101–5
   sixteenth-century definitions of, 11
   and state of the soul, 65, 113–15, 143
   See also edification; spiritual formation
confidentiality, 118
conformity, 41, 42–43, 48
Continental Reformation, 23, 24, 25, 56
conversion, 12, 71–72, 80, 89, 91, 129–31
covenant, 11
Crabb, Larry, 176–77
Cranmer, Thomas, 23, 25
Cromwell, Thomas, 22
Crossman, Samuel, 60, 89–90
culture, 28, 56, 66–68, 73, 115, 144, 157–58, 160
Culverwell, Ezekiel, 20, 128

Davies, Horton, 2
deprivation of living, 25, 30, 31, 32
devotion, private, 11
devotional movement, Puritanism as, 3
diaries, 9n29, 12, 18, 19, 128, 144
   of Lady Margaret Hoby, 141, 149–50
   of John Manningham, 84–85
   of Robert Woodford, 140

Diary (Manningham), 84–85
diligence, 95
dissolution of monasteries, 22
doctrine, 78, 79, 150
Downame, John, 103, 113–14

Earl of Huntingdon. *See* Hastings, Henry
edification, 31, 52, 63, 80–81, 84, 87, 104, 110, 134, 138, 140, 152
Edward VI, 23–24
election, 10
Eliot, John, 18
Elizabethan Settlement (1559), 27–29
Elizabeth I, 26–30, 31, 39–50
Emanuel order of prophesyings, 38
English Reformation, 22, 23, 24, 32
Erasmus, Desiderius, 22
evangelicals, 7, 8, 154, 156, 175, 178–79
exegesis, 14, 56, 76, 78, 84n54
exercises, spiritual, 18, 67, 93, 138, 143, 149
   of ministers, in prophesyings, 33, 35, 36, 38–39, 42, 45, 47–48
experience, 2, 5, 8, 85, 100–101
Exploring Christian Spirituality (Collins, ed.), 4–5
exposition, 78

faith, 2, 9, 15, 59, 95
   public profession of, 12, 89, 130
Faithful Shepherd, The (Bernard), 14, 75
false piety, 8
form of sermons, 77–81
Forty-two Articles of Religion (1553), 24, 27–28
Foster, Richard, 173–74
Fuller, John, 127–28
funeral sermon(s), 85, 136, 144, 148

Gallup, George, 161, 163–64
Geneva Bible, 37, 41n73, 48, 60, 60n22, 76
George, Timothy, 6
Geree, John, 72
Gibson, David, 161–62
Gilby, Anthony, 48
Gleason, Randall C., 7
God
    glory of, 98, 161
    instruction, through Scripture, 64
    knowledge of, 99–100, 104, 110–11, 134, 162, 166, 173; see also biblical literacy
    purposes and plans of, 171
    relationship to, 10, 17, 63
    sovereignty of, 10
    submission to, 65
    will of, 65
godliness, growth of, 10, 54, 59, 72, 85, 89, 91, 98, 142
Goodwin, John, 147
Gouge, William, 137
grace, 12, 74
    means of, 17–19, 20, 31, 52, 89, 92–94
        private, 60–68, 92
        public, 69–81 92–93
        sacraments as, 31
    See also spiritual discipline(s)
Greenham, Richard, 51, 61–62, 71–72, 73, 95, 142
Grindal, Edmund, 19, 43–49

Hageman, Howard G., 4
Hambrick-Stowe, Charles, 3, 9–10, 18
Harley, Lady Brilliana, 113, 141
Harley, Edward, 113
Hastings, Henry (Earl of Huntingdon), 149
Henry VIII, 21–23

Hildersham, Arthur, 84, 145
Hinson, E. Glenn, 10–11
Hoby, Lady Margaret, 141, 149–50
Holt, Bradley, 5
Holy Spirit
    activity of, 14, 58, 92, 167, 170, 173, 176
    doctrine of, in Puritanism, 2, 17
    and illumination, 64–65, 75
    inspiration of and witness to Scripture, 54–55, 57, 58, 64
home meetings, 18–19; see also conference; household
Hooker, Richard, 147
Hooker, Thomas, 127, 128
Hooper, John, 25, 33
household
    conference, 137–42, 168–70
    instruction and worship, 15–16, 87
humanism, 22
hyperbole, 63

idiom, 66–68
illiteracy about Scripture, 161–63, 168
imagery, 64, 66, 67
individualism, 158, 160
infant mortality, 135
information technology, 157
Institutes of the Christian Religion, The (Calvin), 69
interpretation, biblical, 10, 16, 63–64, 70, 74–76, 95, 163, 169, 176
Invitation to Christian Spirituality (Tyson), 4
inward religion, 5
isolation, 157–58

Janeway, James, 136
Jesus, 101, 122, 153, 174, 175

conferencing with disciples, 102–3
questions asked by, 177, 178
See also Christ
Johnston, O. R., 8, 14, 20
Journal, The (Beadle), 127

Kapic, Kelly, 7
Kinnaman, David, 169–70
knowledge of God, 99–100, 104, 110–11, 134, 162, 166, 173; see also biblical literacy

Latimer, Hugh, 25
leaders, training, 175–77
legalism, 8
letters, conference by, 12–13, 113, 120–22, 145
Lewis, Jo, 169
Ley, John, 148
life expectancy, 135
listening, to retain sermon content, 81–83
literacy, 61
literal meaning of Scripture, 63
literary devices in Scripture, 63
liturgical movement, Puritanism as, 2
liturgy, 28, 70
Lives of Thirty-two English Divines (Clarke), 84
logic, 84
longhand, 85
Lord's Day, the, 86
Lovelace, Richard, 5
Luther, Martin, 24, 56
Maas, Robin, 4
Manningham, John, 65, 84–85
manuals, 12, 16, 19, 75, 78, 148
Marrow of Theology, The (Ames), 57
Mary I, 24–26
Mather, Cotton, 127, 150–51

Matthew, Thomas. See Tyndale, William
McGrath, Alister, 6
McPherson, Miller, 157
means of grace, 17–19, 20, 31, 52, 89, 92–94
 private, 60–68, 92
 public, 69–81, 92–93
 sacraments as, 31
 See also spiritual discipline(s)
meditation, 9, 13, 18, 36, 52, 62, 75, 81, 83, 84, 93, 95, 96–97, 156
Meet the Puritans (Beeke and Pederson), 7
memorization, 83, 84, 109–11
metanarrative, 68, 162
metaphors, 66, 67
Methodism, 151
middle way, 28
Miller, Perry, 14
ministers, 14–15, 16, 18–19, 29, 95–96, 100
 care by, 108–9
 and education, 29, 31, 35, 42–43, 48, 126
 responsibility to preach, 70–72
 use of conference by, 89, 108–9, 115–16, 150
 pastoral, 129–37, 166–68
 professional, 125–29, 164–65
ministry of the Word, 14, 93, 108
Mitchel, Jonathan, 12–13, 120–22
mortem obire, 135–37

narratives, 19
New Age practices, 154
New Testament, 22, 28, 32, 33, 56, 61, 101, 102
Nienhuis, David, 169
Nuttall, Geoffrey, 2

O'Donnell, Gabriel, 4
Olds, Jacqueline, 160

Old Testament, 101
opening Scripture. *See* interpretation, biblical
oratorical style of preaching, 84
original languages of Scripture, 76
Owen, John, 13–14, 151

Packer, J. I., 3
parable, 63
parents, religious responsibilities of, 138–39, 168–69
Parker, Matthew, 40–43
Parliament
  authority of, 23
  first, of Elizabeth I, 26–27
  repeal of Protestant reforms by, 24
Paul (apostle), 32, 38, 47, 69, 101, 102, 103, 104, 112, 153, 174
Peace, Richard, 173
Pederson, Randall, 7
Perkins, William, 14, 59, 63, 64, 74, 75, 78, 82, 87, 137, 138
persecution, 25, 30, 66, 107
Philip of Spain, 25
piety. *See* spirituality
pilgrimage. *See* spiritual guidance
Pilgrim's Progress (Bunyan), 12, 107, 138–39, 152
plain style of preaching, 77–78, 83
psalms, 14, 67, 87, 93
politics, 66
practice, 95
Practice of Piety (Bayly), 62
Practice of Piety (Hambrick-Stowe), 9
prayer, 9, 14, 15–16, 18, 36, 37, 62, 67, 80, 93, 95, 116, 147, 149
  as means of grace, 93
preaching, 22, 24, 29–30, 34, 44, 108, 129–30
  as prophesying, 74–76

oratorical style of, 84
plain style of, 77–78, 83
Puritan, 70–72
See also sermons
preconversion experience, 92, 130
preparation, 95
preparation of sermons, 76–77
Preston, John, 17, 71, 77, 80–81, 86
primitive church, 2
proofs, 78–79
prophecy, prophesying, 74–76
prophesyings
  format of, 36–39
  Grindal's defense of, 46–49
  in England, 33–36, 125
  origin of, 32–33
  suppression of, 42–43, 46, 48
prophezei, 33
Protestant Spiritual Traditions (Senn, ed.), 10
public profession of faith, 12, 89, 130
Puritan Devotion (Wakefield), 9
Puritanism
  as devotional movement, 3
  as liturgical movement, 2
  characterizations of, 2–3, 8, 54
  culture as influenced by Scripture, 66–68
  movement and ethos, 6, 28–29, 29n22
  preaching, 70–72; *see also* sermons
  role of women in, 146–53
  social aspects of, 18
  spirituality, 3–7, 14
    in families, 15–16
    in community, 7, 11, 18–19, 88–89, 154
    See also conference
  view of Scripture, 3, 5, 9, 10, 17, 28, 57–60, 148

Subject Index

Puritan Reformed Spirituality (Beeke), 7
Puritans and Puritanism in Europe and America (Bremer and Webster, eds.), 6

quadriga, 63
Quest for Godliness (Packer), 3
questions, well-formatted, 177–78

Ratcliffe, Jane, 148
Reformation
   Catholic, 25, 26
   Continental, 23, 24, 25, 56
   English, 22, 23, 24, 32
Reformed Pastor, The (Baxter), 108
religious commitment, correlated to spiritual training, 170
repeating sermons, 86–88
repentance, 9
retaining content of sermons, 81–89
revelation, 53, 171, 175
Reyner, Edward, 93
rhetorical style of sermons, 14, 77
Ridley, Nicholas, 23, 25
Rogers, John, 114, 143
Rogers, Richard, 61, 83, 92, 96–97, 128–29, 166
Rogers, Timothy, 151
Roman Catholic Church, 2, 21–22, 25, 28, 54–55, 154
Rous, Francis, 107
rule of faith and practice, Scripture as, 58

sacraments, 58
   administration of, 14, 69, 93
   as means of grace, 31
salvation, 24, 44, 47, 56, 59, 69, 72, 130
sanctification. *See* spiritual formation

Schwartz, Richard, 160
Scripture
   authority of, 13, 30, 52, 54–60, 89
   centrality of, 13–15, 20, 148
   English translations of, 22–23
   exegesis of, 14, 56, 76, 78, 84n54
   forms of worship derived from, 24
   illumination of, 64–65
   influence of in daily life, 66–68
   interpretation of, 63–64, 74–76, 95, 163, 169, 176
   perspicuity of, 95
   Puritan view of, 3, 5, 9, 10, 17, 28, 57–60
   reading, 13, 18, 59, 142–43, 166, 171
      as means of grace, 60–68
      private, 60–66, 72–74
   rule of faith and practice, 58
   small-group study of, 8, 95, 166, 171–73
   support for conference, 101–5
   See also preaching; sermons
Seaver, Paul, 141
"secret" exercises, 18, 92
self-deception, 8
self-examination, 10–11, 15, 18, 149
Senn, Frank, 10
sermons, 13–15, 35, 166
   form of, 77–81
   leading to conversion, 131–32
   preparation of, 76–77, 167
   and private Scripture reading, 72–74
   retaining content of, 81–89
      conference, 88–89
      listening, 81–83
      taking notes, 83–86, 142
      repeating, 86–88
   See also preaching

servants, religious instruction of, 139–40, 141
Seven Treatises (Rogers), 92
Shepard, Thomas, 15, 73–74
shorthand, 15, 85n56
Sibbes, Richard, 64, 97, 112, 114–15
Sill, John, 15
small group(s), small group movement, 158
    accommodating perceived needs, 160–61
    biblical illiteracy, 161–63
    creating incremental changes, 159–60
    limited view of God, 161
    little transformation, 163–64
    training leaders, 175–77
Smith, Henry, 65, 81
Smith-Lovin, Lynn, 157
soul(s)
    care of, 8, 10, 100, 120, 144–45, 167, 172, 174
    state of, 65, 113–15, 143
spiritual direction, 164, 173–75
spiritual discipline(s)
    conference as, 8
    definition of, 124
    See also conference; means of grace
spiritual formation, 3–4, 8, 72, 91, 167
    correlation with religious commitment, 170
    public means of, for Puritans, 14
    See also conference, lay; conference, ministerial; edification
spiritual guidance, 8, 10–11, 12–13, 131–34
    provided by women, 150–52
spirituality, 3–7
Spirituality of Western Christendom, The, II (Elder, ed.), 5

Spiritual Traditions for the Contemporary Church (Maas and O'Donnell, eds.), 4
spouses, conference between, 141–42
Spurr, John, 146
Staunton, Edmund, 144, 145–46
stenography, 85n56
Stott, John R. W., 167
study materials, 171–73
Study of Spirituality, The (Jones, Wainwright, and Yarnold, eds.), 5
Sweet, Leonard, 168
symbolism, 64

taking notes on sermons, 15, 83–86, 84n54, 110, 142
Taylor, Justin, 7
text, 78
thanksgiving, 14, 80, 87, 93, 117, 134
theology, 3, 14, 17, 24, 43, 78
    of Geneva Bible, 60–61, 60n22
    Puritan, 53, 57
"things indifferent," 28
Thirsty for God (Holt), 5
Thirty-nine Articles (1562), 27, 31, 56
training leaders, 175–77
transcendent, the, awareness of, 160, 161
trans[in]formational reading and study, 172, 176
transformation, 94, 134, 154, 158, 160, 163–64, 170–71, 172, 174, 176, 178–79
Tregoss, Thomas, 135, 144–45
Trinity, the, 175
tropology, 63
Turner, John, 65, 91, 94
Tyndale, William, 22–23
typology, 64

Subject Index

Tyson, John, 4

Udall, John, 110

Vestments (Vestiarian) controversy, 41
via media, 28, 48
visible saint, 18
visitation of the sick, 135

Wakefield, Gordon, 3, 5, 9
Walker, Lady Anne, 85, 136
Wallington, Nehemiah, 141
Wallington's World (Seaver), 141
Watson, Thomas, 10, 51, 82, 101, 102, 103, 105, 106
Wesley, Charles, 151
Wesley, John, 151, 152
Wesley, Susanna, 151–52
Westminster Confession, 58

White, John, 142
Willard, Dallas, 174
winning of souls. *See* conversion; salvation
wisdom, 75, 95, 173
Withers, George, 35
women, role in Puritanism, 146–53
Woodford, Robert, 140
word-centeredness, 56, 56n9
Word of God. *See* Scripture
worship, 2, 13
  prophesying, in early church, 33
  simplified forms of, 22, 23–24, 28
Wuthnow, Robert, 159, 160–61, 162–63

Younge, Richard, 135